COLLECTOR'S VALUE GUIDE™

X-MEN®

Collector Handbook and Price Guide

PREMIERE EDITION

X-Men®

The Collector's Value Guide™ is not sponsored by, or otherwise affiliated with, Marvel®, TOPPS®, Fleer/Skybox International, Toy Biz®, WIZARDS OF THE COAST® or their licensees.

The individual names of each of the characters are trademarks of Marvel®.

Any opinions expressed are solely those of the authors, and do not necessarily reflect those of Marvel®, TOPPS®, Fleer/Skybox International, Toy Biz®, WIZARDS OF THE COAST® or their licensees.

EDITORIAL
Managing Editor: Jeff Mahony
Associate Editors: Melissa A. Bennett
Jan Cronan
Gia C. Manalio
Paula Stuckart
Contributing Editor: Mike Micciulla
Assistant Editors: Heather N. Carreiro
Jennifer Filipek
Joan C. Wheal
Editorial Assistants: Jennifer Abel
Timothy R. Affleck
Beth Hackett
Christina M. Sette
Steven Shinkaruk

WEB (collectorbee.com)
Web Reporter: Samantha Bouffard
Web Graphic Designer: Ryan Falis

R&D
R&D Specialist: Priscilla Berthiaume
R&D Graphic Designer: Angi Shearstone

ART
Creative Director: Joe T. Nguyen
Assistant Art Director: Lance Doyle
Senior Graphic Designers: Susannah C. Judd
David S. Maloney
Carole Mattia-Slater
David Ten Eyck
Graphic Designers: Jennifer J. Bennett
Sean-Ryan Dudley
Kimberly Eastman
Marla B. Gladstone
Caryn Johnson
Jim MacLeod
Jeremy Maendel
Chery-Ann Poudrier

PRODUCTION
Production Manager: Scott Sierakowski
Product Development Manager: Paul Rasid

ISBN 1-58598-068-4

CHECKERBEE™ and COLLECTOR'S VALUE GUIDE™ are trademarks of CheckerBee, Inc.
Copyright © 2000 by CheckerBee, Inc.
All rights reserved. No part of this book may be reproduced or transmitted in any form or by any means, electronic or mechanical, including photocopying, recording, or by any information storage or retrieval system, without the written permission of the publisher.

CheckerBee PUBLISHING
306 Industrial Park Road
Middletown, CT 06457

Table Of Contents

Introducing The Collector's Value Guide™ • **5**

Comics Through The Years • **6-10**

History Of X-Men® • **11-14**

Creators Of The Comics • **15-17**

X-Men® **Lineup** • **18-23**

X-Men® **On Screen** • **24-27**

X-Men® **On TV** • **28**

X-Men® **In The Cards** • **29-31**

How To Use Your Collector's Value Guide™ • **32**

Value Guide

X-Men® (1963-1981) • **33-57**

Uncanny X-Men® (1981-Present) • **57-106**

X-Men® (1991-Present) • **106-132**

The Age Of Apocalypse • **132-138**

Mini Series • **138-148**

Other X-Men® Comics • **148**

X-Men® Spin Offs • **149-162**

COLLECTOR'S
VALUE GUIDE™

Table Of Contents

X-Men® Action Figures • 163-182

X-Men® Trading Card Game • 183-191

Total Value Of My Collection • 192-194

Secondary Market Overview • 195-197

Other X-Men® Merchandise • 198-200

Comic Book Index & Checklist • 201-204

Action Figure Index & Checklist • 205-206

Trading Card Game Index & Checklist • 207

COLLECTOR'S
VALUE GUIDE™

Introducing The Collector's Value Guide™

X-Men® is heating up! As a result of this summer's motion picture release of *X-Men®: The Movie*, there is a renewed interest in the top-selling comic book series and an explosion of merchandise, including new trading cards, action figures, a trading card game and other memorabilia. These mutant superheroes have been familiar to comic book fans since 1963 and are sure to attract a new following of fans into the new millennium.

This Premiere Edition Collector's Value Guide™ is a great tool to keep track of your X-Men collection. With values for comics, action figures and trading cards, this is your one-stop source for X-Men secondary market information. And that's not all! In this book you will also find:

- A sneak peek into the history of comics and the X-Men
- A spotlight on the creative force behind *X-Men*
- An overview of the newly released feature film and movie merchandise
- Full-color cover photos of the *X-Men* comics along with their original titles, release dates, writers, pencilers, inkers and secondary market values
- Handy checklists for many of the popular spin-off comics, listed with their titles and secondary market values
- Color photos and comprehensive information of over 250 action figures
- A look at the new trading card game from Wizards Of The Coast®
- An examination of other X-Men collectibles

COLLECTOR'S
VALUE GUIDE™

Comics Through The Years

Comics and comic books have been part of the American literary landscape since the turn of the century and have provided a unique perspective of the Great Depression, World Wars I and II, the McCarthy era of the 1950s, the super 60s, the psychedelic 70s and the collector craze of the 1980s and 1990s. This century-old medium began as a single picture in a New York newspaper that caught the attention of discriminating readers.

Strips At The Newsstand

In 1896, a colorful panel featuring a bald-headed, big-eared kid wearing a yellow smock was published in William Randolph Hearst's *New York American* newspaper. Richard Felton Outcault's *The Yellow Kid* is now considered to be the first American comic strip and reprints of these strips, published in book style, were forerunners of the comic book format that we are familiar with today.

Other newspaper strips that experienced popularity during the turn of the century included Rudolf Dirks' *Katzenjammer Kids* and George Herriman's *Krazy Kat*. During the Stock Market crash in 1929 and the Great Depression that followed, Americans were grateful to escape into the world of comics filled with fantastic adventures.

The Hero Explosion

In 1938, a number of "superhero" characters debuted which started the period in comic book history commonly known as the *Golden Age*. DC Comics introduced *Superman* (1938), *Batman* (1939), *The Flash* (1940), *The Green Lantern* (1940) and *Wonder Woman* (1941) while Timely Comics (later to become Marvel Comics)

unveiled *The Sub-Mariner* (1939), *The Human Torch* (1939) and *Captain America* (1941).

Influenced by the war in Europe, American superheroes were shown defending their homeland against German, and later Japanese, villains. In 1943, paper shortages caused by the war prompted a decline in comic book production and by the end of World War II in 1945, the genre was destined to experience other changes as well.

BOMBS AND BLONDE BOMBSHELLS

After the atomic bomb was used against Japan, Americans were intrigued by the possible effects of radioactivity on humans – and superheroes! During the 1940s, several titles showed the American public just how devastating the power of the atom could be.

Female characters became favorites by the mid 1940s with the introduction of Marvel's *Miss America* and others including *Millie The Model, Nellie The Nurse* and *Tessie The Typist*. Teenage girls were demanding realistic heroines who also happened to act heroic. The introduction of women to the comic world also targeted adolescent boys with titles like *The Sea Beauty Namora* and *Venus*. Over time, more skin was revealed and outfits became more form-fitting. Romances became popular with titles including Marvel's *My Love, My Romance, Our Love* and *Young Hearts*.

COWBOYS AND CRIMEFIGHTERS

Western titles made a splash in the late 1940s with nostalgic stories of the Wild West including titles such as *Kid Colt Hero of the West* and *Two-Gun Kid*. Crossovers into romance produced *Cowboy Romances* and *Romances of the West*. Postwar comics also featured "based on actual cases" crime stories with such titles as *All True Crime* and *Crime*

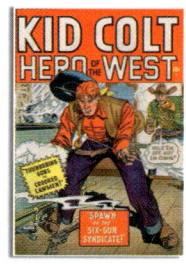

Does Not Pay. Controversy arose as the subject matter in these comics evolved from true-blue crimefighters to adult-only violence.

Comics Code Crackdown

In 1950, William Gaines of EC Comics introduced a series of titles featuring the horrific, the graphic and the shocking. Other pub‑

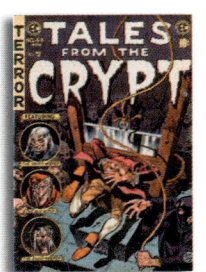

lishers tried to capitalize on EC's success and published their own tales of terror. With the increasing level of violence and questionable behavior infiltrating the comic book storylines and with no laws regulating comic sales to children, a group of citizens began to vocalize their concern.

In 1954, Dr. Fredric Wertham published his book, *Seduction Of The Innocent,* in which he attempted to correlate the violence depicted in comics to the increase in juvenile delinquency. This was taken seriously as U.S. Senate hearings were held to investigate his statements.

In response, comic publishers developed the *Standards Of The Comics Code Authority* themselves instead of waiting for the government to impose regulations on their industry. The standards reflected the wholesome morals of the 1950s and specified certain prohibitions regarding drugs, gore, explicit sex, criminal activity as well as offered suggestions for approved dialogue, costumes and storylines. These self-imposed restrictions caused many publishers to cease production of popular top-sellers and pushed many others into

bankruptcy. The remaining publishers would re-evaluate the appeal of the superheroes to decide whether or not to continue publishing.

A Marvel-ous Revival

The late 1950s proved to be a time of economic struggle for comic book publishers who were forced to let go of many talented artists. The number of titles written decreased dramatically and pub‑

lishers focused on reintroducing old favorites like *The Human Torch* and *The Sub-Mariner*. *The Flash* appeared again, but was a redesign of *The Flash* from the 1940s; *The Atom, Green Lantern, Justice League of America* (formerly *Justice Society of America*) were modernized.

At Marvel, publisher Martin Goodman requested that the writer and artist team of Stan Lee and Jack Kirby come up with a new super team after seeing the success of *Justice League of America* at DC Comics. With *The Fantastic Four*'s popularity, other Marvel heroes appeared in the form of *The Amazing Spider-Man, The Incredible Hulk* and *Thor*. Following these in 1963, another superhero group made its debut: *The X-Men*. This period of resurgence in the popularity of comic superheroes, that was led primarily by the publishing company Marvel Comics, is often referred to as the *Silver Age*.

THE SEVENTIES SLUMP

However, by 1969, the appeal of superheroes was again experiencing a lull. A sharp decline in sales was experienced which may have been due, in part, to an increase in the price of comic books – a jump from 12 to 15 cents per issue. This prompted old characters like Batman to be revamped and led to the introduction of new ones like Conan The Barbarian. *X-Men* went into reprint for almost five years and horror titles attempted a comeback after the Comics Code was revised in response to the anti-drug issues released by Marvel and DC. A trend toward more realistic art and more relevant topics became evident. In 1997, when Marvel acquired the rights to adapt the film *Star Wars*, things started to turn around for the company.

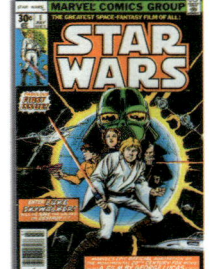

DIVIDE AND CONQUER

By the end of the 1970s, the practice of introducing a superhero into the worlds of other heroes – the crossover – became common. New titles and series were flooding the market and the two power-house publishers, Marvel and DC, were edging the others out of business. During the 1980s, alternative comics found an audience which again pushed the Comics Code envelope. Nudity, sex and violence once again infiltrated the world of comic book heroes and villains. Characters were rewritten to take on an edgy, dark slant with human tendencies and began dealing with more contemporary concerns. In 1984, a black-and-white parody of the typical superhero called *Teenage Mutant Ninja Turtles* was published and became one of the most recognized and licensed super teams of the decade. The Comics Code was again revised in 1989, the same year as the release of the movie *Batman*. Once again, a big screen debut revived interest in the comic book genre and comic books became collectible.

By the 1990s, the comic books themselves became marketing gimmicks offering a variety of covers and designs to attract more readers and sell more copies. Featuring a new artist, Todd MacFarlane, *Spider-Man* #1 was released with multiple covers and in special bags which prompted collectors to make multiple purchases. *X-Force*, a spin-off of the *X-Men* series, and a new series of *X-Men* written by Chris Claremont and drawn by Jim Lee also became collector items.

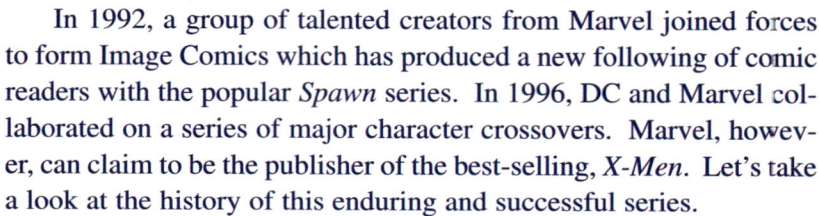

In 1992, a group of talented creators from Marvel joined forces to form Image Comics which has produced a new following of comic readers with the popular *Spawn* series. In 1996, DC and Marvel collaborated on a series of major character crossovers. Marvel, however, can claim to be the publisher of the best-selling, *X-Men*. Let's take a look at the history of this enduring and successful series.

HISTORY OF X-MEN®

The year was 1963. It was a time of transition between the crew-cut and bobby socks era of the late fifties and the rock-and-roll and Viet Nam War era of the late sixties. A postage stamp was a nickel, 15¢ would buy a McDonald's hamburger and a gallon of gas for your dad's Ford Falcon would cost about 50¢. If you found twelve cents in your pocket, it could provide a world of superhero entertainment with a purchase from the spinning comic book rack found at the corner drugstore.

LEE AND KIRBY: THE ORIGINAL X-MEN

Mirroring the Civil Rights Movement of the 1960s, in 1963, writer Stan Lee and artist Jack Kirby created a team of rebellious and isolated adolescents struggling with their super powers and dealing with the fear they cause because they are different. Enrolled in a school run by wheelchair-bound Professor Xavier, the five original students included the winged Angel, the gorilla-like Beast, Cyclops with death-ray eyes, the frosty Iceman and telekinetic Marvel Girl. To introduce the team in *X-Men* issue #1, Lee and Kirby began the new series with action-filled scenes in "The Danger Room," where the teenagers train to fight evil mutants – including Magneto, their first and foremost foe – and to keep the world safe from prejudice.

This new team helped to establish Marvel as one of the comic book publishing powerhouses during the 1960s. Thanks to the inspiration and vision of the Lee and Kirby creative team, the series flourished throughout the decade and enjoyed a revival of new storylines and art provided by the team of

COLLECTOR'S
VALUE GUIDE™

Roy Thomas and Neal Adams. But by March of 1970, the prolific *X-Men* series suffered along with other comic series and until 1975, publication reverted to reprints of old issues.

A GIANT-SIZED COMEBACK

During the mid-seventies, Marvel was experiencing reorganization with a renewed marketing vision. Comic books were now offered in world-wide distribution, which initiated the idea of a new team of international *X-Men* characters. Marvel Editor-In-Chief Roy Thomas turned over the concept to the writer and artist team of Len Wein and Dave Cockrum who created the new characters for the 1975 landmark issue *Giant Size X-Men* #1. The all-new, all-different *X-Men* still included the teenagers' mentor, Dr. X and one of the old team members, Cyclops, but also featured new members from Africa, Canada, Germany and Russia. Cockrum's energetic characterizations of Colossus, Nightcrawler, Storm, and Wolverine quickly established him at Marvel. When Len Wein became Marvel Editor-In-Chief, the writing duties were taken over by Chris Claremont, who joined Cockrum with *X-Men* #94. The team of Claremont and Cockrum re-established the *X-Men* team again in their fight to preserve the human race.

DEATH OF THE DARK ONE

Although the Marvel Universe is a fictional one, the creative team at Marvel insisted on "moral consequences" for Dark Phoenix's actions after Jean Grey was unable to control the evil identity she had taken on. In an emotional and innovative plot twist, Jean Grey, one of the comic's most popular characters, was killed in 1980 in issue #137. John Byrne, the artist, Chris Claremont, the writer, and Jim

Shooter, the editor-in-chief for this infamous saga, helped to catapult the series into an overnight controversial sensation. In 1984, readers were treated to a special issue, *Phoenix: The Untold Story,* a reprint of the original #137, but with a different ending of previously drawn panels in which Jean Grey does not perish. Also included are behind-the-scenes details of the creative team's decisions leading up to the death of Phoenix.

THE X-PLOSION OF THE 80S

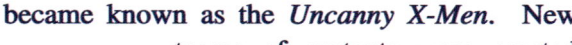

The 1980s also ushered in a new *X-Men* era featuring exciting and imaginative artwork provided by the Marvel creative machine. Although John Byrne moved on to pencil *The Fantastic Four* comic in 1981, other talents such as Jim Lee, John Romita, Jr. and Marc Silvestri stepped in with their own artistic styles. In 1981, the *X-Men* became known as the *Uncanny X-Men*. New teams of mutants were created with spin-offs such as *The New Mutants* in 1983, *X-Factor* in 1986 and *Excalibur* in 1988. (For a list of the more popular *X-Men* spin-off titles, turn to page 149.) Teamed with a powerhouse block of titles including *The Fantastic Four* and *The Avengers*, the *X-Men* titles ensured the popularity of superhero teams for Marvel.

Bag It, Buy It And Mark It With An "X"

To offer comic book readers a variety of *X-Men* and to give the talent at Marvel more exposure, a brand new series of *X-Men* debuted in 1991 which featured the writing wizardry of Chris Claremont and  the artistry of Jim Lee. This much anticipated issue was specially bagged and published with multiple cover designs which only added to its collectibility. Consequently, a record 8 million copies were sold which ensured the continuation of the new teams that were introduced in the series. Jim Lee, Fabian Nicieza, Scott Lobdell, Art Thibert and other writers and artists have since contributed to the continued success of the series. The end of the decade brought news of Chris Claremont's comeback to write *X-Men*. He had been away for nine years.

Let's take a closer look at the creative teams of writers and artists who have had a hand in ensuring the longevity of the *X-Men*.

Creators Of The Comics

Throughout the history of *X-Men* comics, there have been hundreds of creators, including plotters, writers, scripters, pencilers, inkers, letterers and colorists, who brought life to the characters and stories of *X-Men*, from its beginning in 1963 to today. While each person involved has made important contributions, the following people are considered to be the most influential to the evolution of the *X-Men* comic.

Neal Adams

Penciler: *X-Men* #56-63, 65 (1969-1970)
Claim To X-Fame: In collaboration with Roy Thomas, Adams attempted to revive the struggling *X-Men* title with his realistic style, unconventional panel layouts and exciting cover designs. The series, however, was cancelled because of lagging sales and went into reprint from 1970 to 1975.

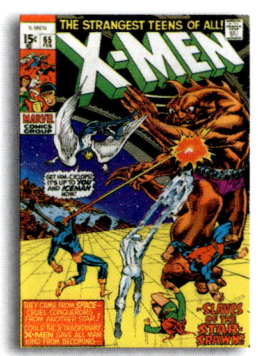

John Byrne

Co-plotter/Penciler: *X-Men* #108-109, #111-143 (1977-1981)
Writer: *Uncanny X-Men* #281-285, 288 (1991-1992)
Claim To X-Fame: Byrne was the penciler for the infamous and popular "Dark Phoenix" saga which ended with Phoenix's death in issue #137. Byrne also helped to create popular characters including Dazzler and Kitty Pryde and also brought the character of Wolverine into more of the storylines.

CHRIS CLAREMONT

Writer: *X-Men* #94-279 (1975-1991), *Uncanny X-Men* #381 (2000), *X-Men* #1-3 (1991), #100 (2000)

Claim To X-Fame: While interning at Marvel, 19-year-old Chris Claremont assisted Roy Thomas in co-plotting *X-Men* #59 in 1969. Claremont then began writing *X-Men* in 1975 and continued for 16 years until 1991. In 1991, he wrote *X-Men* #1 which is currently the best selling comic with 8 million copies sold. He returned to Marvel in 1998 as editorial director and began writing *X-Men* again in June 2000.

DAVE COCKRUM

Penciler: *Giant Size X-Men* #1 (1975), *X-Men* #94-107 (1975-1977), #145-164 (1981-1982)

Claim To X-Fame: Cockrum is known for the development of several new characters and their distinctive costumes, including Colossus, Nightcrawler and Storm who were designed to be an international group of X-Men that included a Russian, a German and an African, among others.

JACK KIRBY

Penciler: *X-Men* #1-11 (1963-1965)

Claim To X-Fame: Born Jacob Kurtzberg in 1917, in 1963, Kirby co-created the original *X-Men* with Stan Lee following a 20-year career of cartoon animation and newspaper strips that began in 1935 at the Max Fleisher Studios. One of the most prolific artists in comic book history, Kirby died in 1994 at the age of 77.

STAN LEE

Writer/Penciler: *X-Men* #1-19 (1963-1966)
Marvel Editor: 1941-1972
Claim To X-Fame: Known to comic book fans as "Stan the Man," Lee co-created the original *X-Men* series in 1963 with artist Jack Kirby. He is considered the driving force behind the Marvel world of comics and continues to make contributions to the comic publishing industry today.

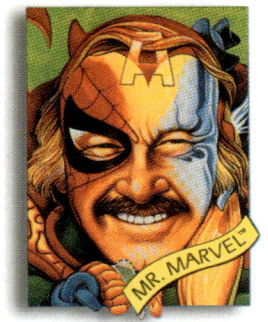

SCOTT LOBDELL

Writer: *Uncanny X-Men* #286-350 (1992-1997), *X-Men* #6-11, #46-50, #56-69 (1992-1997)
Claim To X-Fame: Lobdell was instrumental in introducing the "Age Of Apocalypse" storyline in 1995 which was published when all other existing X-Men titles ceased publication for four months.

ROY THOMAS

Writer: *X-Men* #20-66 (1966-1970)
Marvel Editor-in-Chief: 1972-1974
Claim To X-Fame: Thomas ushered in the new "generation" of *X-Men* creators during his tenure as writer in the late 1960s and editor in the early 1970s. After helping to give new life to the title by collaborating with Neal Adams, Thomas oversaw the reprint years of *X-Men* until 1974.

X-MEN® LINEUP

ARCHANGEL

Real Name: Warren Worthington III

First Appearance: *X-Men* #1

Mutant Power: Archangel possesses the ability to fly with a pair of wings, has enhanced vision and hollow bones.

Before X-Men: Once called Angel, Warren's wings began to sprout in his early teens and he used them for the first time when he rescued a man from a burning building. Unfortunately, he followed this display of heroism with a career as a costumed criminal. Eventually, he was recruited to became one of the original five X-Men.

BEAST

Real Name: Henry "Hank" McCoy

First Appearance: *X-Men* #1

Mutant Power: The Beast has extraordinary strength and agility, aided by his extra-large hands and feet. The oldest member of the X-Men, Beast's intelligence is highly prized by his teammates. An experiment caused him to grow blue fur and claws.

Before X-Men: Hank's father worked in a nuclear plant and risked his life to prevent a meltdown. As a result, radioactive effects manifested themselves in Hank. He excelled at sports, but publicity about his overly-enthusiastic display of power attracted Professor X's attention. Professor X then recruited Hank to become a member of the X-Men.

COLOSSUS

Real Name: Piotr Rasputin

First Appearance: *Giant-Size X-Men* #1

Mutant Power: Colossus has the ability to turn his flesh into organic steel. In this state, his body is protected from almost any physical assault and he doesn't need to eat or even breathe.

Before X-Men: Piotr grew up on a farm in Russia where his mutant ability first manifested itself when an out-of-control tractor was about to crush his sister. He transformed and stopped the tractor which alerted Professor X to his powers. The professor later persuaded Colossus to join the X-Men.

COLLECTOR'S
VALUE GUIDE™

X-Men® Lineup

CYCLOPS

Real Name: Scott Summers

First Appearance: *X-Men* #1

Mutant Power: Cyclops has the ability to shoot powerful optic blasts from his eyes. A born leader, to keep his blasts in check, Scott always wears his special eye gear.

Before X-Men: When their family plane was shot down, Scott's mother strapped him and his brother Alex (later known as Havok) into the only parachute and pushed them from the plane. When the parachute caught fire, Scott used his optic blast to slow their fall. Placed in an orphanage secretly run by Mr. Sinister, Alex was soon adopted, but Scott languished there until he ran away. Scott was then pursued by the U.S. Army before Professor X rescued him.

GAMBIT

Real Name: Remy LeBeau

First Appearance: *Uncanny X-Men* #266

Mutant Power: Gambit has the ability to charge objects with kinetic energy, causing them to explode on contact.

Before X-Men: Remy was raised by the Thieves Guild in New Orleans and planned to marry a woman from the Assassins Guild to end a rivalry. This backfires when Remy is attacked by her brother and kills him in self defense. Remy then strikes out on his own as a thief and meets Storm who recruits him for the X-Men.

ICEMAN

Real Name: Robert "Bobby" Drake

First Appearance: *X-Men* #1

Mutant Power: The Iceman has the ability to lower his body temperature to form a layer of ice around his body and freeze water molecules in the air.

Before X-Men: He first discovered his power in his early teens and used it publicly to protect himself and his girlfriend from a bully. When the story spread, a lynch mob was formed and Bobby was taken into custody by the local sheriff. Cyclops was sent to rescue him and Bobby agreed to join the X-Men.

COLLECTOR'S
VALUE GUIDE™

X-Men® Lineup

Real Name: Cain Marko

First Appearance: *X-Men* #12

Mutant Power: Juggernaut's invulnerability is only weakened by mental attacks. When he is wearing his protective helmet, even mental attacks cannot harm him.

Before Super-Villiany: Cain was Charles Xavier's step-brother and held a great deal of hatred for him. When he and Charles were drafted to serve in the Korean War, Cain stumbled across a hidden cavern during a cowardly act of retreat. Inside this cave, he came into contact with a powerful gem and was transformed into the powerful Juggernaut.

Real Name: Erik Lensherr

First Appearance: *X-Men* #1

Mutant Power: Magneto has the ability to manipulate metal, magnetic fields (including electricity) and even a person's blood flow since it contains iron.

Before Super-Villiany: In a life filled with tragedy, Erik saw his parents die in a German concentration camp and later his own daughter in a fire. After using his power to attack the townspeople in revenge, his frightened wife left and later died giving birth to twins (Quicksilver and The Scarlet Witch). At first Erik and Charles Xavier were friends, committed to human and mutant harmony. But Erik became bitter and was determined to prevent another Holocaust. His reign of terror began.

Real Name: Dr. Nathaniel Essex

First Appearance: *Uncanny X-Men* #221

Mutant Power: Mr. Sinister has the ability to control his molecular structure, does not appear to age and has embarked on a campaign for genetic perfection.

Before Super-Villiany: Nathaniel was a normal human and a doctor in England who predicted that mutations would soon affect humanity. He conducted many experiments with questionable morality. Rejected by his peers and his family, Dr. Essex sought out Apocalypse who transformed him into Mr. Sinister.

COLLECTOR'S VALUE GUIDE™

MYSTIQUE

Real Name: Raven Darkholme

First Appearance: *Ms. Marvel* #18

Mutant Power: Mystique can shape-change into almost any form. She can even transform only part of her body

Before Super-Villiany: Mystique had two children, Nightcrawler (with a Bavarian Count) and Graydon Creed (with Sabretooth). She also served as foster mother to Rogue and also the leader of the Evil Brotherhood of Mutants. Later Mystique was convinced to join the forces of good with *X-Factor*.

NIGHTCRAWLER

Real Name: Kurt Wagner

First Appearance: *Giant-Size X-Men* #1

Mutant Power: Nightcrawler can stick to walls, hide in shadows and teleport short distances. His demon appearance is accompanied by a sulfurous smell.

Before X-Men: Kurt was abandoned in Germany by his mother Mystique and raised by a fortune teller. He fit in quite well as a circus performer but in one town he is pursued by an angry mob. Only Professor X's intervention saves him and he joins up with the X-Men.

PHOENIX

Real Name: Jean Grey (originally known as Marvel Girl)

First Appearance: *X-Men* #1

Mutant Power: Possesses telepathic and telekinetic abilities although her telepathy has been blocked by Professor X.

Before X-Men: Jean's power first became evident as a child when her best friend died and Jean found that she could read her thoughts. As a teenager, Jean would join the X-Men. Some time later, her likeness was assumed by the Phoenix entity as the real Jean Grey was placed in suspended animation. The real Jean was eventually found by The Fantastic Four in a regenerating cocoon and in time, gained some of the Phoenix's power and took on the name.

Real Name: Professor Charles Xavier

First Appearance: *X-Men* #1

Mutant Power: Known as a scholar and defender of mutantkind, Professor X is a mutant himself and possesses the world's most powerful mind.

Before X-Men: Both of Charles' parents worked at a nuclear research center and he believes their exposure to radiation caused his mutation. He first discovered his powers at a young age, began to lose his hair in his teens and eventually lost the use of his legs when he battled Lucifer. He became the founder of Xavier's School for Gifted Youngsters where young mutants are taught to control and refine their powers.

Real Name: unknown

First Appearance: *Avengers Annual* #10

Mutant Power: Rogue absorbs memories and abilities when she makes flesh-to-flesh contact with someone. Consequently, she feels that she must keep her distance from others.

Before X-Men: Rogue was taken in by Mystique who acted as her foster mother. She joined the Brotherhood of Evil Mutants, but eventually sought help from her former enemies, the X-Men. Professor X was persuaded to let her join.

Real Name: Victor Creed

First Appearance: *Iron Fist* #14

Mutant Power: Sabretooth possesses a deadly set of claws, the ability to heal himself and enhanced senses. Similar to Wolverine, he even has adamantium bones and claws.

Before Super-Villainy: Sabretooth was one of the Marauders during the Mutant Massacre and he had a son, Graydon Creed, with Mystique. Victor's relationship with Wolverine stretches back to the Weapon X project which they both participated in and both left.

SENTINELS

Real Name: N/A

First Appearance: *X-Men* #14

Power: The Sentinels can sense mutants, have an arsenal of deadly weapons and can adapt and learn from their experiences.

Before X-Men: Originally created by Bolivar Trask who believed that mutants should be cleansed from the Earth, the Sentinels are perfectly suited to their task, receiving their instructions from a Master Mold. Unfortunately for Bolivar, this artificial intelligence caused his death. Others have since taken over the helm to control the Sentinels.

STORM

Real Name: Ororo Munroe

First Appearance: *Giant-Size X-Men* #1

Mutant Power: Storm has the ability to control the weather.

Before X-Men: Ororo was orphaned when a bomb collapsed her family home in Cairo, killing her parents and burying her under a mountain of debris. This incident causes her to suffer from claustrophobia. Ororo then became a thief for the Shadow King and even attempted to steal Professor X's wallet! Many years later, when Ororo has become a goddess to an African tribe, Xavier crosses her path yet again and offers her a chance to use her powers for a good cause.

WOLVERINE

Real Name: Logan

First Appearance: *Incredible Hulk* #181 after a cameo appearance in *Incredible Hulk* #180

Mutant Power: Wolverine possesses an adamantium skeleton and claws, the ability to heal himself and enhanced senses.

Before X-Men: Logan was part of a top-secret government program in Canada called Weapon X. After escaping this program, Logan wandered the Canadian wilderness until he was discovered and went to work for the Canadian government. Later, he jumped at the chance to join the X-Men which would provide him with greater personal freedom.

COLLECTOR'S
VALUE GUIDE™

X-Men® On Screen

Talk about summer blockbusters! The much anticipated release of director Bryan Singer's movie adaptation of *X-Men* has proved to be one of the highest grossing opening weekends ever. Rivaling the debuts of *The Lost World: Jurassic Park*, *Star Wars: Episode One* and *Mission Impossible II*, *X-Men* earned $57.5 million in its weekend premiere, the most any movie has ever earned during a three-day opening in July. Distributed by Twentieth Century Fox, the multi-million dollar adaptation of the number one-selling comic book series had been followed closely with Internet updates on the film's progress. According to reviews and editorials, everyone – including a wide range of comic book, action movie and Patrick Stewart fans – seems to be extremely pleased with the result.

Actors With Powerful Attitude

Dozens of super powered characters have come and gone during the years of X-Men, but only a select few appear in the film – including Professor X, Cyclops, Jean Grey, Storm and Wolverine. The wheel-chair bound Professor X is played by Patrick Stewart of Star Trek fame, reportedly the only actor who was ever considered for the part. The new and upcoming Australian actor, Hugh Jackman, takes the popular role of the ferocious loner – Wolverine. Halle Berry shoots lightning bolts across the screen as she plays the weather-controlling Storm. Cyclops, the character who can kill you with one look, is played by James Marsden. Oscar award winner Anna Paquin plays Rogue, while Famke Janssen takes the role of Jean Grey.

COLLECTOR'S
VALUE GUIDE™

What X-Men story would be complete without those evil mutant villains to stir up trouble? The line-up of villains include Magneto, Sabretooth, Toad and the shape-shifting Mystique. Sir Ian McKellan takes the role of the evil mastermind Magneto, while the glamorous super model, Rebecca Romijn-Stamos plays the sneaky and mysterious Mystique. Ray Park flicks an amazing tongue and jumps around the screen as he plays the role of Toad. Wrestler Tyler Mane takes on an animalistic role as the beast-like mutant, Sabretooth. Caught in the middle of the mutant fracas is the unwitting character of conservative Senator Kelly, played by Bruce Davison. But don't worry, X-fans, if your favorite mutant does not appear in this movie, he or she may appear in the second or third parts of the X-Men trilogy which are tentatively scheduled for future production.

Super Heroic Measures

The movie's plot is centered upon the character of Wolverine, as he reluctantly encounters the X-Men at the Xavier School for Mutants, and Rogue, as she first discovers her uncontrollable power. The central conflict of the movie focuses on the mutant forces of good versus evil. While the students of Xavier's school, run by Professor X, are eager to use their superhuman powers to help mankind, The Brotherhood of Evil Mutants, headed by Magneto, awaits the day that they will take over the world. Besides being action-packed, full of adventure and tinged with a comedic salute to its comic book forebears, the movie portrays the isolated and lonely feeling of being different than everyone else, especially focusing on Wolverine and Rogue, who have not yet learned to deal with their special powers.

GET THE X-PERIENCE

Even before the *X-Men* movie hit theaters across America in July, the phenomenon fueled one of the biggest hype machines in years. And with it, of course, came all of the movie-related merchandise. In addition to newly designed action figures associated with the film, there is everything from T-shirts and leather jackets to shooters and martini glasses available for the fan looking for the latest in X.

X-fanatics all across America love the new line of X-Men T-shirts made especially for the summer 2000 flick. Graphitti Designs™ has created numerous T-shirts and long sleeve shirts that display the *X-Men* movie logo and the mutants who make up the *X-Men* team. To wear over your *X-Men* T-shirt is a variety of fashionable denim and leather jackets displaying the X-Men logo. *X-Men* movie hats will also accentuate your outfit, along with *X-Men* movie belt buckles, buttons, dog tags, lapel pins and watches. If you are going for the eXtra "cool" look, Oakley™ makes a special style of sunglasses similar to the eye gear worn by Cyclops. If you are dressed in formal wear, yet still want to sport the *X-Men*, a variety of cuff link and tie sets are on the market. The *X-Men* Xavier Academy ring will also keep you in style and looking like a true fan.

If decorating your body in *X-Men* apparel is not enough, perhaps the variety of *X-Men* movie banners and posters will accommodate your decorating needs. Find a place on your wall for the movie "DNA" Photo Set or the movie Room Decor Kit by Diamond Comic Distributors, Inc. Clear off a spot on the fridge for the *X-Men* Heroes and Villains Magnet Sets, also by Diamond Comic Distributors, Inc.

If you are a true *X-Men* fan, you are eXcited about X-Men on screen and want to celebrate in *X-Men* style. Check out the wide range of glassware by Diamond Comic Distributors, Inc. You can find shooters and shot glasses that feature each movie character, along with the *X-Men* movie logo. Some hot items include the *X-Men* Movie Metallic Tri-Logo Shot Set and the Metallic Logo Martini Glass.

FUN X-MEN STUFF!

The *X-Men* fun continues even when the movie is over. Planning to buy the movie soundtrack? If so, keep it safe in the *X-Men* movie CD holder. There is also a nylon beltbag, lunchbag and book bag, decorated with images from the film. Keep your extra pocket change in the cool new *X-Men* Animatronic Battle Bank. Maybe you can enen save enough to see the movie twice. Carry your keys safely on an *X-Men* acrylic key chain and open up your letters with a Wolverine Claw Letter Opener. Watch the time fly by with the *X-Men* Electronic Animatronic Clock. For all die-hard Cyclops fans, the Movie Cyclops Visor is the perfect way to look just like your favorite mutant.

THE X- CLUB

If the movie was not enough for you, there is now an *X-Men* collectors club. It is operated and maintained by Collectible Concepts Group, Inc. and is easy to join. All you have to do is visit their Internet site at X-Menclub.com and sign up. As a member, you will receive an *X-Men* Club Kit which includes a personalized membership certificate, a personalized mutant ID card, a high quality computer wrist rest, discount coupons on *X-Men* merchandise and exclusive club movie character posters. Also, you will receive free newsletters featuring club news, hot offers and special events. Sign up soon and join the Mutant Revolution!

X-Men® On TV

The X-Men made their television debut in 1989 during the *Marvel Action Hour*. A half-hour animated pilot called "Pryde of the X-Men" was launched but was never developed into a series. It featured narration by Stan Lee and characters such as Wolverine, Professor X and Storm. This pilot was later released on video and a musical recording is planned that will feature the original score, new songs inspired by the show and interviews with Stan Lee.

In 1992, the X-Men finally got their own animated series. It ran for five seasons on Fox with a total of 76 episodes. The show followed the comics closely with storylines like the "Phoenix Saga." The team throughout the show's run consisted of Beast, Cyclops, Gambit, Jean Grey (Marvel Girl), Jubilee, Rogue, Storm, Wolverine and Professor X. In February of 1996, Fox aired a two-hour, live-action television pilot called "Generation X," based on the spin-off comic of the same name, but this never developed into a series.

Young fans can look forward to the Kids WB animated series, "X-Men Evolution," to be aired in the fall of 2000. The show will feature Cyclops, Jean Grey, Kitty Pryde (Shadowcat), Nightcrawler and Rogue as teenagers attending the Xavier Institute. Storm and Wolverine will also appear in the series, serving as adult mentors working with Professor X. Also appearing are Mystique, who serves as the school's principal, and Spike, a brand new character, who is Storm's nephew. Marvel and Film Roman Inc. are co-producing the show and are planning 13 episodes for the first season.

X-Men® In The Cards

X-men fans have the opportunity to hold their favorite (and even not so favorite) characters in the palm of their hands. Since 1991, there have been several sets of trading cards available. In conjunction with the *X-Men* movie, TOPPS® has released a brand new set of cards. TOPPS is also releasing a Special Collector's Edition of the set featuring different chase cards, four movie memorabilia cards and cards autographed by the movie's leading stars.

Below you will find a chronological list of popular trading card sets from the most recent to the oldest. With each set, you will find the manufacturer, release date, number of cards in the set, a listing of chase (C) and promotional (P) cards and a secondary market value for the complete set, as well as the special cards (listed as "N/E" if no value has been established).

X-Men The Movie Trading Cards (TOPPS, 2000)

Set of 72 cards . . . . .New!
Clear-Cling (C, set/12) . . . . .New!
X-Foil (C, set/10) . . . . .New!
Cyclops (P) . . . . .New!
Magneto (P) . . . . .New!
Mutants Among Us (P) . . . . .New!
Storm (P) . . . . .New!
Wolverine (P) .New!

X-Men '97 Timelines (Fleer/SkyBox, 1997)

Set of 82 cards $25
Deadpool Party (C, set/9) $30
New Recruits (C, set/8) $25
Wanted (C, set/4) $40

COLLECTOR'S
VALUE GUIDE™

ULTRA X-MEN (FLEER, 1995)

Set of 150 cards	$23
Hunters & Stalkers (gold, C, set/9)	N/E
Hunters & Stalkers (rainbow, C, set/9)	$20
Hunters & Stalkers (silver, C, set/9)	N/E
Sinister Observations (C, set/10)	$52
Suspended Animation (C, set/10)	$36
Wolverine (P)	$24

ULTRA X-MEN CHROMIUM (FLEER, 1995)

Set of 100 cards	$30
Alternate X (C, set/20)	$35
Cyclops (P)	$4
Gold Signature (C, set/100)	$100
Lethal Weapons (C, set/9)	$40
Wolverine (P)	$4

ULTRA X-MEN (FLEER, 1994)

Set of 150 cards	$28
3-Card Triptych Panel (P)	$15
Fatal Attractions (C, set/6)	$38
Red Foil/Team Triptych (Blue Team, C, set/3)	$25
Red Foil/Team Triptych (Gold Team, C, set/3)	$25
Silver X-Overs (C, set/6)	$80
Team Portraits (C, set/9)	$30
X-Men's Greatest Battles (C, set/6)	$42

COLLECTOR'S
VALUE GUIDE

X-Men Series 2 (SkyBox, 1993)

Set of 100 cards $20
   30th Anniversary Gold Foil (C, set/9) $42
   Hologram (C, set/3) $35
   Juggernaut (P) $3
   Wolverine 3D Hologram (C) $45

X-Men Series 1 (Impel, 1992)

Set of 100 cards $30
   Hologram (C, set/5) $30
   Jim Lee Autographed Card (C) $115

X-Men (Comic Images, 1991)

Set of 90 cards $22
   Jim Lee Autographed Card (C) $130

X-Men Covers Set 2 (Comic Images, 1990)

Set of 45 cards $20

X-Men Covers Set 1 (Comic Images, 1990)

Set of 90 cards $28

COLLECTOR'S
VALUE GUIDE™

How To Use Your Collector's Value Guide™

1. Find your X-Men.

Comics: Comics are listed in numerical order with the original *X-Men* first, followed by the *Uncanny X-Men* and then the second *X-Men* series. Each on-going series is followed by annuals and then one-shots. At the end of these sections, you will find the "Age Of Apocalypse" comics followed by mini series, all of which are listed in alphabetical order within their category. These comics are listed with the issue's title, release date and writer, penciler and inker. If there is more than one story within the comic, only the information for the larger story is given. Next, there is a checklist featuring the larger spin-off comics with their titles and values.

Action Figures: Action figures are listed in alphabetical order by character name with their series, size and year of release. Variations and re-issues, with values, are listed if applicable.

Trading Card Game: The trading cards are listed in alphabetical order with their name, card number, card type, rarity and the deck(s) in which the card is available. This section is followed by a listing of the cards that will soon be available in booster packs.

2. Record the price that you paid for each piece you have in the spaces provided.

3. Add the values for your X-Men on that page and write it in the appropriate box at the bottom of the page. Then do the same with the secondary market values. Pieces that do not yet have established secondary market values are listed as "N/E."

4. Transfer the totals from each page to the "Total Value Of My Collection" worksheets on pages 192-194. Add all of the totals together to determine the overall value of your collection. Use a pencil so you can change the totals as your collection grows!

Collector's Value Guide™ — X-Men®

X-MEN® COMIC BOOKS

In 1963, Marvel began publishing a comic book series featuring a team of teenage mutants with hidden powers who are feared by and isolated from the general public. These mutants of *X-Men* comics have achieved phenomenal success with their popularity over the past 37 years.

The original *X-Men* began in 1963. In 1981, the name of the comic changed to *Uncanny X-Men* and the series continues under that name today. In 1991, a new series with the same name of *X-Men* began and also continues today alongside *Uncanny X-Men*.

For those fans that just can't get enough of those mutants, not only are there these two on-going series, but also bonus annual issues, one-shots, *Age Of Apocalypse* comics and mini series.

#-1
The Boy Who Saw Tomorrow
(Flashback Issue)
July 1997
Scott Lobdell
Bryan Hitch
Paul Neary

Orig. Retail	Price Paid	Value
$1.95		$2.50

#-1
The Boy Who Saw Tomorrow (American Entertainment Cover)
July 1997
Scott Lobdell
Bryan Hitch
Paul Neary

Orig. Retail	Price Paid	Value
$1.95		$5.25

#1
X-Men

September 1963
Stan Lee
Jack Kirby
Paul Reinman

Orig. Retail	Price Paid	Value
12¢		$6,500

COLLECTOR'S **Value Guide**™

	Price Paid	Total Value
Page Totals:		

Collector's Value Guide™ — X-Men®

#2
No One Can Stop The Vanisher!

November 1963

Stan Lee
Jack Kirby
Paul Reinman

Orig. Retail	Price Paid	Value
12¢		$1,750

#3
Beware of the Blob!

January 1964

Stan Lee
Jack Kirby
Paul Reinman

Orig. Retail	Price Paid	Value
12¢		$725

#4
The Brotherhood Of Evil Mutants

March 1964

Stan Lee
Jack Kirby
Paul Reinman

Orig. Retail	Price Paid	Value
12¢		$600

#5
Trapped: One X-Man!

May 1964

Stan Lee
Jack Kirby
Paul Reinman

Orig. Retail	Price Paid	Value
12¢		$455

#6
Sub-Mariner! Joins The Evil Mutants

July 1964

Stan Lee
Jack Kirby
Chic Stone

Orig. Retail	Price Paid	Value
12¢		$300

#7
The Return Of The Blob

September 1964

Stan Lee
Jack Kirby
Chic Stone

Orig. Retail	Price Paid	Value
12¢		$300

Page Totals:	Price Paid	Total Value

COLLECTOR'S VALUE GUIDE™

Collector's Value Guide™ — X-Men®

#8
The Uncanny Threat Of . . . Unus The Untouchable!
November 1964

Stan Lee
Jack Kirby
Chic Stone

Orig. Retail	Price Paid	Value
12¢		$300

#9
Enter The Avengers!

January 1965

Stan Lee
Jack Kirby
Chic Stone

Orig. Retail	Price Paid	Value
12¢		$300

#10
The Coming Of . . . Ka-Zar!

March 1965

Stan Lee
Jack Kirby
Chic Stone

Orig. Retail	Price Paid	Value
12¢		$300

#11
The Triumph Of Magneto!

May 1965

Stan Lee
Jack Kirby
Chic Stone

Orig. Retail	Price Paid	Value
12¢		$250

#12
The Origin Of Professor X!

July 1965

Stan Lee
Jack Kirby/Alex Toth
Vince Colletta

Orig. Retail	Price Paid	Value
12¢		$350

#13
Where Walks The Juggernaut!

September 1965

Stan Lee
Jack Kirby/Jay Gavin
Joe Sinnott

Orig. Retail	Price Paid	Value
12¢		$245

Page Totals: Price Paid / Total Value

Value Guide — X-Men® (1963-1981)

Collector's Value Guide™ — X-Men®

#14
Among Us Stalk . . . The Sentinels!

November 1965

Stan Lee
Jack Kirby/Jay Gavin
Vince Colletta

Orig. Retail	Price Paid	Value
12¢		$245

#15
Prisoners Of The Mysterious Master Mold!

December 1965

Stan Lee
Jack Kirby/Jay Gavin
Dick Ayers

Orig. Retail	Price Paid	Value
12¢		$245

#16
The Supreme Sacrifice!

January 1966

Stan Lee
Jack Kirby/Jay Gavin
Dick Ayers

Orig. Retail	Price Paid	Value
12¢		$150

#17
. . . And None Shall Survive!

February 1966

Stan Lee
Jack Kirby/Jay Gavin
Dick Ayers

Orig. Retail	Price Paid	Value
12¢		$140

#18
If Iceman Should Fail – !

March 1966

Stan Lee
Jay Gavin
Dick Ayers

Orig. Retail	Price Paid	Value
12¢		$140

#19
Lo! Now Shall Appear – The Mimic!

April 1966

Stan Lee
Jay Gavin
Dick Ayers

Orig. Retail	Price Paid	Value
12¢		$135

Page Totals: Price Paid _____ Total Value _____

COLLECTOR'S VALUE GUIDE™

Collector's Value Guide™ — X-Men®

#20
I, Lucifer . . .

May 1996
Roy Thomas
Jay Gavin
Dick Ayers

Orig. Retail	Price Paid	Value
12¢		$135

#21
From Whence Comes . . . Dominus?

June 1966
Roy Thomas
Jay Gavin
Dick Ayers

Orig. Retail	Price Paid	Value
12¢		$105

#22
Divided – We Fall!

July 1966
Roy Thomas
Jay Gavin
Dick Ayers

Orig. Retail	Price Paid	Value
12¢		$105

#23
To Save A City

August 1966
Roy Thomas
Werner Roth
Dick Ayers

Orig. Retail	Price Paid	Value
12¢		$100

#24
The Plague Of The Locust

September 1966
Roy Thomas
Werner Roth
Dick Ayers

Orig. Retail	Price Paid	Value
12¢		$100

#25
The Power And The Pendant

October 1966
Roy Thomas
Werner Roth
Dick Ayers

Orig. Retail	Price Paid	Value
12¢		$100

Value Guide — X-Men® (1963-1981)

COLLECTOR'S VALUE GUIDE™

Page Totals: | Price Paid | Total Value

Collector's Value Guide™ — X-Men®

#26
Holocaust

November 1966

Roy Thomas
Werner Roth
Dick Ayers

Orig. Retail	Price Paid	Value
12¢		$100

#27
Re-Enter: The Mimic

December 1966

Roy Thomas
Werner Roth
Dick Ayers

Orig. Retail	Price Paid	Value
12¢		$100

#28
The Wail Of
The Banshee

January 1967

Roy Thomas
Werner Roth
Dick Ayers

Orig. Retail	Price Paid	Value
12¢		$150

#29
When Titans Clash

February 1967

Roy Thomas
Werner Roth
John Tartaglione

Orig. Retail	Price Paid	Value
12¢		$100

#30
The Warlock Wakes

March 1967

Roy Thomas
Jack Sparling
John Tartaglione

Orig. Retail	Price Paid	Value
12¢		$100

#31
We Must Destroy The
Cobalt Man!

April 1967

Roy Thomas
Werner Roth
John Tartaglione

Orig. Retail	Price Paid	Value
12¢		$75

Page Totals: Price Paid / Total Value

COLLECTOR'S
VALUE GUIDE™

Collector's Value Guide™ — X-Men®

#32
Beware The Juggernaut, My Son

May 1967

Roy Thomas
Werner Roth
John Tartaglione

Orig. Retail	Price Paid	Value
12¢		$75

#33
Into The Crimson Cosmos

June 1967

Roy Thomas
Werner Roth
John Tartaglione

Orig. Retail	Price Paid	Value
12¢		$75

#34
War In A World Of Darkness

July 1967

Roy Thomas
Dan Adkins
Dan Adkins

Orig. Retail	Price Paid	Value
12¢		$75

#35
Along Came A Spider

August 1967

Roy Thomas
Werner Roth
Dan Adkins

Orig. Retail	Price Paid	Value
12¢		$120

#36
Mekano Lives

September 1967

Roy Thomas
Ross Andru
George Bell

Orig. Retail	Price Paid	Value
12¢		$75

#37
We, The Jury

October 1967

Roy Thomas
Ross Andru
Don Heck

Orig. Retail	Price Paid	Value
12¢		$70

Value Guide — X-Men® (1963-1981)

COLLECTOR'S VALUE GUIDE™

Page Totals:	Price Paid	Total Value

Collector's Value Guide™ — X-Men®

#38
The Sinister Shadow Of Doomsday!

November 1967

Roy Thomas
Don Heck
George Bell

Orig. Retail	Price Paid	Value
12¢		$80

#39
The Fateful Finale

December 1967

Roy Thomas
Don Heck
Vince Colletta

Orig. Retail	Price Paid	Value
12¢		$70

#40
The Mark Of The Monster

January 1968

Roy Thomas
Don Heck
George Tuska

Orig. Retail	Price Paid	Value
12¢		$70

#41
Now Strikes The Sub-Human

February 1968

Roy Thomas
Don Heck
George Tuska

Orig. Retail	Price Paid	Value
12¢		$65

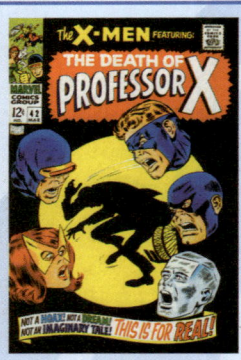

#42
If I Should Die

March 1968

Roy Thomas
Don Heck
George Tuska

Orig. Retail	Price Paid	Value
12¢		$65

#43
The Torch Is Passed

April 1968

Roy Thomas
George Tuska
John Tartaglione

Orig. Retail	Price Paid	Value
12¢		$65

Page Totals: Price Paid __ Total Value __

COLLECTOR'S VALUE GUIDE™

Collector's Value Guide™ — X-Men®

#44
Red Raven, Red Raven

May 1968

Roy Thomas
Don Heck/Werner Roth
John Tartaglione

Orig. Retail	Price Paid	Value
12¢		$65

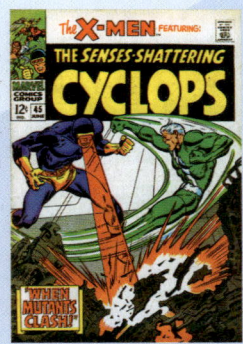

#45
When Mutants Clash

June 1968

Gary Friedrich
Don Heck/Werner Roth
John Tartaglione

Orig. Retail	Price Paid	Value
12¢		$65

#46
The End Of The X-Men

July 1968

Gary Friedrich
Don Heck/Werner Roth
John Tartaglione

Orig. Retail	Price Paid	Value
12¢		$65

#47
The Warlock Wears
Three Faces

August 1968

Gary Friedrich/Arnold Drake
Don Heck/Werner Roth
John Tartaglione

Orig. Retail	Price Paid	Value
12¢		$65

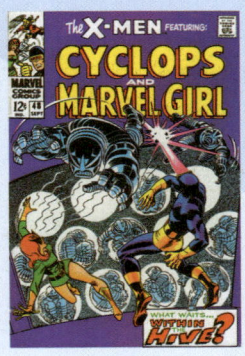

#48
Beware Computo,
Commander Of The
Robot Hive

September 1968

Arnold Drake
Don Heck/Werner Roth
John Verpoorten

Orig. Retail	Price Paid	Value
12¢		$65

#49
Who Dares Defy
The Demi-Men?

October 1968

Arnold Drake
Don Heck/Werner Roth
John Tartaglione

Orig. Retail	Price Paid	Value
12¢		$65

Page Totals:	Price Paid	Total Value

Collector's Value Guide™ — X-Men®

#50
City Of Mutants

November 1968

Arnold Drake
Jim Steranko
John Tartaglione

Orig. Retail	Price Paid	Value
12¢		$65

#51
The Devil Had A Daughter

December 1968

Arnold Drake
Jim Steranko
John Tartaglione

Orig. Retail	Price Paid	Value
12¢		$65

#52
The Twilight Of The Mutants

January 1969

Arnold Drake
Don Heck/Werner Roth
John Tartaglione

Orig. Retail	Price Paid	Value
12¢		$55

#53
The Rage Of Blastaar

February 1969

Arnold Drake
Barry Smith
Michael Dee

Orig. Retail	Price Paid	Value
12¢		$75

#54
Wanted: Dead Or Alive – Cyclops

March 1969

Arnold Drake
Don Heck/Werner Roth
Vince Colletta

Orig. Retail	Price Paid	Value
12¢		$75

#55
The Living Pharaoh

April 1969

Roy Thomas
Don Heck/Werner Roth
Vince Colletta

Orig. Retail	Price Paid	Value
12¢		$70

Page Totals: Price Paid | Total Value

COLLECTOR'S VALUE GUIDE™

Collector's Value Guide™ — X-Men®

#56
What Is The Power?

May 1969

Roy Thomas
Neal Adams
Tom Palmer

Orig. Retail	Price Paid	Value
12¢		$65

#57
The Sentinels Live

June 1969

Roy Thomas
Neal Adams
Tom Palmer

Orig. Retail	Price Paid	Value
12¢		$65

#58
Mission: Murder

July 1969

Roy Thomas
Neal Adams
Tom Palmer

Orig. Retail	Price Paid	Value
15¢		$95

#59
Do Or Die, Baby

August 1969

Roy Thomas/Chris Claremont
Neal Adams
Tom Palmer

Orig. Retail	Price Paid	Value
15¢		$65

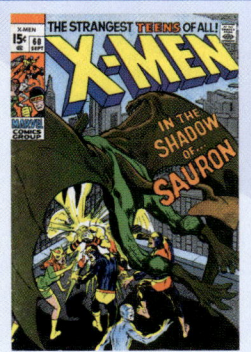

#60
In The Shadow Of Sauron

September 1969

Roy Thomas
Neal Adams
Tom Palmer

Orig. Retail	Price Paid	Value
15¢		$65

#61
Monsters Also Weep

October 1969

Roy Thomas
Neal Adams
Tom Palmer

Orig. Retail	Price Paid	Value
15¢		$60

COLLECTOR'S VALUE GUIDE™

Page Totals:	Price Paid	Total Value

Value Guide — X-Men® (1963-1981)

Collector's Value Guide™ — X-Men®

#62
Strangers In A Savage Land

November 1969

Roy Thomas
Neal Adams
Tom Palmer

Orig. Retail	Price Paid	Value
15¢		$60

#63
War In The World Below

December 1969

Roy Thomas
Neal Adams
Tom Palmer

Orig. Retail	Price Paid	Value
15¢		$60

#64
The Coming Of Sunfire

January 1970

Roy Thomas
Don Heck
Tom Palmer

Orig. Retail	Price Paid	Value
15¢		$60

#65
Before I'd Be Slave

February 1970

Dennis O'Neil
Neal Adams
Tom Palmer

Orig. Retail	Price Paid	Value
15¢		$60

#66
The Mutants And The Monster

March 1970

Roy Thomas
Sal Buscema
Sam Grainger

Orig. Retail	Price Paid	Value
15¢		$60

#67
Reprint of *X-Men* #12 and #13

December 1970

Various
Various
Various

Orig. Retail	Price Paid	Value
25¢		$35

Page Totals:	Price Paid	Total Value

COLLECTOR'S VALUE GUIDE™

Collector's Value Guide™ — X-Men®

#68
Reprint of *X-Men* #14 and #15

February 1971

Various
Various
Various

Orig. Retail	Price Paid	Value
25¢		$35

#69
Reprint of *X-Men* #16 and #19

April 1971

Various
Various
Various

Orig. Retail	Price Paid	Value
25¢		$45

#70
Reprint of *X-Men* #17 and #18

June 1971

Various
Various
Various

Orig. Retail	Price Paid	Value
25¢		$45

#71
Reprint of *X-Men* #20

August 1971

Roy Thomas
Jay Gavin
Dick Ayers

Orig. Retail	Price Paid	Value
15¢		$35

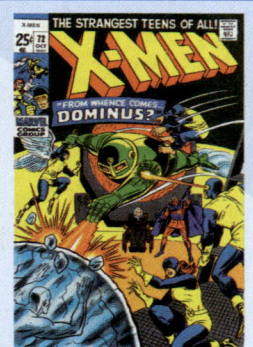

#72
Reprint of *X-Men* #21 and #24

October 1971

Various
Various
Various

Orig. Retail	Price Paid	Value
25¢		$35

#73
Reprint of *X-Men* #25

December 1971

Roy Thomas
Werner Roth
Dick Ayers

Orig. Retail	Price Paid	Value
20¢		$32

Value Guide — X-Men® (1963-1981)

COLLECTOR'S VALUE GUIDE™

Page Totals:	Price Paid	Total Value

Collector's Value Guide™ — X-Men®

#74
Reprint of *X-Men* #26

February 1972

Roy Thomas
Werner Roth
Dick Ayers

Orig. Retail	Price Paid	Value
20¢		$32

#75
Reprint of *X-Men* #27

April 1972

Roy Thomas
Werner Roth
Dick Ayers

Orig. Retail	Price Paid	Value
20¢		$32

#76
Reprint of *X-Men* #28

June 1972

Roy Thomas
Werner Roth
Dick Ayers

Orig. Retail	Price Paid	Value
20¢		$32

#77
Reprint of *X-Men* #29

August 1972

Roy Thomas
Werner Roth
John Tartaglione

Orig. Retail	Price Paid	Value
20¢		$32

#78
Reprint of *X-Men* #30

October 1972

Roy Thomas
Jack Sparling
John Tartaglione

Orig. Retail	Price Paid	Value
20¢		$32

#79
Reprint of *X-Men* #31

December 1972

Roy Thomas
Werner Roth
John Tartaglione

Orig. Retail	Price Paid	Value
20¢		$32

Page Totals:	Price Paid	Total Value

COLLECTOR'S VALUE GUIDE™

Collector's Value Guide™ — X-Men®

#80
Reprint of *X-Men* #32

February 1973
Roy Thomas
Werner Roth
John Tartaglione

Orig. Retail	Price Paid	Value
20¢		$32

#81
Reprint of *X-Men* #33

April 1973
Roy Thomas
Werner Roth
John Tartaglione

Orig. Retail	Price Paid	Value
20¢		$32

#82
Reprint of *X-Men* #34

June 1973
Roy Thomas
Dan Adkins
Dan Adkins

Orig. Retail	Price Paid	Value
20¢		$32

#83
Reprint of *X-Men* #35

August 1973
Roy Thomas
Werner Roth
Dan Adkins

Orig. Retail	Price Paid	Value
20¢		$32

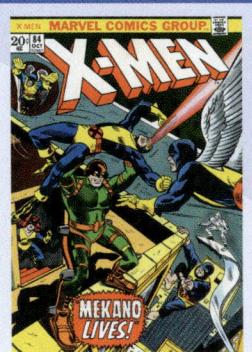

#84
Reprint of *X-Men* #36

October 1973
Roy Thomas
Ross Andru
George Bell

Orig. Retail	Price Paid	Value
20¢		$32

#85
Reprint of *X-Men* #37

December 1973
Roy Thomas
Ross Andru
Don Heck

Orig. Retail	Price Paid	Value
20¢		$32

Value Guide — X-Men® (1963-1981)

	Price Paid	Total Value
Page Totals:		

Collector's Value Guide™ — X-Men®

#86
Reprint of *X-Men* #38 and *Amazing Adult Fantasy* #2
February 1974
Various
Various
Various

Orig. Retail	Price Paid	Value
20¢		$32

#87
Reprint of *X-Men* #39 and *Amazing Adult Fantasy* #10
April 1974
Various
Various
Various

Orig. Retail	Price Paid	Value
20¢		$32

#88
Reprint of *X-Men* #40
June 1974
Roy Thomas
Don Heck
George Tuska

Orig. Retail	Price Paid	Value
25¢		$32

#89
Reprint of *X-Men* #41 and *Amazing Adult Fantasy* #11
August 1974
Various
Various
Various

Orig. Retail	Price Paid	Value
25¢		$32

#90
Reprint of *X-Men* #42 and *Amazing Adult Fantasy* #7
October 1974
Various
Various
Various

Orig. Retail	Price Paid	Value
25¢		$32

#91
Reprint of *X-Men* #43 and *Amazing Adult Fantasy* #7
December 1974
Various
Various
Various

Orig. Retail	Price Paid	Value
25¢		$30

Page Totals: Price Paid | Total Value

COLLECTOR'S VALUE GUIDE™

Collector's Value Guide™ — X-Men®

#92
Reissue of *X-Men* #44 and *Mystery Tales* #30

February 1975
Various
Various
Various

Orig. Retail	Price Paid	Value
25¢		$30

#93
Reissue of *X-Men* #45 and *Journey Into Mystery* #74

April 1975
Various
Various
Various

Orig. Retail	Price Paid	Value
25¢		$30

#94
The Doomsmith Scenario!

August 1975
Len Wein/Chris Claremont
Dave Cockrum
Bob McCleod

Orig. Retail	Price Paid	Value
25¢		$490

#95
Warhunt!

October 1975
Len Wein/Chris Claremont
Dave Cockrum
Sam Grainger

Orig. Retail	Price Paid	Value
25¢		$115

#96
Night Of The Demon!

December 1975
Chris Claremont/Bill Mantlo
Dave Cockrum
Sam Grainger

Orig. Retail	Price Paid	Value
25¢		$80

#97
My Brother, My Enemy!

February 1976
Chris Claremont
Dave Cockrum
Sam Grainger

Orig. Retail	Price Paid	Value
25¢		$75

COLLECTOR'S VALUE GUIDE™

Page Totals:	Price Paid	Total Value

Collector's Value Guide™ — X-Men®

#98
Merry Christmas, X-Men . . .

April 1976

Chris Claremont
Dave Cockrum
Sam Grainger

Orig. Retail	Price Paid	Value
25¢		$75

#99
Deathstar, Rising!

June 1976

Chris Claremont
Dave Cockrum
Frank Chiaramonte

Orig. Retail	Price Paid	Value
25¢		$75

#100
Greater Love Hath No X-Man . . .

August 1976

Chris Claremont
Dave Cockrum
Dave Cockrum

Orig. Retail	Price Paid	Value
25¢		$85

#101
Like A Phoenix, From The Ashes!

October 1976

Chris Claremont
Dave Cockrum
Frank Chiaramonte

Orig. Retail	Price Paid	Value
30¢		$70

#102
Who Will Stop The Juggernaut?

December 1976

Chris Claremont
Dave Cockrum
Sam Grainger

Orig. Retail	Price Paid	Value
30¢		$37

#103
The Fall Of The Tower

February 1977

Chris Claremont
Dave Cockrum
Sam Grainger

Orig. Retail	Price Paid	Value
30¢		$37

Page Totals:

Price Paid	Total Value

COLLECTOR'S VALUE GUIDE™

Collector's Value Guide™ — X-Men®

#104
The Gentleman's Name Is Magneto

April 1977

Chris Claremont
Dave Cockrum
Sam Grainger

Orig. Retail	Price Paid	Value
30¢		$37

#105
Phoenix Unleashed!

June 1977

Chris Claremont
Dave Cockrum
Bob Layton

Orig. Retail	Price Paid	Value
30¢		$37

#106
Dark Shroud Of The Past!

August 1977

Bill Mantlo/Chris Claremont
Bob Brown/Dave Cockrum
Tom Sutton

Orig. Retail	Price Paid	Value
30¢		$37

#107
Where No X-Man Has Gone Before!

October 1977

Chris Claremont
Dave Cockrum
Dan Green

Orig. Retail	Price Paid	Value
30¢		$37

#108
Armageddon Now!

December 1977

Chris Claremont
John Byrne
Terry Austin

Orig. Retail	Price Paid	Value
35¢		$70

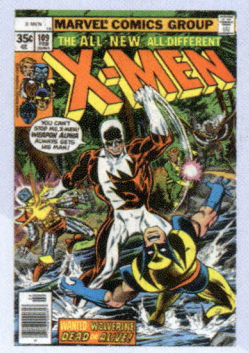

#109
Home Are The Heroes!

February 1978

Chris Claremont
John Byrne
Terry Austin

Orig. Retail	Price Paid	Value
35¢		$50

COLLECTOR'S VALUE GUIDE™

Page Totals:	Price Paid	Total Value

Collector's Value Guide™ — X-Men®

#110
The "X" - Sanction!

April 1978

Chris Claremont
T. DeZuniga/D. Cockrum
Tony DeZuniga

Orig. Retail	Price Paid	Value
35¢		$37

#111
Mindgames!

June 1978

Chris Claremont
John Byrne
Terry Austin

Orig. Retail	Price Paid	Value
35¢		$35

#112
Magneto Triumphant!

August 1978

Chris Claremont
John Byrne
Terry Austin

Orig. Retail	Price Paid	Value
35¢		$32

#113
Showdown!

September 1978

Chris Claremont/John Byrne
John Byrne
Terry Austin

Orig. Retail	Price Paid	Value
35¢		$32

#114
Desolation

October 1978

Chris Claremont/John Byrne
John Byrne
Terry Austin

Orig. Retail	Price Paid	Value
35¢		$32

#115
Visions Of Death!

November 1978

Chris Claremont/John Byrne
John Byrne
Terry Austin

Orig. Retail	Price Paid	Value
35¢		$32

Page Totals:	Price Paid	Total Value

COLLECTOR'S VALUE GUIDE™

Collector's Value Guide™ — X-Men®

#116
To Save The
Savage Land

December 1978

Chris Claremont/John Byrne
John Byrne
Terry Austin

Orig. Retail	Price Paid	Value
35¢		$32

#117
Psi War

January 1979

Chris Claremont/John Byrne
John Byrne
Terry Austin

Orig. Retail	Price Paid	Value
35¢		$37

#118
The Submergence
Of Japan!

February 1979

Chris Claremont/John Byrne
John Byrne
Ric Villamonte

Orig. Retail	Price Paid	Value
35¢		$32

#119
'Twas The Night Before
Christmas . . .

March 1979

Chris Claremont/John Byrne
John Byrne
Terry Austin

Orig. Retail	Price Paid	Value
35¢		$32

#120
Wanted: Wolverine!
Dead Or Alive!

April 1979

Chris Claremont/John Byrne
John Byrne
Terry Austin

Orig. Retail	Price Paid	Value
35¢		$55

#121
Shoot-Out At The
Stampede!

May 1979

Chris Claremont/John Byrne
John Byrne
Terry Austin

Orig. Retail	Price Paid	Value
40¢		$60

COLLECTOR'S VALUE GUIDE™

Page Totals:	Price Paid	Total Value

Collector's Value Guide™ — X-Men®

#122
Cry For The Children!

June 1979

Chris Claremont/John Byrne
John Byrne
Terry Austin

Orig. Retail	Price Paid	Value
40¢		$30

#123
Listen – Stop Me If You've Heard It – But This One Will Kill You!

July 1979

Chris Claremont/John Byrne
John Byrne/Terry Austin
Terry Austin

Orig. Retail	Price Paid	Value
40¢		$30

#124
He Only Laughs When I Hurt!

August 1979

Chris Claremont/John Byrne
John Byrne
Terry Austin

Orig. Retail	Price Paid	Value
40¢		$30

#125
There's Something Awful On Muir Island!

September 1979

Chris Claremont
John Byrne
Terry Austin

Orig. Retail	Price Paid	Value
40¢		$30

#126
How Sharper Than A Serpent's Tooth . . . !

October 1979

Chris Claremont
John Byrne
Terry Austin

Orig. Retail	Price Paid	Value
40¢		$30

#127
The Quality Of Hatred!

November 1979

Chris Claremont/John Byrne
John Byrne
Terry Austin

Orig. Retail	Price Paid	Value
40¢		$30

Page Totals:	Price Paid	Total Value

COLLECTOR'S VALUE GUIDE™

Collector's Value Guide™ — X-Men®

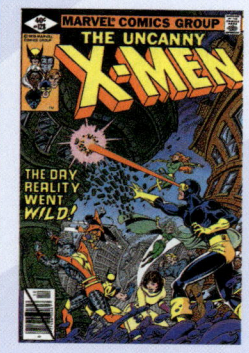

#128
The Action Of The Tiger!

December 1979

Chris Claremont/John Byrne
John Byrne
Terry Austin

Orig. Retail	Price Paid	Value
40¢		$30

#129
God Spare The Child . . .

January 1980

Chris Claremont/John Byrne
John Byrne
Terry Austin

Orig. Retail	Price Paid	Value
40¢		$40

#130
Dazzler

February 1980

Chris Claremont/John Byrne
John Byrne
Terry Austin

Orig. Retail	Price Paid	Value
40¢		$32

#131
Run For Your Life!

March 1980

Chris Claremont/John Byrne
John Byrne
Terry Austin

Orig. Retail	Price Paid	Value
40¢		$28

#132
And Hellfire Is Their Name!

April 1980

Chris Claremont/John Byrne
John Byrne
Terry Austin

Orig. Retail	Price Paid	Value
40¢		$28

#133
Wolverine: Alone

May 1980

Chris Claremont/John Byrne
John Byrne
Terry Austin

Orig. Retail	Price Paid	Value
40¢		$28

Value Guide — X-Men® (1963-1981)

COLLECTOR'S VALUE GUIDE™

Page Totals:	Price Paid	Total Value

Collector's Value Guide™ — X-Men®

#134
Too Late, The Heroes!

June 1980

Chris Claremont/John Byrne
John Byrne
Terry Austin

Orig. Retail	Price Paid	Value
40¢		$28

#135
Dark Phoenix

July 1980

Chris Claremont/John Byrne
John Byrne
Terry Austin

Orig. Retail	Price Paid	Value
40¢		$28

#136
Child Of Light And Darkness!

August 1980

Chris Claremont/John Byrne
John Byrne
Terry Austin

Orig. Retail	Price Paid	Value
40¢		$26

#137
The Fate Of The Phoenix

September 1980

Chris Claremont/John Byrne
John Byrne
Terry Austin

Orig. Retail	Price Paid	Value
75¢		$28

#138
Elegy

October 1980

Chris Claremont/John Byrne
John Byrne
Terry Austin

Orig. Retail	Price Paid	Value
50¢		$23

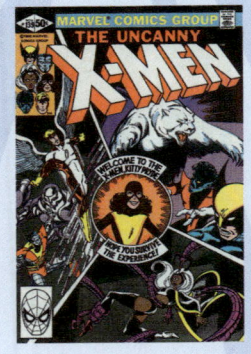

#139
...Something Wicked This Way Comes!

November 1980

Chris Claremont/John Byrne
John Byrne
Terry Austin

Orig. Retail	Price Paid	Value
50¢		$35

Page Totals:	Price Paid	Total Value

COLLECTOR'S VALUE GUIDE™

Collector's Value Guide™ — X-Men®

#140
Rage!

December 1980
Chris Claremont/John Byrne
John Byrne
Terry Austin

Orig. Retail	Price Paid	Value
50¢		$32

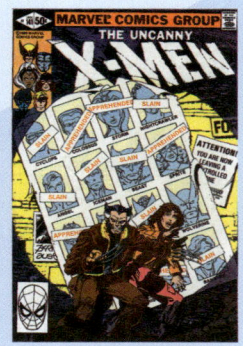

#141
Days Of Future Past

January 1981
Chris Claremont/John Byrne
John Byrne
Terry Austin

Orig. Retail	Price Paid	Value
50¢		$35

#142
Mind Out Of Time!

February 1981
Chris Claremont/John Byrne
John Byrne
Terry Austin

Orig. Retail	Price Paid	Value
50¢		$30

#143
Demon

March 1981
Chris Claremont/John Byrne
John Byrne
Terry Austin

Orig. Retail	Price Paid	Value
50¢		$11

#144
Even In Death . . .

April 1981
Chris Claremont
Brent Anderson
Josef Rubinstein

Orig. Retail	Price Paid	Value
50¢		$7

#145
Kidnapped!

May 1981
Chris Claremont
Dave Cockrum
Josef Rubinstein

Orig. Retail	Price Paid	Value
50¢		$7

Value Guide — Uncanny X-Men® (1981-Present)

COLLECTOR'S VALUE GUIDE™

Page Totals:	Price Paid	Total Value

Collector's Value Guide™ — X-Men®

#146
Murderworld!

June 1981
Chris Claremont
Dave Cockrum
Josef Rubinstein

Orig. Retail	Price Paid	Value
50¢		$7

#147
Rogue Storm!

July 1981
Chris Claremont
Dave Cockrum
Josef Rubinstein

Orig. Retail	Price Paid	Value
50¢		$7

#148
Cry, Mutant!

August 1981
Chris Claremont
Dave Cockrum
Josef Rubinstein

Orig. Retail	Price Paid	Value
50¢		$7

#149
And The Dead Shall Bury The Living!

September 1981
Chris Claremont
Dave Cockrum
Josef Rubinstein

Orig. Retail	Price Paid	Value
50¢		$7

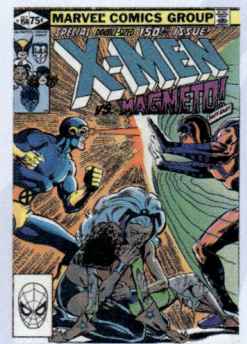

#150
I, Magneto . . .

October 1981
Chris Claremont
Dave Cockrum
J. Rubinstein/B. Wiacek

Orig. Retail	Price Paid	Value
75¢		$9

#151
X-Men Minus One!

November 1981
Chris Claremont
Jim Sherman/Bob McLeod
Josef Rubinstein

Orig. Retail	Price Paid	Value
50¢		$5.50

Page Totals:

Price Paid	Total Value

COLLECTOR'S VALUE GUIDE™

Collector's Value Guide™ — X-Men®

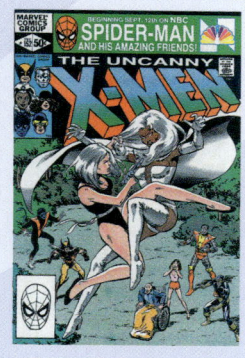

#152
The Hellfire Gambit

December 1981

Chris Claremont
Bob McLeod
Josef Rubinstein

Orig. Retail	Price Paid	Value
50¢		$5.50

#153
Kitty's Fairy Tale

January 1982

Chris Claremont
Dave Cockrum
Josef Rubinstein

Orig. Retail	Price Paid	Value
60¢		$5.50

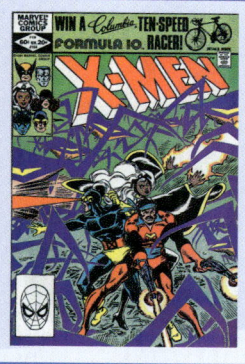

#154
Reunion

February 1982

Chris Claremont
Dave Cockrum
B. Wiacek/J. Rubinstein

Orig. Retail	Price Paid	Value
60¢		$5.50

#155
First Blood

March 1982

Chris Claremont
Dave Cockrum
Bob Wiacek

Orig. Retail	Price Paid	Value
60¢		$5.50

#156
Pursuit

April 1982

Chris Claremont
Dave Cockrum
Bob Wiacek

Orig. Retail	Price Paid	Value
60¢		$5.50

#157
Hide - 'N' - Seek

May 1982

Chris Claremont
Dave Cockrum
Bob Wiacek

Orig. Retail	Price Paid	Value
60¢		$5.50

Page Totals: | Price Paid | Total Value |

Collector's Value Guide™ — X-Men®

#158
The Life That Late I Led . . .

June 1982

Chris Claremont
Dave Cockrum
Bob Wiacek

Orig. Retail	Price Paid	Value
60¢		$9

#159
Night Screams!

July 1982

Chris Claremont
Bill Sienkiewicz
Bob Wiacek

Orig. Retail	Price Paid	Value
60¢		$5.50

#160
Chutes And Ladders!

August 1982

Chris Claremont
Brent Anderson
Bob Wiacek

Orig. Retail	Price Paid	Value
60¢		$5.50

#161
Gold Rush

September 1982

Chris Claremont
Dave Cockrum
Bob Wiacek

Orig. Retail	Price Paid	Value
60¢		$5.50

#162
Beyond The Farthest Star

October 1982

Chris Claremont
Dave Cockrum
Bob Wiacek

Orig. Retail	Price Paid	Value
60¢		$9

#163
Rescue Mission

November 1982

Chris Claremont
Dave Cockrum
Bob Wiacek

Orig. Retail	Price Paid	Value
60¢		$5.50

Page Totals: Price Paid / Total Value

COLLECTOR'S VALUE GUIDE™

Collector's Value Guide™ — X-Men®

#164
Binary Star!

December 1982
Chris Claremont
Dave Cockrum
Bob Wiacek

Orig. Retail	Price Paid	Value
60¢		$6.25

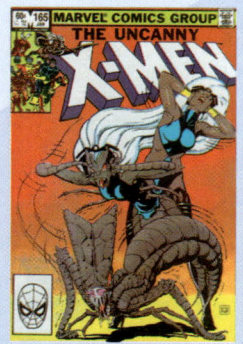

#165
Transfigurations

January 1983
Chris Claremont
Paul Smith
Bob Wiacek

Orig. Retail	Price Paid	Value
60¢		$5.25

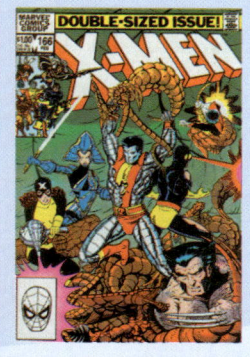

#166
Live Free Or Die!

February 1983
Chris Claremont
Paul Smith
Bob Wiacek

Orig. Retail	Price Paid	Value
$1		$5.25

#167
The Goldilocks
Syndrome

March 1983
Chris Claremont
Paul Smith
Bob Wiacek

Orig. Retail	Price Paid	Value
60¢		$4.25

#168
Professor Xavier
Is A Jerk!

April 1983
Chris Claremont
Paul Smith
Bob Wiacek

Orig. Retail	Price Paid	Value
60¢		$5.25

#169
Catacombs

May 1983
Chris Claremont
Paul Smith
Bob Wiacek

Orig. Retail	Price Paid	Value
60¢		$5.25

Value Guide — Uncanny X-Men® (1981-Present)

COLLECTOR'S
VALUE GUIDE™

Page Totals:	Price Paid	Total Value

Collector's Value Guide™ — X-Men®

#170
Dancin' In The Dark

June 1983
Chris Claremont
Paul Smith
Bob Wiacek

Orig. Retail	Price Paid	Value
60¢		$4.25

#171
Rogue

July 1983
Chris Claremont
Walt Simonson
Bob Wiacek

Orig. Retail	Price Paid	Value
60¢		$8.25

#172
Scarlet In Glory

August 1983
Chris Claremont
Paul Smith
Bob Wiacek

Orig. Retail	Price Paid	Value
60¢		$5.25

#173
To Have And Have Not

September 1983
Chris Claremont
Paul Smith
Bob Wiacek

Orig. Retail	Price Paid	Value
60¢		$4.25

#174
Romances

October 1983
Chris Claremont
Paul Smith
Bob Wiacek

Orig. Retail	Price Paid	Value
60¢		$4.25

#175
Phoenix

November 1983
Chris Claremont
Paul Smith/John Romita, Jr.
Bob Wiacek/Paul Smith

Orig. Retail	Price Paid	Value
$1		$6.50

Page Totals: Price Paid ___ Total Value ___

COLLECTOR'S VALUE GUIDE™

Collector's Value Guide™ — X-Men®

#176
Decisions

December 1983

Chris Claremont
John Romita, Jr.
Bob Wiacek

Orig. Retail	Price Paid	Value
60¢		$4.25

#177
Sanction

January 1984

Chris Claremont
John Romita, Jr.
John Romita, Sr.

Orig. Retail	Price Paid	Value
60¢		$4.25

#178
Hell Hath No Fury . . .

February 1984

Chris Claremont
John Romita, Jr.
Bob Wiacek/Brett Breeding

Orig. Retail	Price Paid	Value
60¢		$4.25

#179
What Happened To Kitty?

March 1984

Chris Claremont
John Romita, Jr.
Dan Green

Orig. Retail	Price Paid	Value
60¢		$4.25

#180
Whose Life Is It, Anyway?

April 1984

Chris Claremont
John Romita, Jr.
Dan Green/Bob Wiacek

Orig. Retail	Price Paid	Value
60¢		$4.25

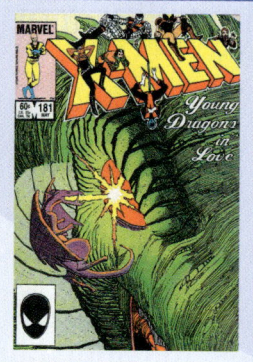

#181
Tokyo Story

May 1984

Chris Claremont
John Romita, Jr.
Dan Green

Orig. Retail	Price Paid	Value
60¢		$4.25

COLLECTOR'S VALUE GUIDE™

	Price Paid	Total Value
Page Totals:		

Value Guide — Uncanny X-Men® (1981-Present)

Collector's Value Guide™ — X-Men®

Value Guide — Uncanny X-Men® (1981-Present)

#182
Madness

June 1984

Chris Claremont
John Romita, Jr.
Dan Green

Orig. Retail	Price Paid	Value
60¢		$4.25

#183
He'll Never Make Me Cry

July 1984

Chris Claremont
John Romita, Jr.
Dan Green

Orig. Retail	Price Paid	Value
60¢		$4.25

#184
The Past... Of Future Days

August 1984

Chris Claremont
John Romita, Jr.
Dan Green

Orig. Retail	Price Paid	Value
60¢		$6.25

#185
Public Enemy!

September 1984

Chris Claremont
John Romita, Jr.
Dan Green

Orig. Retail	Price Paid	Value
60¢		$4.25

#186
Lifedeath

October 1984

Chris Claremont
Barry Windsor-Smith
Terry Austin

Orig. Retail	Price Paid	Value
$1		$5.25

#187
Wraithkill!

November 1984

Chris Claremont
John Romita, Jr.
Dan Green

Orig. Retail	Price Paid	Value
60¢		$4.25

Page Totals:	Price Paid	Total Value

COLLECTOR'S VALUE GUIDE™

Collector's Value Guide™ — X-Men®

#188
Legacy Of The Lost

December 1984

Chris Claremont
John Romita, Jr.
Dan Green

Orig. Retail	Price Paid	Value
60¢		$4.25

#189
Two Girls Out To Have Fun

January 1985

Chris Claremont
John Romita, Jr.
Steve Leialoha

Orig. Retail	Price Paid	Value
60¢		$4.25

#190
An Age Undreamed Of

February 1985

Chris Claremont
John Romita, Jr.
Dan Green

Orig. Retail	Price Paid	Value
60¢		$4.25

#191
Raiders Of The Lost Temple!

March 1985

Chris Claremont
John Romita, Jr.
Dan Green

Orig. Retail	Price Paid	Value
60¢		$4.25

#192
Fun 'N' Games

April 1985

Chris Claremont
John Romita, Jr.
Dan Green

Orig. Retail	Price Paid	Value
65¢		$4.25

#193
Warhunt 2

May 1985

Chris Claremont
John Romita, Jr.
Dan Green

Orig. Retail	Price Paid	Value
$1.25		$7.50

COLLECTOR'S VALUE GUIDE™

Page Totals:	Price Paid	Total Value

Collector's Value Guide™ — X-Men®

#194
Juggernaut's Back In Town!

June 1985

Chris Claremont
John Romita, Jr.
Dan Green/Steve Leialoha

Orig. Retail	Price Paid	Value
65¢		$4.25

#195
It Was A Dark And Stormy Night . . . !

July 1985

Chris Claremont
John Romita, Jr.
Dan Green

Orig. Retail	Price Paid	Value
65¢		$4.25

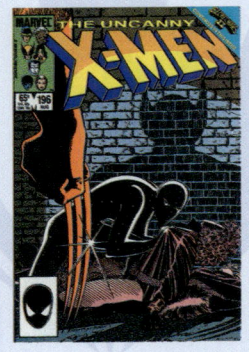

#196
What Was That?!!

August 1985

Chris Claremont
John Romita, Jr.
Dan Green

Orig. Retail	Price Paid	Value
65¢		$4.25

#197
To Save Arcade?!?

September 1985

Chris Claremont
John Romita, Jr.
Dan Green

Orig. Retail	Price Paid	Value
65¢		$4.25

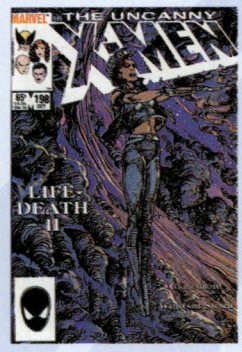

#198
Lifedeath: From The Heart Of Darkness

October 1985

Chris Claremont
Barry Windsor-Smith
Barry Windsor-Smith

Orig. Retail	Price Paid	Value
65¢		$4.25

#199
The Spiral Path

November 1985

Chris Claremont
John Romita, Jr.
Dan Green

Orig. Retail	Price Paid	Value
65¢		$4.25

Page Totals:	Price Paid	Total Value

Collector's Value Guide™ — X-Men®

#200
The Trial Of Magneto

December 1985

Chris Claremont
John Romita, Jr.
Dan Green

Orig. Retail	Price Paid	Value
$1.25		$8

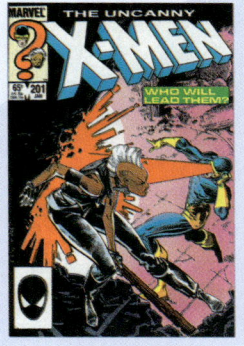

#201
Duel

January 1986

Chris Claremont
Rick Leonardi
Whilce Portacio

Orig. Retail	Price Paid	Value
65¢		$10

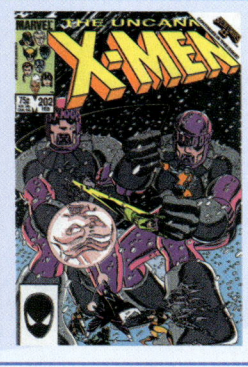

#202
X-Men . . . I've Gone To Kill – The Beyonder!

February 1986

Chris Claremont
John Romita, Jr.
Al Williamson

Orig. Retail	Price Paid	Value
75¢		$4.25

#203
Crossroads

March 1986

Chris Claremont
John Romita, Jr.
Al Williamson

Orig. Retail	Price Paid	Value
75¢		$4.25

#204
What Happened To Nightcrawler?

April 1986

Chris Claremont
June Brigman
Whilce Portacio

Orig. Retail	Price Paid	Value
75¢		$4.25

#205
Wounded Wolf

May 1986

Chris Claremont
Barry Windsor-Smith
Barry Windsor-Smith

Orig. Retail	Price Paid	Value
75¢		$11

COLLECTOR'S VALUE GUIDE™

	Price Paid	Total Value
Page Totals:		

Collector's Value Guide™ — X-Men®

#206
Freedom Is A Four Letter Word!

June 1986

Chris Claremont
John Romita, Jr.
Dan Green

Orig. Retail	Price Paid	Value
75¢		$4.25

#207
Ghosts

July 1986

Chris Claremont
John Romita, Jr.
Dan Green

Orig. Retail	Price Paid	Value
75¢		$5.25

#208
Retribution

August 1986

Chris Claremont
John Romita, Jr.
Dan Green

Orig. Retail	Price Paid	Value
75¢		$4.25

#209
Salvation

September 1986

Chris Claremont
John Romita, Jr.
P. Craig Russell

Orig. Retail	Price Paid	Value
75¢		$4.25

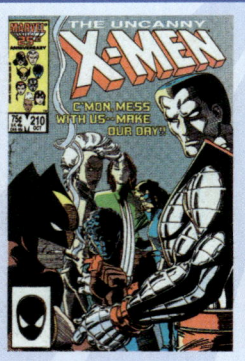

#210
The Morning After

October 1986

Chris Claremont
John Romita, Jr.
Dan Green

Orig. Retail	Price Paid	Value
75¢		$10

#211
Massacre

November 1986

Chris Claremont
John Romita, Jr./Bret Blevins
Al Williamson

Orig. Retail	Price Paid	Value
75¢		$10

Page Totals: Price Paid ___ Total Value ___

COLLECTOR'S VALUE GUIDE™

Collector's Value Guide™ — X-Men®

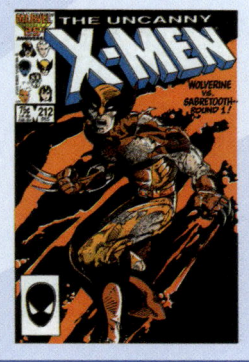

#212
The Last Run

December 1986
Chris Claremont
Rick Leonardi
Dan Green

Orig. Retail	Price Paid	Value
75¢		$12

#213
Psylocke

January 1987
Chris Claremont
Alan Davis
Paul Neary

Orig. Retail	Price Paid	Value
75¢		$13

#214
With Malice Toward All!

February 1987
Chris Claremont
Barry Windsor-Smith
Bob Wiacek

Orig. Retail	Price Paid	Value
75¢		$4.25

#215
Old Soldiers

March 1987
Chris Claremont
Alan Davis
Dan Green

Orig. Retail	Price Paid	Value
75¢		$4.25

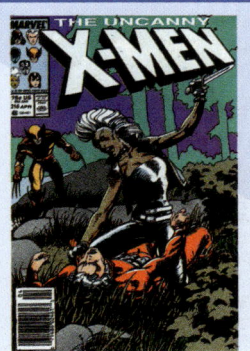

#216
Crucible

April 1987
Chris Claremont
Jackson Guice
Dan Green

Orig. Retail	Price Paid	Value
75¢		$4.25

#217
Folly's Gambit

May 1987
Chris Claremont
Jackson Guice
Steve Leialoha

Orig. Retail	Price Paid	Value
75¢		$4.25

Value Guide — Uncanny X-Men® (1981-Present)

Page Totals:	Price Paid	Total Value

Collector's Value Guide™ — X-Men®

#218
Charge Of The Light Brigade

June 1987

Chris Claremont
Marc Silvestri
Dan Green

Orig. Retail	Price Paid	Value
75¢		$4.25

#219
Where Duty Lies

July 1987

Chris Claremont
Bret Blevins
Dan Green

Orig. Retail	Price Paid	Value
75¢		$4.25

#220
Unfinished Business

August 1987

Chris Claremont
Marc Silvestri
Dan Green

Orig. Retail	Price Paid	Value
75¢		$4.25

#221
Death By Drowning!

September 1987

Chris Claremont
Marc Silvestri
Dan Green

Orig. Retail	Price Paid	Value
75¢		$6.50

#222
Heartbreak!

October 1987

Chris Claremont
Marc Silvestri
Dan Green

Orig. Retail	Price Paid	Value
75¢		$8

#223
Omens & Portents

November 1987

Chris Claremont
Kerry Gammill
Dan Green

Orig. Retail	Price Paid	Value
75¢		$4.25

Page Totals: | Price Paid | Total Value |

COLLECTOR'S VALUE GUIDE™

Collector's Value Guide™ — X-Men®

#224
The Dark Before The Dawn

December 1987

Chris Claremont
Marc Silvestri
Bob Wiacek

Orig. Retail	Price Paid	Value
75¢		$4.25

#225
False Dawn

January 1988

Chris Claremont
Marc Silvestri
Dan Green

Orig. Retail	Price Paid	Value
75¢		$5

#226
Go Tell The Spartans

February 1988

Chris Claremont
Marc Silvestri
Dan Green

Orig. Retail	Price Paid	Value
$1.25		$5

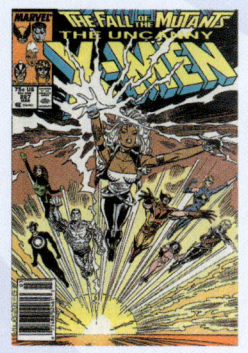

#227
The Belly Of The Beast!

March 1988

Chris Claremont
Marc Silvestri
Dan Green

Orig. Retail	Price Paid	Value
75¢		$5

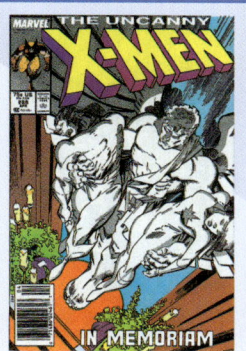

#228
Deadly Games!

April 1988

Chris Claremont
Rick Leonardi
Terry Austin

Orig. Retail	Price Paid	Value
75¢		$4.50

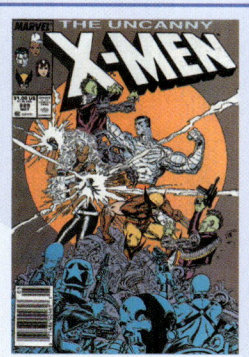

#229
Down Under

May 1988

Chris Claremont
Marc Silvestri
Dan Green

Orig. Retail	Price Paid	Value
$1		$4.50

Page Totals:	Price Paid	Total Value

Collector's Value Guide™ — X-Men®

#230
'Twas The Night . . .

June 1988

Chris Claremont
Marc Silvestri
Joe Rubinstein

Orig. Retail	Price Paid	Value
$1		$4.50

#231
. . . Dressed For Dinner!

July 1988

Chris Claremont
Rick Leonardi
Dan Green

Orig. Retail	Price Paid	Value
$1		$4.50

#232
Earthfall

August 1988

Chris Claremont
Marc Silvestri
Dan Green

Orig. Retail	Price Paid	Value
$1		$4.50

#233
Dawn Of Blood

Early September 1988

Chris Claremont
Marc Silvestri
Dan Green

Orig. Retail	Price Paid	Value
$1		$4.50

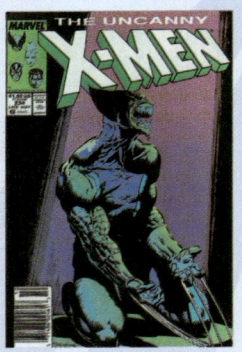

#234
Glory Day

Late September 1988

Chris Claremont
Marc Silvestri
Josef Rubinstein

Orig. Retail	Price Paid	Value
$1		$4.50

#235
Welcome To Genosha

Early October 1988

Chris Claremont
Rick Leonardi
P. Craig Russell

Orig. Retail	Price Paid	Value
$1		$4.50

Page Totals:	Price Paid	Total Value

COLLECTOR'S
VALUE GUIDE™

Collector's Value Guide™ — X-Men®

#236
Busting Loose!

Late October 1988

Chris Claremont
Marc Silvestri
Dan Green

Orig. Retail	Price Paid	Value
$1		$4.50

#237
Who's Human?

Early November 1988

Chris Claremont
Rick Leonardi
Terry Austin

Orig. Retail	Price Paid	Value
$1		$4.50

#238
Gonna Be A Revolution

Late November 1988

Chris Claremont
Marc Silvestri
Dan Green

Orig. Retail	Price Paid	Value
$1		$4.50

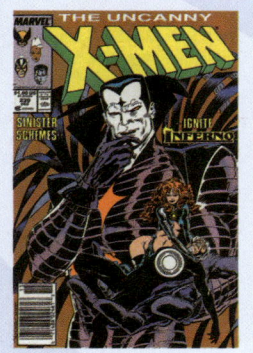

#239
Vanities

December 1988

Chris Claremont
Marc Silvestri
Dan Green

Orig. Retail	Price Paid	Value
$1		$4.50

#240
Strike The Match

January 1989

Chris Claremont
Marc Silvestri
Dan Green

Orig. Retail	Price Paid	Value
$1		$4.50

#241
Fan The Flame

February 1989

Chris Claremont
Marc Silvestri
Dan Green

Orig. Retail	Price Paid	Value
$1		$4.50

COLLECTOR'S VALUE GUIDE™

Page Totals:	Price Paid	Total Value

Collector's Value Guide™ — X-Men®

#242
Burn!

March 1989
Chris Claremont
Marc Silvestri
Dan Green

Orig. Retail	Price Paid	Value
$1.50		$4.50

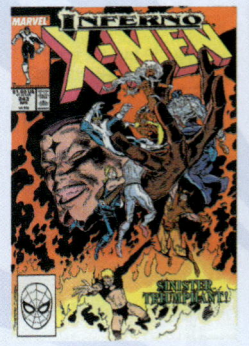

#243
Ashes

April 1989
Chris Claremont
Marc Silvestri
Hilary Barta

Orig. Retail	Price Paid	Value
$1		$4.25

#244
Ladies' Night

May 1989
Chris Claremont
Marc Silvestri
Dan Green

Orig. Retail	Price Paid	Value
$1		$14

#245
Men!

June 1989
Chris Claremont
Rob Liefeld
Dan Green

Orig. Retail	Price Paid	Value
$1		$4.25

#246
The Day Of Other Lights!

July 1989
Chris Claremont
Marc Silvestri
Dan Green

Orig. Retail	Price Paid	Value
$1		$4.25

#247
The Light That Failed

August 1989
Chris Claremont
Marc Silvestri
Dan Green

Orig. Retail	Price Paid	Value
$1		$4.25

Page Totals: Price Paid _____ Total Value _____

COLLECTOR'S VALUE GUIDE™

Collector's Value Guide™ — X-Men®

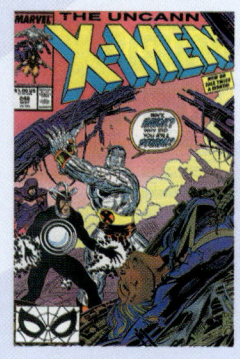

#248
The Cradle Will Fall!

September 1989
Chris Claremont
Jim Lee
Dan Green

Orig. Retail	Price Paid	Value
$1		$13

#248
The Cradle Will Fall!
(2nd Printing)

June 1992
Chris Claremont
Jim Lee
Dan Green

Orig. Retail	Price Paid	Value
$1.25		$1.50

#249
The Dane Curse

Early October 1989
Chris Claremont
Marc Silvestri
Dan Green

Orig. Retail	Price Paid	Value
$1		$4.25

#250
The Shattered Star

Late October 1989
Chris Claremont
Marc Silvestri
Steve Leialoha

Orig. Retail	Price Paid	Value
$1		$4.25

#251
Fever Dream

Early November 1989
Chris Claremont
Marc Silvestri
Dan Green

Orig. Retail	Price Paid	Value
$1		$4.25

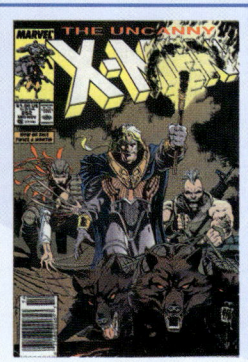

#252
Where's Wolverine?!?

Mid November 1989
Chris Claremont
Rick Leonardi
Kent Williams

Orig. Retail	Price Paid	Value
$1		$4.25

Value Guide — Uncanny X-Men® (1981-Present)

Collector's Value Guide™

Page Totals:	Price Paid	Total Value

Collector's Value Guide™ — X-Men®

#253
Storm Warnings!

Late November 1989

Chris Claremont
Marc Silvestri
Steve Leialoha

Orig. Retail	Price Paid	Value
$1		$4.50

#254
Here We Go Again!

Early December 1989

Chris Claremont
Marc Silvestri
Dan Green

Orig. Retail	Price Paid	Value
$1		$4.50

#255
Crash & Burn

Mid December 1989

Chris Claremont
Marc Silvestri
Dan Green

Orig. Retail	Price Paid	Value
$1		$4.50

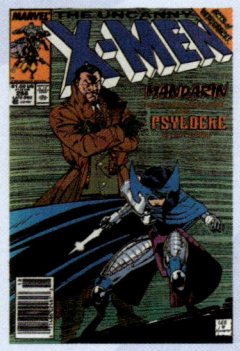

#256
The Key That Breaks The Locke

Late December 1989

Chris Claremont
Jim Lee
Scott Williams

Orig. Retail	Price Paid	Value
$1		$8

#257
I Am Lady Mandarin

January 1990

Chris Claremont
Jim Lee
Josef Rubinstein

Orig. Retail	Price Paid	Value
$1		$8

#258
Broken Chains

February 1990

Chris Claremont
Jim Lee
Scott Williams

Orig. Retail	Price Paid	Value
$1		$8

Page Totals: Price Paid ___ Total Value ___

COLLECTOR'S VALUE GUIDE™

Collector's Value Guide™ — X-Men®

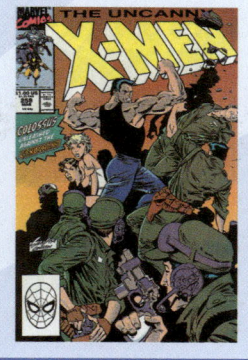

#259
Dream A Little Dream

March 1990
Chris Claremont
Marc Silvestri
Dan Green

Orig. Retail	Price Paid	Value
$1		$5

#260
Star 90

April 1990
Chris Claremont
Marc Silvestri
Dan Green

Orig. Retail	Price Paid	Value
$1		$4.25

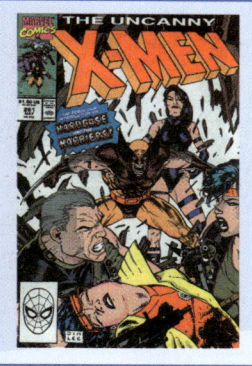

#261
Harriers Hunt

May 1990
Chris Claremont
Marc Silvestri
Dan Green

Orig. Retail	Price Paid	Value
$1		$4.25

#262
Scary Monsters

June 1990
Chris Claremont
Kieron Dwyer
Josef Rubinstein

Orig. Retail	Price Paid	Value
$1		$4.25

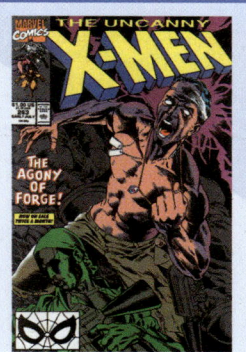

#263
The Lower Depths

Early July 1990
Chris Claremont
Bill Jaaska
Josef Rubinstein

Orig. Retail	Price Paid	Value
$1		$4.25

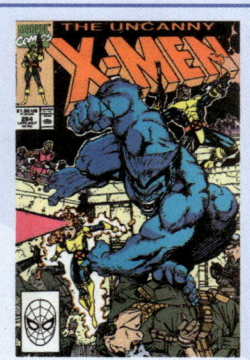

#264
Hot Pursuit

Late July 1990
Chris Claremont
Mike Collins
Josef Rubinstein

Orig. Retail	Price Paid	Value
$1		$4.25

COLLECTOR'S VALUE GUIDE™

	Price Paid	Total Value
Page Totals:		

Value Guide — Uncanny X-Men® (1981-Present)

Collector's Value Guide™ — X-Men®

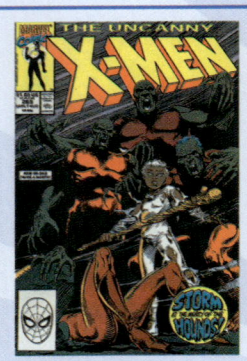

#265
Storm

Early August 1990
Chris Claremont
Bill Jaaska
Joe Rubinstein

Orig. Retail	Price Paid	Value
$1		$4.25

#266
Gambit: Out Of The Frying Pan

Late August 1990
Chris Claremont
Mike Collins
Josef Rubinstein

Orig. Retail	Price Paid	Value
$1		$26

#267
Nanny: Into The Fire

Early September 1990
Chris Claremont
Jim Lee
W. Portacio/S. Williams

Orig. Retail	Price Paid	Value
$1		$14

#268
Madripoor Knights

Late September 1990
Chris Claremont
Jim Lee
Scott Williams

Orig. Retail	Price Paid	Value
$1		$12

#268
Madripoor Knights
(2nd Printing)

Late September 1990
Chris Claremont
Jim Lee
Scott Williams

Orig. Retail	Price Paid	Value
$1		$2.50

#269
Rogue Redux

October 1990
Chris Claremont
Jim Lee
Art Thibert

Orig. Retail	Price Paid	Value
$1		$4.25

Page Totals: Price Paid ___ Total Value ___

COLLECTOR'S VALUE GUIDE™

Collector's Value Guide™ — X-Men®

#270
First Strike

November 1990

Chris Claremont
Jim Lee
Art Thibert/Scott Williams

Orig. Retail	Price Paid	Value
$1		$8

#270
**First Strike
(2nd Printing,
Gold Version)**

November 1990

Chris Claremont
Jim Lee
Art Thibert/Scott Williams

Orig. Retail	Price Paid	Value
$1		$3

#271
Flashpoint!

December 1990

Chris Claremont
Jim Lee
Scott Williams

Orig. Retail	Price Paid	Value
$1		$4.50

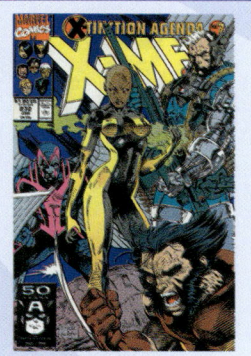

#272
Capital Crimes

January 1991

Chris Claremont
Jim Lee
Scott Williams

Orig. Retail	Price Paid	Value
$1		$4.50

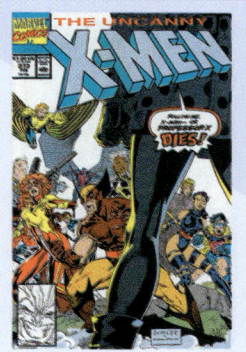

#273
**Too Many Mutants!
Or Whose House Is
This, Anyway?**

February 1991

Chris Claremont
Various
Scott Williams

Orig. Retail	Price Paid	Value
$1		$4.25

#274
Crossroads

March 1991

Chris Claremont
Jim Lee
Scott Williams

Orig. Retail	Price Paid	Value
$1		$4.25

Page Totals: Price Paid _____ Total Value _____

Collector's Value Guide™ — X-Men®

#275
The Path Not Taken!

April 1991

Chris Claremont
Jim Lee
Scott Williams

Orig. Retail	Price Paid	Value
$1.50		$4

#275
The Path Not Taken!
(2nd Printing, Gold Version)

April 1991

Chris Claremont
Jim Lee
Scott Williams

Orig. Retail	Price Paid	Value
N/A		$2.25

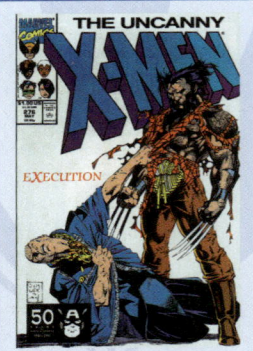

#276
Double Death

May 1991

Chris Claremont
Jim Lee
Scott Williams

Orig. Retail	Price Paid	Value
$1		$3

#277
Free Charley

June 1991

Chris Claremont
Jim Lee
Scott Williams

Orig. Retail	Price Paid	Value
$1		$3

#278
The Battle of Muir Isle

July 1991

Chris Claremont
Paul Smith
Hilary Barta

Orig. Retail	Price Paid	Value
$1		$3

#279
Bad To The Bone

August 1991

C. Claremont/F. Nicieza
Andy Kubert
Scott Williams

Orig. Retail	Price Paid	Value
$1		$3

Page Totals: | Price Paid | Total Value |

COLLECTOR'S VALUE GUIDE™

Collector's Value Guide™ — X-Men®

#280
One Step Back –
Two Steps Forward

September 1991

Fabian Nicieza
Andy Kubert/Steven Butler
Various

Orig. Retail	Price Paid	Value
$1		$3

#281
Fresh Upstart

October 1991

J. Lee/W. Portacio/J. Byrne
Whilce Portacio
Art Thibert

Orig. Retail	Price Paid	Value
$1		$4.25

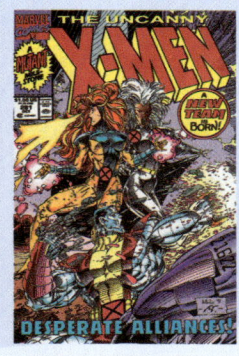

#281
Fresh Upstart
(2nd Printing,
Red Logo)

October 1991

J. Lee/W. Portacio/J. Byrne
Whilce Portacio
Art Thibert

Orig. Retail	Price Paid	Value
$1		$2.25

#282
Payback

November 1991

Whilce Portacio/John Byrne
Whilce Portacio
Art Thibert

Orig. Retail	Price Paid	Value
$1		$8.50

#282
Payback
(2nd Printing)

November 1991

Whilce Portacio/John Byrne
Whilce Portacio
Art Thibert

Orig. Retail	Price Paid	Value
$1		$2.25

#283
Bishop's Crossing

December 1991

Whilce Portacio/John Byrne
Whilce Portacio
Art Thibert

Orig. Retail	Price Paid	Value
$1		$8

COLLECTOR'S VALUE GUIDE™

Page Totals:	Price Paid	Total Value

Value Guide — Uncanny X-Men® (1981-Present)

Collector's Value Guide™ — X-Men®

#284
Into The Void

January 1992

Whilce Portacio/John Byrne
Whilce Portacio
Art Thibert

Orig. Retail	Price Paid	Value
$1		$3.25

#285
Down The Rabbit Hole

February 1992

W. Portacio/J. Byrne/J. Lee
Whilce Portacio
Art Thibert/Al Milgrom

Orig. Retail	Price Paid	Value
$1.25		$3.25

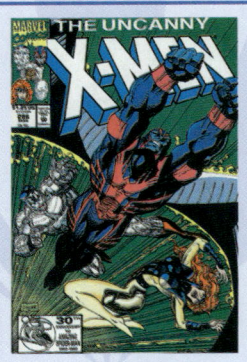

#286
Close Call!

March 1992

J. Lee/W. Portacio/S. Lobdell
Jim Lee/Whilce Portacio
Art Thibert

Orig. Retail	Price Paid	Value
$1.25		$3.25

#287
Bishop To King's Five!

April 1992

Jim Lee/Scott Lobdell
John Romita, Jr.
Various

Orig. Retail	Price Paid	Value
$1.25		$3.50

#288
Time And Place

May 1992

Lee/Portacio/Byrne/Lobdell
Andy Kubert
Bill Sienkiewicz

Orig. Retail	Price Paid	Value
$1.25		$3.25

#289
Knots

June 1992

Scott Lobdell
Whilce Portacio
Scott Williams

Orig. Retail	Price Paid	Value
$1.25		$3.25

Page Totals:	Price Paid	Total Value

COLLECTOR'S
VALUE GUIDE™

Collector's Value Guide™ — X-Men®

#290
Frayed

July 1992

Scott Lobdell
Whilce Portacio
Scott Williams

Orig. Retail	Price Paid	Value
$1.25		$3.25

#291
Underbelly

August 1992

Scott Lobdell
Tom Raney
Hilary Barta

Orig. Retail	Price Paid	Value
$1.25		$3.25

#292
. . . The Morlocks Take Manhattan!

September 1992

Scott Lobdell
Rurik Tyler/Tom Raney
Josef Rubinstein/Al Milgrom

Orig. Retail	Price Paid	Value
$1.25		$3.25

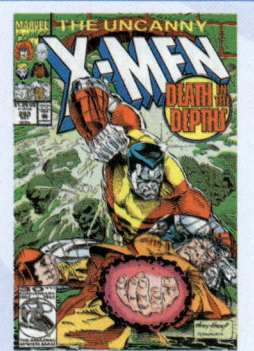

#293
The Last Morlock Story!

October 1992

Scott Lobdell
Rurik Tyler/Tom Raney
Joe Rubinstein

Orig. Retail	Price Paid	Value
$1.25		$3.25

#294
Overture

November 1992

Scott Lobdell
Brandon Peterson
Terry Austin

Orig. Retail	Price Paid	Value
$1.50		$3.25

#295
Familiar Refrain

December 1992

Scott Lobdell
Brandon Peterson
Terry Austin

Orig. Retail	Price Paid	Value
$1.50		$3.25

COLLECTOR'S VALUE GUIDE™

	Price Paid	Total Value
Page Totals:		

Collector's Value Guide™ — X-Men®

#296
Crescendo

January 1993

Scott Lobdell
Brandon Peterson
Terry Austin

Orig. Retail	Price Paid	Value
$1.50		$3.25

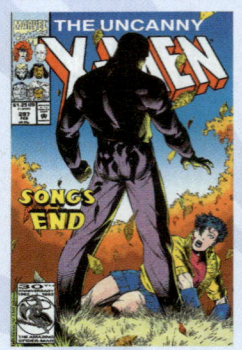

#297
Up And Around

February 1993

Scott Lobdell
Brandon Peterson
Dan Panosian

Orig. Retail	Price Paid	Value
$1.25		$3.25

#298
. . . For The Children!

March 1993

Scott Lobdell
Brandon Peterson
Al Milgrom

Orig. Retail	Price Paid	Value
$1.25		$3.25

#299
Nightlines

April 1993

Scott Lobdell
Brandon Peterson
Dan Panosian

Orig. Retail	Price Paid	Value
$1.25		$3.50

#300
Legacies

May 1993

Scott Lobdell
John Romita, Jr.
Dan Green

Orig. Retail	Price Paid	Value
$3.95		$6

#301
Dominion!

June 1993

Scott Lobdell
John Romita, Jr.
Dan Green

Orig. Retail	Price Paid	Value
$1.25		$3

Page Totals: Price Paid Total Value

COLLECTOR'S
Value Guide™

Collector's Value Guide™ — X-Men®

#302
Province

July 1993

Scott Lobdell
John Romita, Jr.
Dan Green/Dan Panosian

Orig. Retail	Price Paid	Value
$1.25		$3

#303
Going Through
The Motions

August 1993

Scott Lobdell
Richard Bennett
Richard Bennett/Dan Green

Orig. Retail	Price Paid	Value
$1.25		$3

#303
Going Through
The Motions
(Gold Cover)

August 1993

Scott Lobdell
Richard Bennett
Richard Bennett/Dan Green

Orig. Retail	Price Paid	Value
N/A		$8

#304
. . . For What I
Have Done

September 1993

Scott Lobdell
Various
Various

Orig. Retail	Price Paid	Value
$3.95		$6

#305
The Measure Of
The Man

October 1993

Scott Lobdell
Jan Duuresma
Jose Marzan

Orig. Retail	Price Paid	Value
$1.25		$3

#306
Mortal Coils

November 1993

Scott Lobdell
John Romita, Jr.
Dan Green

Orig. Retail	Price Paid	Value
$1.25		$3

	Price Paid	Total Value
Page Totals:		

Collector's Value Guide™ — X-Men®

#307
Night And Fog

December 1993
Scott Lobdell
John Romita, Jr.
Dan Green

Orig. Retail	Price Paid	Value
$1.25		$2.75

#308
Mixed Blessings

January 1994
Scott Lobdell
John Romita, Jr.
Dan Green/Al Vey

Orig. Retail	Price Paid	Value
$1.25		$2.75

#309
When Tigers Come At Night!

February 1994
Scott Lobdell
John Romita, Jr.
Dan Green/Jon Holdredge

Orig. Retail	Price Paid	Value
$1.25		$2.75

#310
...Show Me The Way To Go Home...

March 1994
Scott Lobdell
John Romita, Jr.
Dan Green

Orig. Retail	Price Paid	Value
$1.95		$3.25

#311
Putting The Cat Out

April 1994
Scott Lobdell
John Romita, Jr.
Dan Green/Al Vey

Orig. Retail	Price Paid	Value
$1.25		$2.75

#312
Romp

May 1994
Scott Lobdell
Joe Madureira
Dan Green/Harry Candelario

Orig. Retail	Price Paid	Value
$1.50		$3.50

Page Totals:	Price Paid	Total Value

COLLECTOR'S VALUE GUIDE™

Collector's Value Guide™ — X-Men®

#313
Hands Across The Water

June 1994
Scott Lobdell
Joe Madureira
Dan Green

Orig. Retail	Price Paid	Value
$1.50		$3

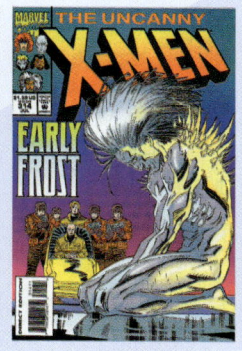

#314
Early Frost

July 1994
Scott Lobdell
Lee Weeks
Bill Sienkiewicz

Orig. Retail	Price Paid	Value
$1.50		$2.75

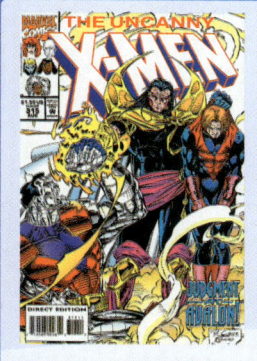

#315
Peers

August 1994
Scott Lobdell
Roger Cruz
Various

Orig. Retail	Price Paid	Value
$1.50		$3

#316
Encounter

September 1994
Scott Lobdell
Joe Madureira
Terry Austin/Dan Green

Orig. Retail	Price Paid	Value
$1.50		$2.25

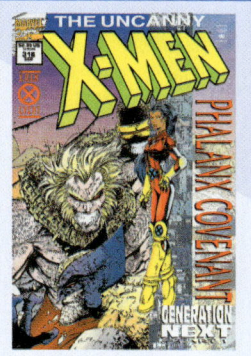

#316
Encounter
(Foil Cover)

September 1994
Scott Lobdell
Joe Madureira
Terry Austin/Dan Green

Orig. Retail	Price Paid	Value
$2.95		$4.50

#317
Enter Freely And Of Your Own Will

October 1994
Scott Lobdell
Joe Madureira
Dan Green

Orig. Retail	Price Paid	Value
$1.50		$2.25

COLLECTOR'S VALUE GUIDE™

	Price Paid	Total Value
Page Totals:		

Collector's Value Guide™ — X-Men®

#317
Enter Freely And Of Your Own Will (Foil Cover)
October 1994
Scott Lobdell
Joe Madureira
Dan Green

Orig. Retail	Price Paid	Value
$2.95		$4.25

#318
Moving Day
November 1994
Scott Lobdell
Roger Cruz
Tim Townsend

Orig. Retail	Price Paid	Value
$1.50		$2.25

#318
Moving Day (Deluxe Edition)
November 1994
Scott Lobdell
Roger Cruz
Tim Townsend

Orig. Retail	Price Paid	Value
$1.95		$3

#319
Untapped Potential

December 1994
Scott Lobdell
Steve Epting
Dan Green/Tim Townsend

Orig. Retail	Price Paid	Value
N/A		$2.25

#319
Untapped Potential (Deluxe Edition)

December 1994
Scott Lobdell
Steve Epting
Dan Green/Tim Townsend

Orig. Retail	Price Paid	Value
$1.95		$3

#320
The Son Rises In The East

January 1995
Mark Waid
Roger Cruz
Tim Townsend

Orig. Retail	Price Paid	Value
$1.50		$2.25

Page Totals: Price Paid _____ Total Value _____

COLLECTOR'S VALUE GUIDE™

Collector's Value Guide™ — X-Men®

#320
The Son Rises In The East (Deluxe Edition)

January 1995

Mark Waid
Roger Cruz
Tim Townsend

Orig. Retail	Price Paid	Value
$1.95		$3.50

#320
The Son Rises In The East (Gold Edition, *Wizard* Exclusive)

January 1995

Mark Waid
Roger Cruz
Tim Townsend

Orig. Retail	Price Paid	Value
N/A		$8.50

#321
Auld Lang Syne

February 1995

Scott Lobdell/Mark Waid
Ron Garney
Various

Orig. Retail	Price Paid	Value
$1.50		$2.25

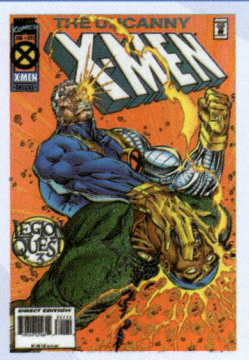

#321
Auld Lang Syne (Deluxe Edition w/Card)

February 1995

Scott Lobdell/Mark Waid
Ron Garney
Various

Orig. Retail	Price Paid	Value
$1.95		$3

#322
Dark Walk

July 1995

Scott Lobdell
Tom Grummett
Various

Orig. Retail	Price Paid	Value
$1.95		$5

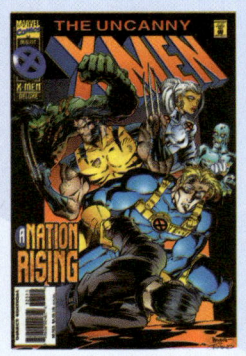

#323
A Nation Rising

August 1995

Scott Lobdell
Bryan Hitch
Cam Smith

Orig. Retail	Price Paid	Value
$1.95		$2.75

Collector's Value Guide™

	Price Paid	Total Value
Page Totals:		

Collector's Value Guide™ — X-Men®

#324
Deadly Messengers

September 1995
Scott Lobdell
Roger Cruz
Various

Orig. Retail	Price Paid	Value
$1.95		$2.75

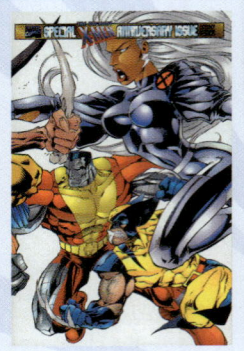

#325
Generation Of Evil

October 1995
Scott Lobdell
Joe Madureira
Tim Townsend/Matt Ryan

Orig. Retail	Price Paid	Value
$3.95		$4.75

#326
The Nature Of Evil

November 1995
Scott Lobdell
Joe Madureira
Tim Townsend

Orig. Retail	Price Paid	Value
$1.95		$2.75

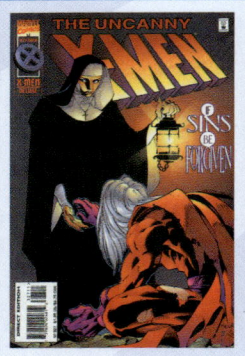

#327
Whispers On The Wind

December 1995
Scott Lobdell
Roger Cruz
Tim Townsend/Al Milgrom

Orig. Retail	Price Paid	Value
$1.95		$2.75

#328
Precipice

January 1996
Scott Lobdell
Joe Madureira
Tim Townsend

Orig. Retail	Price Paid	Value
$1.95		$2.75

#329
Warriors Of The Ebon Night

February 1996
Scott Lobdell/Jeph Loeb
Joe Madureira
Tim Townsend

Orig. Retail	Price Paid	Value
$1.95		$2.75

Page Totals:	Price Paid	Total Value

COLLECTOR'S VALUE GUIDE™

Collector's Value Guide™ — X-Men®

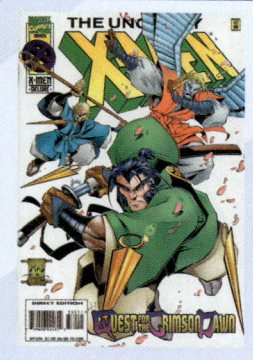

#330
Quest For The Crimson Dawn

March 1996

Scott Lobdell/Jeph Loeb
Joe Madureira
Tim Townsend

Orig. Retail	Price Paid	Value
$1.95		$2.75

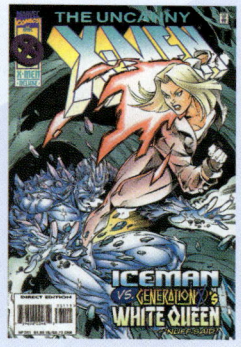

#331
The Splinter Of Our Discontent

April 1996

Scott Lobdell
Bryan Hitch
Paul Neary

Orig. Retail	Price Paid	Value
$1.95		$2.75

#332
The Road To Casablanca

May 1996

Scott Lobdell
Joe Madureira
Tim Townsend

Orig. Retail	Price Paid	Value
$1.95		$2.75

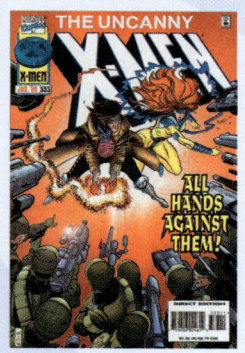

#333
The Other Shoe . . .

June 1996

Scott Lobdell
Pascual Ferry
Various

Orig. Retail	Price Paid	Value
$1.95		$3

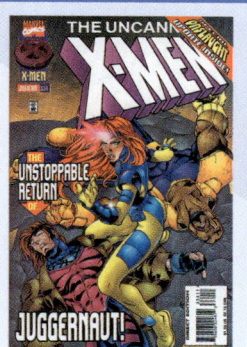

#334
Dark Horizon

July 1996

Scott Lobdell
Joe Madureira
Tim Townsend

Orig. Retail	Price Paid	Value
$1.95		$3

#335
– Apocalypse Lives!

August 1996

Scott Lobdell
Joe Madureira
Tim Townsend

Orig. Retail	Price Paid	Value
$1.95		$3

COLLECTOR'S VALUE GUIDE

Page Totals: | Price Paid | Total Value |

Collector's Value Guide™ — X-Men®

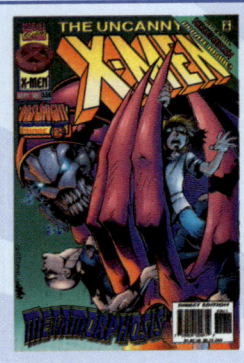

#336
Voice As Deep As Thunder

September 1996
Scott Lobdell
Joe Madureira
Various

Orig. Retail	Price Paid	Value
$1.95		$3

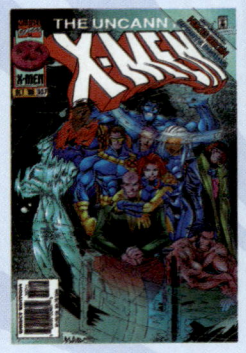

#337
Know Thy Enemy

October 1996
Scott Lobdell
Joe Madureira
Tim Townsend/Vince Russell

Orig. Retail	Price Paid	Value
$1.95		$3

#338
A Hope Reborn A Past Reclaimed

November 1996
Scott Lobdell
J. Madureira/S. Larroca
Tim Townsend/Vince Russell

Orig. Retail	Price Paid	Value
$1.95		$3

#339
Fight And Flight!

December 1996
Scott Lobdell
Adam Hubert/Cedric Nocon
J. Delperdang/S. Hanna

Orig. Retail	Price Paid	Value
$1.99		$3

#340
Relativity

January 1997
Scott Lobdell
Joe Madureira
Tim Townsend

Orig. Retail	Price Paid	Value
$1.95		$3

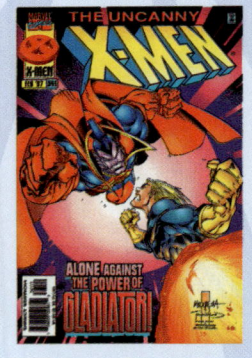

#341
When Strikes A Gladiator!

February 1997
Scott Lobdell
Joe Madureira
Tim Townsend

Orig. Retail	Price Paid	Value
$1.95		$3

Page Totals: Price Paid / Total Value

COLLECTOR'S VALUE GUIDE™

Collector's Value Guide™ — X-Men®

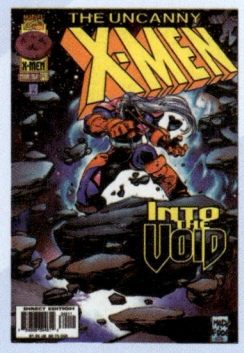

#342
– Did I Miss Something?!

March 1997

Scott Lobdell
Joe Madureira
Tim Townsend

Orig. Retail	Price Paid	Value
$1.95		$4

#342
– Did I Miss Something?!
(Variant Cover)

March 1997

Scott Lobdell
Joe Madureira
Tim Townsend

Orig. Retail	Price Paid	Value
$1.95		$15

#343
Where No X-Man Has Gone Before!

April 1997

Scott Lobdell
Joe Madureira
Tim Townsend

Orig. Retail	Price Paid	Value
$1.95		$3

#344
Casualties Of War

May 1997

Scott Lobdell
Melvin Rubi
Various

Orig. Retail	Price Paid	Value
$1.95		$3

#345
Moving On

June 1997

Scott Lobdell/Ben Raab
Joe Madureira/Melvin Rubi
Various

Orig. Retail	Price Paid	Value
$1.95		$4.25

#346
The Story Of The Year!

August 1997

Scott Lobdell
Joe Madureira
Tim Townsend

Orig. Retail	Price Paid	Value
$1.99		$3

Value Guide — Uncanny X-Men® (1981-Present)

Page Totals: | Price Paid | Total Value |

Collector's Value Guide™ — X-Men®

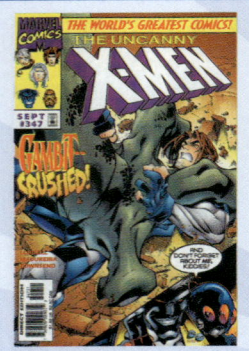

#347
Big Night

September 1997

Scott Lobdell
Joe Madureira
Various

Orig. Retail	Price Paid	Value
$1.99		$2.75

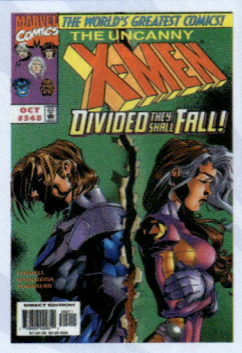

#348
Because, I Said So

October 1997

Scott Lobdell
Joe Madureira
Various

Orig. Retail	Price Paid	Value
$1.99		$2.75

#349
The Crawl

November 1997

Scott Lobdell
Chris Bachalo
Various

Orig. Retail	Price Paid	Value
$1.99		$2.75

#350
Trials & Errors

December 1997

Steve Seagle
Joe Madureira/Andy Smith
T. Townsend/Russell/Panosian

Orig. Retail	Price Paid	Value
$2.99		$3.75

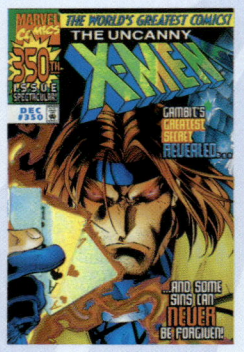

#350
Trials & Errors
(Prismatic Cover)

December 1997

Steve Seagle
Joe Madureira/Andy Smith
T. Townsend/Russell/Panosian

Orig. Retail	Price Paid	Value
N/A		$16

#351
Hours & Minutes

January 1998

Steve Seagle
Ed Benes
Ed Benes

Orig. Retail	Price Paid	Value
$1.99		$3

Page Totals: Price Paid _____ Total Value _____

Collector's Value Guide™ — X-Men®

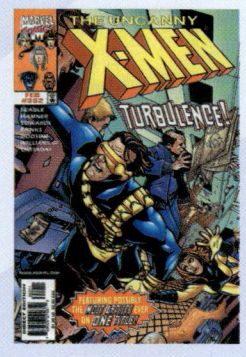

#352
In Sin Air

February 1998

Steve Seagle
Various
Various

Orig. Retail	Price Paid	Value
$1.99		$3

#353
Blackbirds

March 1998

Scott Lobdell
Chris Bachalo
Tim Townsend

Orig. Retail	Price Paid	Value
$1.99		$2.75

#354
Prehistory

April 1998

Scott Lobdell
Chris Bachalo
Tim Townsend

Orig. Retail	Price Paid	Value
$1.99		$2.75

#354
Prehistory
(Variant Cover)

April 1998

Scott Lobdell
Chris Bachalo
Tim Townsend

Orig. Retail	Price Paid	Value
$1.99		$5.50

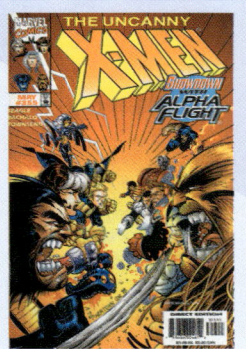

#355
North & South

May 1998

Steve Seagle
Chris Bachalo
Various

Orig. Retail	Price Paid	Value
$1.99		$2.75

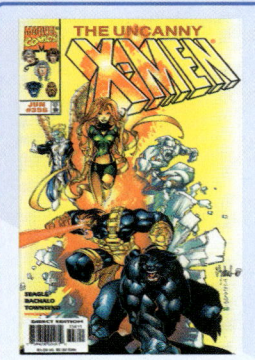

#356
Reunion

June 1998

Steve Seagle
Chris Bachalo
Tim Townsend

Orig. Retail	Price Paid	Value
$1.99		$2.75

Page Totals: | Price Paid | Total Value |

Collector's Value Guide™ — X-Men®

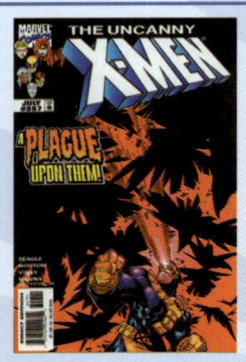

#357
The Sky Is Falling

July 1998

Steve Seagle
Dan Norton
Dexter Vines/Scott Hanna

Orig. Retail	Price Paid	Value
$1.99		$2.75

#358
Lost In Space

August 1998

Steve Seagle/Joseph Harris
Chris Bachalo
Tim Townsend

Orig. Retail	Price Paid	Value
$1.99		$2.75

#359
Power Play

September 1998

Joe Kelly/Steve Seagle
Chris Bachalo/Ryan Benjamin
Various

Orig. Retail	Price Paid	Value
$1.99		$2.75

#360
Children Of The Atom

October 1998

Steve Seagle
Chris Bachalo
Various

Orig. Retail	Price Paid	Value
$2.99		$3.50

#360
Children Of The Atom
(Dynamic Forces Exclusive Cover)

October 1998

Steve Seagle
Chris Bachalo
Various

Orig. Retail	Price Paid	Value
$2.99		$8

#360
Children Of The Atom
(Prismatic Cover)

October 1998

Steve Seagle
Chris Bachalo
Various

Orig. Retail	Price Paid	Value
$2.99		$4.75

Page Totals: Price Paid _____ Total Value _____

COLLECTOR'S VALUE GUIDE™

Collector's Value Guide™ — X-Men®

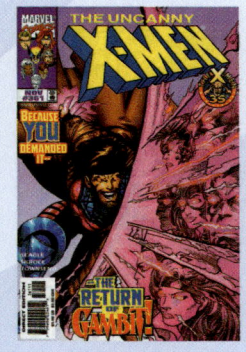

#361
Thieves In The Temple

November 1998

Steve Seagle
Steve Skroce
Various

Orig. Retail	Price Paid	Value
$1.99		$3

#362
Meltdown

December 1998

Steve Seagle
Chris Bachalo
Art Thibert/Tim Townsend

Orig. Retail	Price Paid	Value
$1.99		$3

#363
When You're Unwanted

Early January 1999

Steve Seagle
Chris Bachalo
Art Thibert/Tim Townsend

Orig. Retail	Price Paid	Value
$1.99		$3

#364
Escape From Alcatraz

Late January 1999

Steve Seagle/Ralph Macchio
Leinil Francis Yu
Tim Townsend/Tadeo

Orig. Retail	Price Paid	Value
$1.99		$3

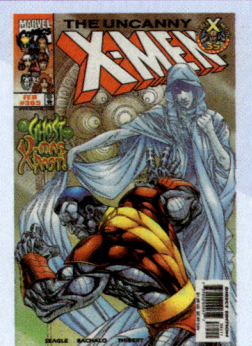

#365
Ghost Of X-Mas Past!

February 1998

Steve Seagle
Chris Bachalo
Various

Orig. Retail	Price Paid	Value
$1.99		$2.75

#366
The Shot Heard Round The World

March 1999

Fabian Nicieza
Leinil Francis Yu
Various

Orig. Retail	Price Paid	Value
$1.99		$2.75

Page Totals: | Price Paid | Total Value |

Collector's Value Guide™ — X-Men®

#367
Disturbing Behavior

April 1999

Alan Davis/Fabian Nicieza
Leinil Francis Yu
Livesay/Vines

Orig. Retail	Price Paid	Value
$1.99		$2.25

#368
Mansions In Heaven

May 1999

Alan Davis/Joe Casey
Adam Kubert
Tim Townsend

Orig. Retail	Price Paid	Value
$1.99		$2.25

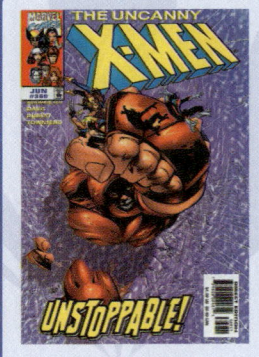

#369
Collision Course

June 1999

Alan Davis/Terry Kavanaugh
Adam Kubert
Tim Townsend

Orig. Retail	Price Paid	Value
$1.99		$2.25

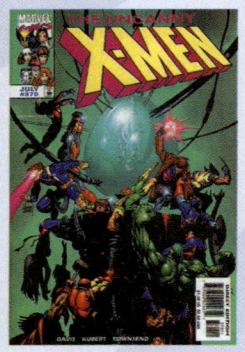

#370
History Repeats

July 1999

Alan Davis/Terry Kavanaugh
Adam Kubert
Tim Townsend

Orig. Retail	Price Paid	Value
$1.99		$2.25

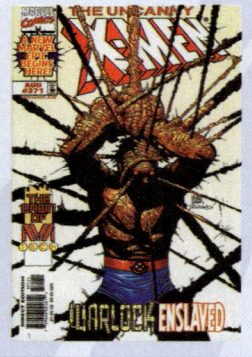

#371
Rage Against The Machine

August 1999

Alan Davis/Terry Kavanaugh
Jimmy Cheung
Mark Morales

Orig. Retail	Price Paid	Value
$1.99		$2

#372
Dream's End

September 1999

Alan Davis/Terry Kavanaugh
Adam Kubert
Batt

Orig. Retail	Price Paid	Value
$1.99		$2

Page Totals: Price Paid _____ Total Value _____

COLLECTOR'S VALUE GUIDE™

Collector's Value Guide™ — X-Men®

#373
Beauty & The Beast Part One: Broken Mirrors
October 1999
Alan Davis/Terry Kavanaugh
Adam Kubert/Rob Jensen
Various

Orig. Retail	Price Paid	Value
$1.99		$2.25

#374
Beauty And The Beast Part Two: You Can't Go Home Again
November 1999
Alan Davis/Jay Faerber
Tom Raney
Scott Hanna

Orig. Retail	Price Paid	Value
$1.99		$2.25

#375
I Am Not Now, Nor Have I Ever Been . . .
December 1999
Alan Davis/Terry Kavanaugh
Adam Kubert
Batt/Tim Townsend

Orig. Retail	Price Paid	Value
$2.99		$3.50

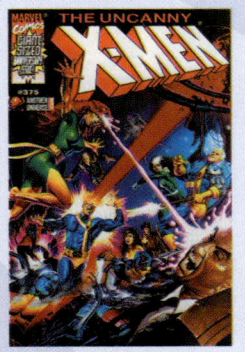

#375
I Am Not Now, Nor Have I Ever Been . . . (Variant Cover)
December 1999
Alan Davis/Terry Kavanaugh
Adam Kubert
Batt/Tim Townsend

Orig. Retail	Price Paid	Value
$2.99		$12

#376
Filling In The Blanks

January 2000
Alan Davis/Terry Kavanaugh
Roger Cruz
Various

Orig. Retail	Price Paid	Value
$1.99		$2

#377
The End Of The World As We Know It

February 2000
Alan Davis/Terry Kavanaugh
Tom Raney
Scott Hanna

Orig. Retail	Price Paid	Value
$1.99		$2.50

Collector's Value Guide™

Page Totals:	Price Paid	Total Value

Value Guide — Uncanny X-Men® (1981-Present)

Collector's Value Guide™ — X-Men®

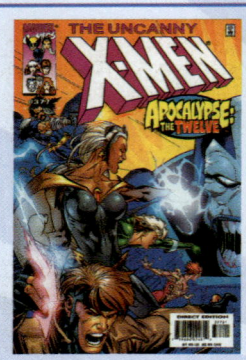

#377
The End Of The World As We Know It (Variant Cover)
February 2000

Alan Davis/Terry Kavanaugh
Tom Raney
Scott Hanna

Orig. Retail	Price Paid	Value
$1.99		$3.50

#378
First & Last

March 2000

Alan Davis/Terry Kavanaugh
Adam Kubert/Graham Nolan
Tim Townsend /J. Palmiotti

Orig. Retail	Price Paid	Value
$1.99		$2

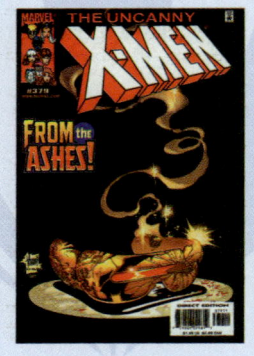

#379
What Dreams May Come . . .

April 2000

Alan Davis
Tom Raney
Scott Hanna

Orig. Retail	Price Paid	Value
$1.99		$2

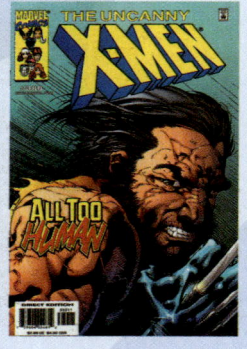

#380
Heaven's Shadow

May 2000

Alan Davis/Terry Kavanaugh
Tom Raney
Scott Hanna

Orig. Retail	Price Paid	Value
$2.99		$3

#381
Night Of Masques

June 2000

Chris Claremont
Adam Kubert
Tim Townsend

Orig. Retail	Price Paid	Value
$2.25		$2.50

#381
Night Of Masques (Variant Cover)

June 2000

Chris Claremont
Adam Kubert
Tim Townsend

Orig. Retail	Price Paid	Value
$2.25		$2.50

Page Totals: Price Paid _____ Total Value _____

COLLECTOR'S VALUE GUIDE™

Collector's Value Guide™ — X-Men®

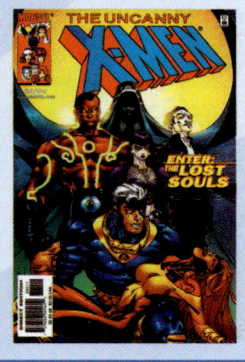

#382
Lost Souls

July 2000

Chris Claremont
Tom Raney
Scott Hanna

Orig. Retail	Price Paid	Value
$2.25		$2.50

#383
Moscow Knights

August 2000

Chris Claremont
Adam Kubert
Tim Townsend/Dan Panosian

Orig. Retail	Price Paid	Value
$2.99		$3

Future Releases
_____
_____
_____
_____
_____
_____
_____
_____
_____
_____
_____

Annual #1
Reprint of X-Men #9 and #11

December 1970

Various
Various
Various

Orig. Retail	Price Paid	Value
25¢		$65

Annual #2
Reprint of X-Men #22 and #23

November 1971

Roy Thomas
Jay Gavin
Dick Ayers

Orig. Retail	Price Paid	Value
25¢		$55

Annual #3
A Fire In The Sky; Rogue In The House; Land Of Shadow, Dawn Of Death

1979

Chris Claremont
George Perez
Terry Austin

Orig. Retail	Price Paid	Value
75¢		$20

	Price Paid	Total Value
Page Totals:		

Collector's Value Guide™ — X-Men®

Value Guide — Uncanny X-Men® (1981–Present)

Annual #4
Nightcrawler's Inferno

1980

Chris Claremont
John Romita, Jr.
Bob McLeod

Orig. Retail	Price Paid	Value
75¢		$14

Annual #5
Ou, La La – Badoon; The Sundered Realm; And Now – Armageddon; The Passing Of The Dream

1981

Chris Claremont
Brent Anderson
Bob McLeod

Orig. Retail	Price Paid	Value
75¢		$10

Annual #6
Blood Feud

1982

Chris Claremont
Bill Sienkiewicz
Bob Wiacek

Orig. Retail	Price Paid	Value
$1		$10

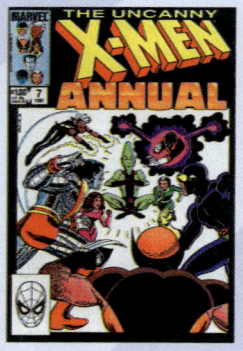

Annual #7
Scavenger Hunt

1983

Chris Claremont
Michael Golden/Bret Blevins
Various

Orig. Retail	Price Paid	Value
$1		$10

Annual #8
The Adventures Of Lockheed The Space Dragon And His Pet Girl Kitty

1984

Chris Claremont/Mary Jo Duffy
Steve Leialoha
Steve Leialoha

Orig. Retail	Price Paid	Value
$1		$10

Annual #9
There's No Place Like Home

1985

Chris Claremont
Arthur Adams
Various

Orig. Retail	Price Paid	Value
$1.25		$12

Page Totals: Price Paid _____ Total Value _____

COLLECTOR'S VALUE GUIDE™

Collector's Value Guide™ — X-Men®

Annual #10
Performance

1986

Chris Claremont
Arthur Adams
Terry Austin

Orig. Retail	Price Paid	Value
$1.25		$12

Annual #11
Lost In The Funhouse

1987

Chris Claremont
Alan Davis
Paul Neary

Orig. Retail	Price Paid	Value
$1.25		$6

Annual #12
Resurrection!

1988

Chris Claremont
Arthur Adams
Bob Wiacek

Orig. Retail	Price Paid	Value
$1.75		$6

Annual #13
Double Cross

1989

Terry Austin
Mike Vosburg
Mike Vosburg

Orig. Retail	Price Paid	Value
$2		$6

Annual #14
You Must Remember This

1990

Chris Claremont
Arthur Adams
Various

Orig. Retail	Price Paid	Value
$2		$10

Annual #15
Kings Of Pain

1991

Fabian Nicieza
Tom Raney
Josef Rubinstein/Art Nichols

Orig. Retail	Price Paid	Value
$2		$4.50

Value Guide — Uncanny X-Men® (1981-Present)

Page Totals:

Price Paid	Total Value

Collector's Value Guide™ — X-Men®

Annual #16
The Masters Of Inevitability

1992

Fabian Nicieza
Jae Lee
Jan Harps/Josef Rubinstein

Orig. Retail	Price Paid	Value
$2.25		$3.50

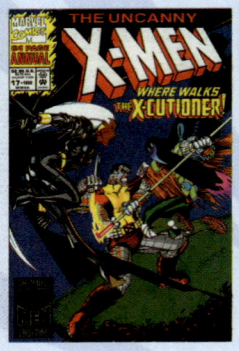

Annual #17
The Gift Goodbye

1993

Scott Lobdell
Jason Pearon
Mark Farmer

Orig. Retail	Price Paid	Value
$2.95		$3.50

Annual #18
Trust Is A Two-Edged Sword

1994

Glenn Herdling
Ian Churchill
Hilary Barta/Bud LaRosa

Orig. Retail	Price Paid	Value
N/A		$3.25

Uncanny X-Men Annual '95
Growing Pains

1995

Terry Kavanaugh
Bryan Hitch
Bob Mcleod

Orig. Retail	Price Paid	Value
$3.95		$4.50

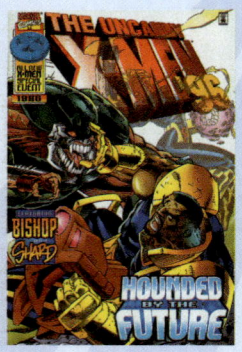

Uncanny X-Men Annual '96
Destiny's Child

1996

T. Kavanaugh/H. Mackie
D. Perrin/N. Gnazzo
A. Thibert/H. Candelario

Orig. Retail	Price Paid	Value
$2.95		$3.25

Uncanny X-Men Annual '97
Rifts

1997

Jorge Gonzalez
Duncan Rouleau
Troy Hubbs

Orig. Retail	Price Paid	Value
$2.99		$3.25

Page Totals: Price Paid _____ Total Value _____

COLLECTOR'S VALUE GUIDE™

Collector's Value Guide™ — X-Men®

Uncanny X-Men Fantastic Four Annual
N/A
1998
N/A

Orig. Retail	Price Paid	Value
N/A		$3

Uncanny X-Men Annual
Utopia Perdida

1999
Ben Raab
Anthony Williams
Troy Hubbs/Scott Koblish

Orig. Retail	Price Paid	Value
$3.50		$4

Giant Size X-Men #1
Second Genesis

1975
Len Wein/Chris Claremont
Dave Cockrum
Dave Cockrum/Peter Iro

Orig. Retail	Price Paid	Value
50¢		$550

Giant Size X-Men #2
The Sentinels Live

1975
Roy Thomas
Neal Adams
Tom Palmer

Orig. Retail	Price Paid	Value
50¢		$50

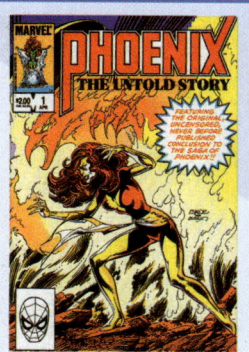

Phoenix: The Untold Story
The Fate Of The Phoenix!

April 1984
Chris Claremont/John Byrne
John Byrne
Terry Austin

Orig. Retail	Price Paid	Value
$2		$12

Pint-Sized X-Babies
Murderama

August 1998
Ruben Diaz
J.J. Kirby
Various

Orig. Retail	Price Paid	Value
$2.99		$3.50

Page Totals: Price Paid | Total Value

Collector's Value Guide™ — X-Men®

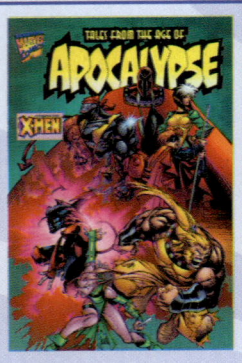

Tales From The Age Of Apocalypse
By The Light

1996
Scott Lobdell/Ralph Macchio
Joe Bennett
Joe Pimentel

Orig. Retail	Price Paid	Value
$5.95		$6.25

X-Babies Reborn
N/A

N/A
N/A

Orig. Retail	Price Paid	Value
N/A		$4

Yearbook 1999
X-Men Class Of '99

February 2000
Michael Raicht
N/A
N/A

Orig. Retail	Price Paid	Value
$2.99		$6.25

X-Men®
(1991-Present)

This next section highlights the second series of the *X-Men* comics which began in 1991 and continues today. The issues in the on-going series will appear first and are followed by the annuals and then the one-shots (in alphabetical order).

#-1
I Had A Dream

July 1997
Scott Lobdell
Carlos Pacheco
Art Thibert

Orig. Retail	Price Paid	Value
$1.95		$2.50

#-1
I Had A Dream
(*Wizard* Exclusive, signed by S. Lee)

July 1997
Scott Lobdell
Carlos Pacheco
Art Thibert

Orig. Retail	Price Paid	Value
N/A		$22

Page Totals: | Price Paid | Total Value |

Collector's Value Guide™ — X-Men®

#0
I Had A Dream
(*Wizard* Exclusive)

July 1997

Scott Lobdell
Carlos Pacheco
Art Thibert

Orig. Retail	Price Paid	Value
N/A		$3.50

#1/2
I Had A Dream
(*Wizard* Exclusive)

July 1997

Scott Lobdell
Carlos Pacheco
Art Thibert

Orig. Retail	Price Paid	Value
N/A		$12

#1
Rubicon

October 1991

Chris Claremont/Jim Lee
Jim Lee
Scott Williams

Orig. Retail	Price Paid	Value
$1.50		$4.25

#1
Rubicon
(Variant Cover)

October 1991

Chris Claremont/Jim Lee
Jim Lee
Scott Williams

Orig. Retail	Price Paid	Value
$1.50		$4.25

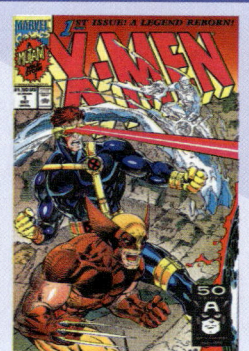

#1
Rubicon
(Variant Cover)

October 1991

Chris Claremont/Jim Lee
Jim Lee
Scott Williams

Orig. Retail	Price Paid	Value
$1.50		$4.25

#1
Rubicon
(Variant Cover)

October 1991

Chris Claremont/Jim Lee
Jim Lee
Scott Williams

Orig. Retail	Price Paid	Value
$1.50		$4.25

COLLECTOR'S
VALUE GUIDE™

Page Totals:	Price Paid	Total Value

Collector's Value Guide™ — X-Men®

#1
Rubicon
(Deluxe Edition)

October 1991

Chris Claremont/Jim Lee
Jim Lee
Scott Williams

Orig. Retail	Price Paid	Value
N/A		$5.25

#2
Firestorm

November 1991

Chris Claremont
Jim Lee
Scott Williams

Orig. Retail	Price Paid	Value
$1		$4.50

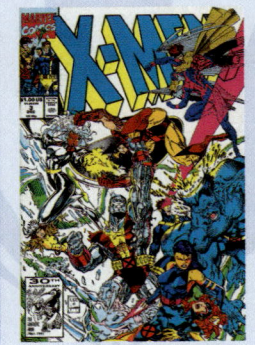

#3
Fallout!

December 1991

Chris Claremont
Jim Lee
Scott Williams

Orig. Retail	Price Paid	Value
$1		$4.50

#4
The Resurrection
And The Flesh

January 1992

Jim Lee
John Byrne
Scott Williams

Orig. Retail	Price Paid	Value
$1		$4.50

#5
Blowback

February 1992

Jim Lee/John Byrne
Jim Lee
Various

Orig. Retail	Price Paid	Value
$1.25		$4.50

#6
Farther Still

March 1992

Jim Lee/Scott Lobdell
Jim Lee
Art Thibert

Orig. Retail	Price Paid	Value
$1.25		$4.50

Page Totals:	Price Paid	Total Value

COLLECTOR'S VALUE GUIDE™

Collector's Value Guide™ — X-Men®

#7
Inside . . . Out!

April 1992
Jim Lee/Scott Lobdell
Jim Lee
Art Thibert

Orig. Retail	Price Paid	Value
$1.25		$4.50

#8
Tooth And Claw

May 1992
Jim Lee/Scott Lobdell
Jim Lee
Jim Lee/Art Thibert

Orig. Retail	Price Paid	Value
$1.25		$4.25

#9
The Not So Big Easy

June 1992
Jim Lee/Scott Lobdell
Jim Lee
Jim Lee/Art Thibert

Orig. Retail	Price Paid	Value
$1.25		$4.25

#10
Where Happy Little
Bluebirds Fly . . .

July 1992
Jim Lee
Scott Lobdell
Scott Williams/Bob Wiacek

Orig. Retail	Price Paid	Value
$1.25		$4.25

#11
The X-Men Vs. The
X-Men! (Again)

August 1992
Jim Lee
Scott Lobdell
Bob Wiacek

Orig. Retail	Price Paid	Value
$1.25		$3.50

#12
Broken Mirrors

September 1992
Fabian Nicieza
Art Thibert
Dan Panosian/Trevor Scott

Orig. Retail	Price Paid	Value
$1.25		$3.50

COLLECTOR'S VALUE GUIDE

Page Totals:	Price Paid	Total Value

Value Guide — X-Men® (1991-Present)

Collector's Value Guide™ — X-Men®

#13
Hazardous Territory

October 1992

Fabian Nicieza
Art Thibert
Dan Panosian

Orig. Retail	Price Paid	Value
$1.25		$3.50

#14
Fingers On The Trigger

November 1992

Fabian Nicieza
Andy Kubert
Mark Pennington

Orig. Retail	Price Paid	Value
$1.50		$3.50

#15
The Camel's Back

December 1992

Fabian Nicieza
Andy Kubert
Mark Pennington

Orig. Retail	Price Paid	Value
$1.50		$3.50

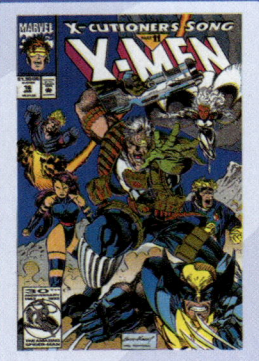

#16
Conflicting Cathexes

January 1993

Fabian Nicieza
Andy Kubert
A. Kubert/M. Pennington

Orig. Retail	Price Paid	Value
$1.50		$3.50

#17
Waiting For The Ripening

February 1993

Fabian Nicieza
Andy Kubert
Mark Pennington

Orig. Retail	Price Paid	Value
$1.25		$3.25

#18
The Crops Mature

March 1993

Fabian Nicieza
Andy Kubert
M. Pennington/D. Panosian

Orig. Retail	Price Paid	Value
$1.25		$3.25

Page Totals: Price Paid | Total Value

Collector's Value Guide™ — X-Men®

#19
Harvest Of The Innocent

April 1993

Fabian Nicieza
Andy Kubert
Various

Orig. Retail	Price Paid	Value
$1.25		$3.25

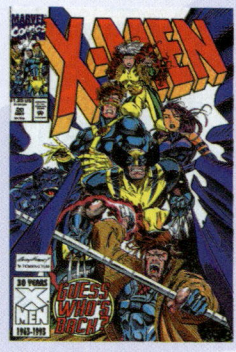

#20
Digging In The Dirt

May 1993

Fabian Nicieza
Andy Kubert
M. Pennington/B. Wiacek

Orig. Retail	Price Paid	Value
$1.25		$3.25

#21
The Puzzle Box

June 1993

Fabian Nicieza
Brandon Peterson
Dan Panosian

Orig. Retail	Price Paid	Value
$1.25		$3.25

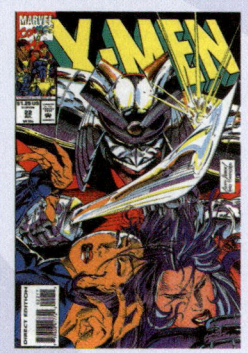

#22
The Mask Behind The Facade

July 1993

Fabian Nicieza
Andy Kubert
Mark Pennington

Orig. Retail	Price Paid	Value
$1.25		$3.25

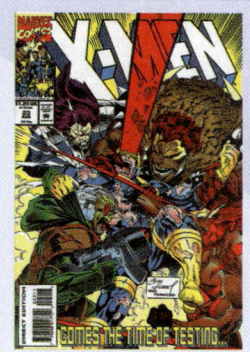

#23
Leaning Towards Oneself

August 1993

Fabian Nicieza
Andy Kubert
Mark Pennington

Orig. Retail	Price Paid	Value
$1.25		$3.25

#24
Between Hope And Sorrow

September 1993

Fabian Nicieza
Andy Kubert
Various

Orig. Retail	Price Paid	Value
$1.25		$3.25

Value Guide — X-Men® (1991-Present)

Collector's Value Guide™

Page Totals:	Price Paid	Total Value

Collector's Value Guide™ — X-Men®

#25
Dreams Fade

October 1993

Fabian Nicieza
Andy Kubert
Matt Ryan

Orig. Retail	Price Paid	Value
$3.50		$14

#25
Dreams Fade
(Black & White Cover)

October 1993

Fabian Nicieza
Andy Kubert
Matt Ryan

Orig. Retail	Price Paid	Value
$3.50		$18

#25
Dreams Fade
(Gold Cover)

October 1993

Fabian Nicieza
Andy Kubert
Matt Ryan

Orig. Retail	Price Paid	Value
$3.50		$35

#26
Civil Disobedience!

November 1993

Fabian Nicieza
Andy Kubert
Matt Ryan

Orig. Retail	Price Paid	Value
$1.25		$3

#27
A Song Of Mourning A Cry Of Joy

December 1993

Fabian Nicieza
Richard Bennett
Bob Wiacek/Scott Hanna

Orig. Retail	Price Paid	Value
$1.25		$3

#28
Devil In The House

January 1994

Fabian Nicieza
Andy Kubert
Matt Ryan

Orig. Retail	Price Paid	Value
$1.25		$3

Page Totals:	Price Paid	Total Value

Collector's Value Guide™ — X-Men®

#29
Return To Hellfire!

February 1994

Fabian Nicieza
Andy Kubert
Matt Ryan

Orig. Retail	Price Paid	Value
$1.25		$3

#30
The Ties That Bind

March 1994

Fabian Nicieza
Andy Kubert
Matt Ryan

Orig. Retail	Price Paid	Value
$1.95		$5

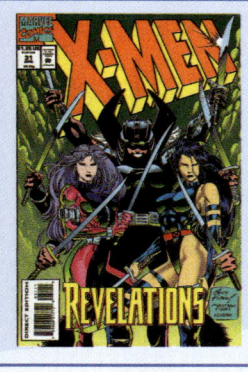

#31
The Butterfly And The Hawk

April 1994

Fabian Nicieza
Andy Kubert
Matt Ryan

Orig. Retail	Price Paid	Value
$1.25		$2.75

#32
The Leopards And The Cats

May 1994

Fabian Nicieza
Andy Kubert
Matt Ryan

Orig. Retail	Price Paid	Value
$1.50		$2.75

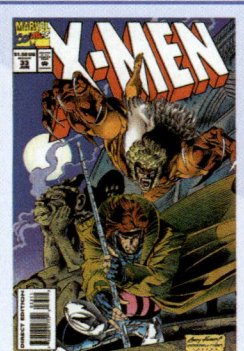

#33
The Hearts Of Thieves

June 1994

Fabian Nicieza
Andy Kubert
Matt Ryan

Orig. Retail	Price Paid	Value
$1.50		$2.75

#34
Life And Consequences

July 1994

Fabian Nicieza
Andy Kubert
Matt Ryan

Orig. Retail	Price Paid	Value
$1.50		$2.75

Value Guide — X-Men® (1991-Present)

COLLECTOR'S VALUE GUIDE™

Page Totals:	Price Paid	Total Value

Collector's Value Guide™ — X-Men®

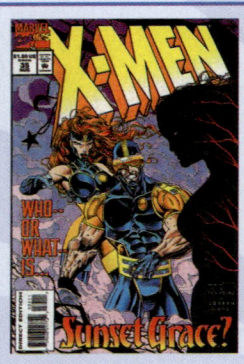

#35
Sunset Grace

August 1994

Fabian Nicieza
Liam Sharp
Robin Riggs

Orig. Retail	Price Paid	Value
$1.50		$2.75

#36
Drop The Leash

September 1994

Fabian Nicieza
Andy Kubert
Matt Ryan

Orig. Retail	Price Paid	Value
$1.50		$2.50

#36
Drop The Leash
(Foil Cover)

September 1994

Fabian Nicieza
Andy Kubert
Matt Ryan

Orig. Retail	Price Paid	Value
$2.95		$5

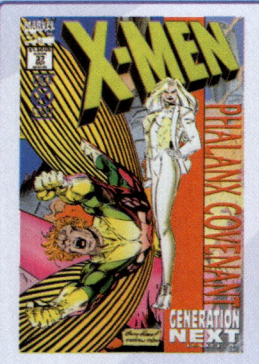

#37
The Currents Shift

October 1994

Fabian Nicieza
Andy Kubert
Matt Ryan/Sellers

Orig. Retail	Price Paid	Value
$1.50		$2.50

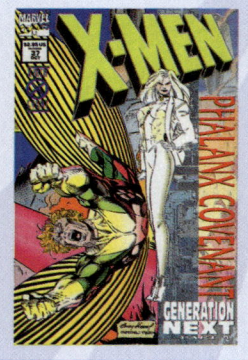

#37
The Currents Shift
(Foil Cover)

October 1994

Fabian Nicieza
Andy Kubert
Matt Ryan/Sellers

Orig. Retail	Price Paid	Value
$2.95		$5

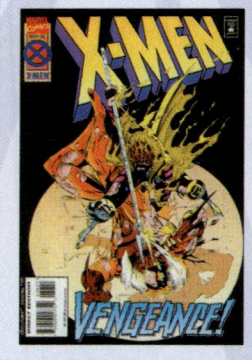

#38
Smoke And Mirrors

November 1994

Fabian Nicieza
Andy Kubert
Matt Ryan

Orig. Retail	Price Paid	Value
$1.95		$2

Page Totals:	Price Paid	Total Value

COLLECTOR'S
VALUE GUIDE™

Collector's Value Guide™ — X-Men®

#38
Smoke And Mirrors
(Deluxe Cover)

November 1994

Fabian Nicieza
Andy Kubert
Matt Ryan

Orig. Retail	Price Paid	Value
$1.95		$2.75

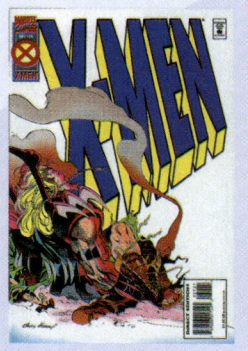

#39
Birds Of A Feather

December 1994

Fabian Nicieza
Terry Dodson
Matt Ryan

Orig. Retail	Price Paid	Value
$1.50		$2

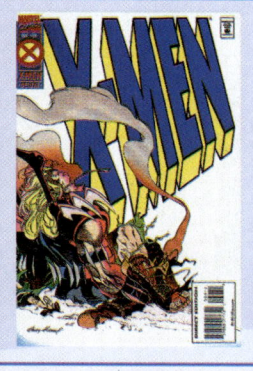

#39
Birds Of A Feather
(Deluxe Cover)

December 1994

Fabian Nicieza
Terry Dodson
Matt Ryan

Orig. Retail	Price Paid	Value
$1.95		$2.75

#40
The Killing Time

January 1995

Fabian Nicieza
Andy Kubert
Matt Ryan

Orig. Retail	Price Paid	Value
$1.95		$2

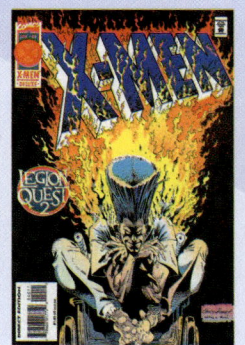

#40
The Killing Time
(Deluxe Cover)

January 1995

Fabian Nicieza
Andy Kubert
Matt Ryan

Orig. Retail	Price Paid	Value
$1.95		$3.25

#41
Dreams Die!

February 1995

Fabian Nicieza
Ron Garney/Andy Kubert
Matt Ryan

Orig. Retail	Price Paid	Value
$1.95		$2

Page Totals:	Price Paid	Total Value

Collector's Value Guide™ — X-Men®

#41
Dreams Die!
(Deluxe Cover)

February 1995
Fabian Nicieza
Ron Garney/Andy Kubert
Matt Ryan

Orig. Retail	Price Paid	Value
$1.95		$2.75

#42
Heaven Can Wait

July 1995
Fabian Nicieza
Paul Smith
Matt Ryan

Orig. Retail	Price Paid	Value
$1.95		$2.50

#43
Falling From Grace

August 1995
Fabian Nicieza
Paul Smith
Matt Ryan/Cam Smith

Orig. Retail	Price Paid	Value
$1.95		$2.50

#44
Lost And Found

September 1995
Fabian Nicieza
Andy Kubert
Matt Ryan

Orig. Retail	Price Paid	Value
$1.95		$2.50

#45
The Enemy Of
My Enemy . . .

October 1995
Fabian Nicieza
Andy Kubert
Cam Smith

Orig. Retail	Price Paid	Value
$3.95		$4.75

#46
They're Baaack . . .

November 1995
Scott Lobdell
Andy Kubert
Cam Smith

Orig. Retail	Price Paid	Value
$1.95		$2.75

Page Totals: | Price Paid | Total Value |

Collector's Value Guide™ — X-Men®

#47
Big Trouble In Little Italy!

December 1995

Scott Lobdell
Andy Kubert
Cam Smith/Jesse Delperdang

Orig. Retail	Price Paid	Value
$1.95		$2.75

#48
Five Card Studs

January 1996

Scott Lobdell
Luke Ross
Andy Lanning

Orig. Retail	Price Paid	Value
$1.95		$2.75

#49
Eyes Of A New York Woman

February 1996

Scott Lobdell/Mark Waid
Jeff Matsuda
Dan Panosian

Orig. Retail	Price Paid	Value
$1.95		$2.75

#50
Full Court Press

March 1996

Scott Lobdell
Andy Kubert
Cam Smith

Orig. Retail	Price Paid	Value
$3.95		$4.25

#50
Full Court Press (American Entertainment Exclusive)

March 1996

Scott Lobdell
Andy Kubert
Cam Smith

Orig. Retail	Price Paid	Value
N/A		$10

#50
Full Court Press (Deluxe Cover)

March 1996

Scott Lobdell
Andy Kubert
Cam Smith

Orig. Retail	Price Paid	Value
N/A		$5

Collector's Value Guide™

Page Totals:	Price Paid	Total Value

Collector's Value Guide™ — X-Men®

#50
Full Court Press (Gold Cover)

March 1996

Scott Lobdell
Andy Kubert
Cam Smith

Orig. Retail	Price Paid	Value
N/A		$35

#51
Deathbound Train

April 1996

Mark Waid
Pascual Ferry
Various

Orig. Retail	Price Paid	Value
$1.95		$2.75

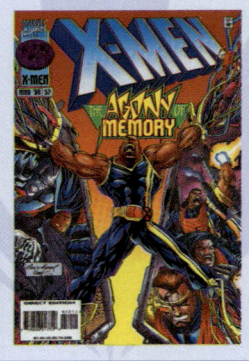

#52
Collector's Item

May 1996

Mark Waid
Andy Kubert
Cam Smith

Orig. Retail	Price Paid	Value
$1.95		$2.75

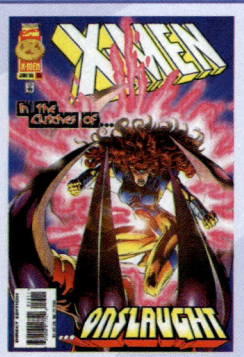

#53
False Fronts

June 1996

Mark Waid
Andy Kubert
Cam Smith/John Dell

Orig. Retail	Price Paid	Value
$1.95		$5

#54
Inquiring Minds

July 1996

Mark Waid
Andy Kubert
Dan Panosian

Orig. Retail	Price Paid	Value
$1.95		$28

#54
Inquiring Minds (Prismatic Cover)

July 1996

Mark Waid
Andy Kubert
Dan Panosian

Orig. Retail	Price Paid	Value
N/A		$3

Page Totals: Price Paid / Total Value

COLLECTOR'S VALUE GUIDE™

Collector's Value Guide™ — X-Men®

#54
Inquiring Minds (Silver Cover)

July 1996

Mark Waid
Andy Kubert
Dan Panosian

Orig. Retail	Price Paid	Value
N/A		$28

#55
Invasion

August 1996

Mark Waid
Andy Kubert
Dan Panosian

Orig. Retail	Price Paid	Value
$1.95		$2.75

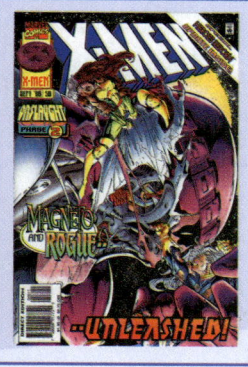

#56
Twilight Of The Gods

September 1996

Scott Lobdell/Mark Waid
Andy Kubert
Art Thibert

Orig. Retail	Price Paid	Value
$1.95		$2.75

#57
Man

October 1996

Scott Lobdell
Andy Kubert
Art Thibert

Orig. Retail	Price Paid	Value
$1.95		$2.75

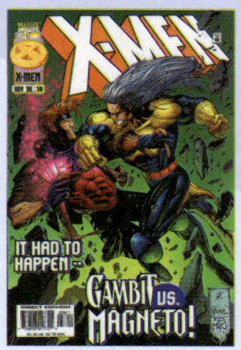

#58
Testament

November 1996

Scott Lobdell/Ralph Macchio
Bernard Chang
Jon Holdredge

Orig. Retail	Price Paid	Value
$1.95		$2.75

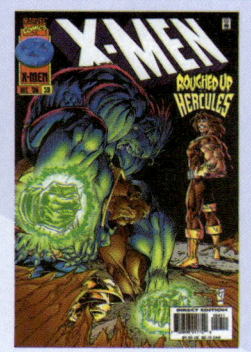

#59
Touched

December 1996

Scott Lobdell/Ralph Macchio
Andy Kubert
Art Thibert

Orig. Retail	Price Paid	Value
$1.95		$2.75

Page Totals:

Price Paid	Total Value

Collector's Value Guide™ — X-Men®

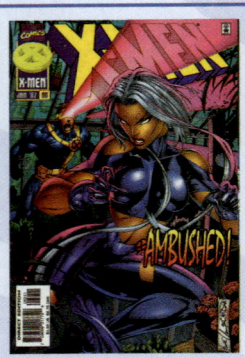

#60
Night

January 1997

Scott Lobdell/Ralph Macchio
Cedric Nocon
Chad Hunt

Orig. Retail	Price Paid	Value
$1.95		$2.75

#61
Bolt

February 1997

Scott Lobdell
Cedric Nocon
Chad Hunt

Orig. Retail	Price Paid	Value
$1.95		$2.75

#62
Games Of Deceit &
Death, Part 1 Of 3

March 1997

Ben Raab
Carlos Pacheco
Art Thibert

Orig. Retail	Price Paid	Value
$1.95		$2.75

#62
Games Of Deceit &
Death, Part 1 Of 3
(Variant Cover)
March 1997

Scott Lobdell/Ben Raab
Carlos Pacheco
Art Thibert

Orig. Retail	Price Paid	Value
N/A		$12

#63
Games Of Deceit &
Death, Part 2 Of 3

April 1997

Scott Lobdell/Ben Raab
Carlos Pacheco
Art Thibert

Orig. Retail	Price Paid	Value
$1.95		$2.75

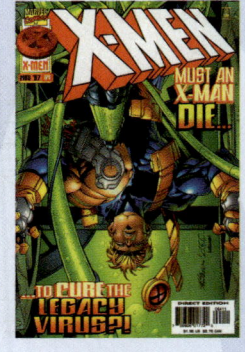

#64
Games Of Deceit &
Death, Part 3 Of 3

May 1997

Scott Lobdell/Ben Raab
Carlos Pacheco
Arthur Edward Thibert

Orig. Retail	Price Paid	Value
$1.95		$2.75

Page Totals: Price Paid | Total Value

COLLECTOR'S VALUE GUIDE™

Collector's Value Guide™ — X-Men®

#65
First Blood

June 1997

Scott Lobdell
Carlos Pacheco
Art Thibert

Orig. Retail	Price Paid	Value
$1.95		$2.75

#66
Start Spreadin' The News . . .

August 1997

Scott Lobdell
Carlos Pacheco
Art Thibert

Orig. Retail	Price Paid	Value
$1.99		$2.50

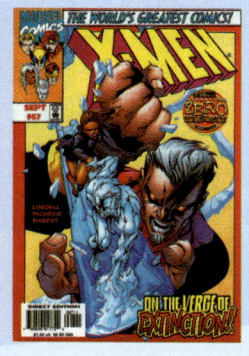

#67
The End Of Days

September 1997

Scott Lobdell
Carlos Pacheco
Art Thibert

Orig. Retail	Price Paid	Value
$1.99		$2.50

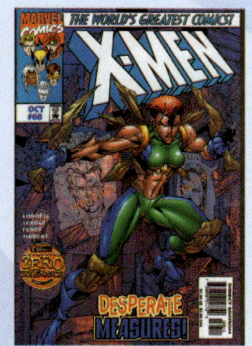

#68
Heart Of The Matter

October 1997

Scott Lobdell/Steve Seagle
Pascual Ferry
Art Thibert

Orig. Retail	Price Paid	Value
$1.99		$2.50

#69
Last Exit

November 1997

Scott Lobdell
C. Pacheco/S. Larroca
Art Thibert

Orig. Retail	Price Paid	Value
$1.99		$2.50

#70
Homecoming

December 1997

Joe Kelly
Carlos Pacheco
Art Thibert/Dell

Orig. Retail	Price Paid	Value
$2.99		$4.75

COLLECTOR'S VALUE GUIDE™

Page Totals:	Price Paid	Total Value

Collector's Value Guide™ — X-Men®

#71
A House In Order

January 1998
Joe Kelly
Carlos Pacheco
Art Thibert

Orig. Retail	Price Paid	Value
$1.99		$3.75

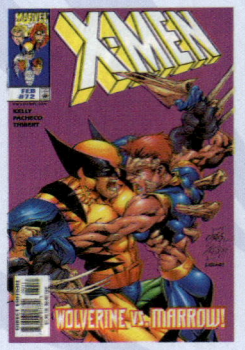

#72
Life Lessons

February 1998
Joe Kelly
Carlos Pacheco
Art Thibert

Orig. Retail	Price Paid	Value
$1.99		$2.75

#73
The Elements Within Us

March 1998
Joe Kelly/Joe Casey
Jeff Johnson
Dan Panosian

Orig. Retail	Price Paid	Value
$1.99		$2.50

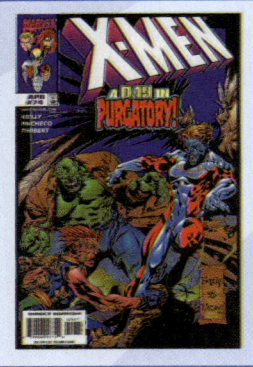

#74
Rituals

April 1998
Joe Kelly
Carlos Pacheco
Art Thibert

Orig. Retail	Price Paid	Value
$1.99		$2.50

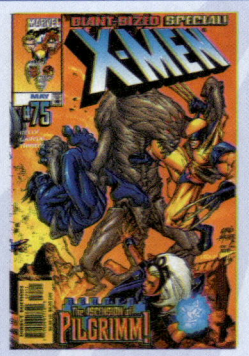

#75
Anatomy Of A Monster

May 1998
Joe Kelly
German Garcia
Various

Orig. Retail	Price Paid	Value
$2.99		$3.50

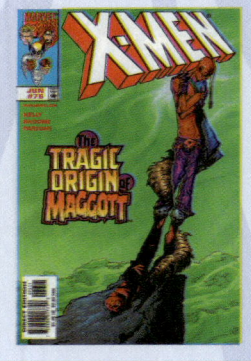

#76
A Boykie And His Dinges

June 1998
Joe Kelly
Matt Broome
Sean Parsons/Aaron Sowd

Orig. Retail	Price Paid	Value
$1.99		$2.50

Page Totals: Price Paid | Total Value

Collector's Value Guide™ — X-Men®

#77
Stormfront Part 1

July 1998
Joe Kelly
German Garcia
Art Thibert

Orig. Retail	Price Paid	Value
$1.99		$2.50

#78
Stormfront Part 2

July 1998
Joe Kelly
German Garcia
Art Thibert

Orig. Retail	Price Paid	Value
$1.99		$2.50

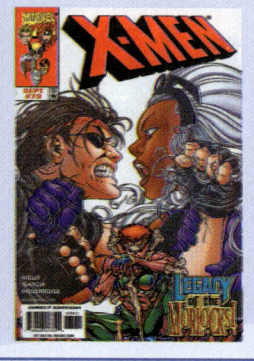

#79
Little Morlock Lost

September 1998
Joe Kelly
German Garcia
Various

Orig. Retail	Price Paid	Value
$1.99		$2.50

#80
Children Of The Atom

October 1998
Joe Kelly
Brandon Peterson
Art Thibert

Orig. Retail	Price Paid	Value
$2.99		$4

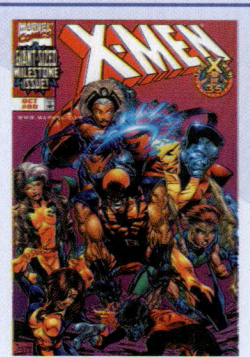

#80
Children Of The Atom
(Dynamic Forces
Exclusive Cover)

October 1998
Joe Kelly
Brandon Peterson
Art Thibert

Orig. Retail	Price Paid	Value
N/A		$7

#80
Children Of The Atom
(Foil Cover)

October 1998
Joe Kelly
Brandon Peterson
Art Thibert

Orig. Retail	Price Paid	Value
$3.99		$5

Page Totals: Price Paid — Total Value

Value Guide — X-Men® (1991-Present)

Collector's Value Guide™ — X-Men®

#81
Jack Of Hearts Queen Of Death!

November 1998

Joe Kelly
Adam Kubert
Mark Farmer

Orig. Retail	Price Paid	Value
$1.99		$2.75

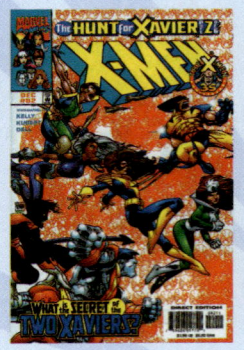

#82
The Hunt For Charly Part 2

December 1998

Joe Kelly
Adam Kubert
John Dell/Jesse Delperdang

Orig. Retail	Price Paid	Value
$1.99		$2.75

#83
Tomb Of Ice

January 1999

Joe Kelly
Adam Kubert
Various

Orig. Retail	Price Paid	Value
$1.99		$2.75

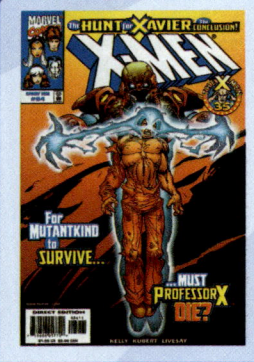

#84
Dream's End!

Early February 1999

Joe Kelly
Adam Kubert/Pascual Ferry
Matt Banning/Pascual Ferry

Orig. Retail	Price Paid	Value
$1.99		$2.75

#85
A Tale Of Two Mutants

Late February 1999

Joe Kelly
Alan Davis
Mark Farmer

Orig. Retail	Price Paid	Value
$1.99		$2.75

#86
Thanks For The Memories

March 1999

Fabian Nicieza/Alan Davis
Alan Davis
Mark Farmer

Orig. Retail	Price Paid	Value
$1.99		$2.75

Page Totals: Price Paid | Total Value

COLLECTOR'S VALUE GUIDE™

Collector's Value Guide™ — X-Men®

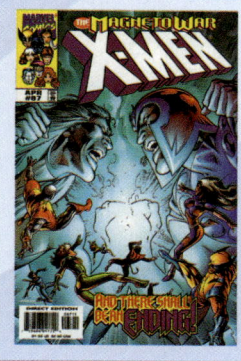

#87
No Surrender!

April 1999

Fabian Nicieza/Alan Davis
Alan Davis
Mark Farmer

Orig. Retail	Price Paid	Value
$1.99		$2.25

#88
A World Apart

May 1999

Joe Casey/Alan Davis
Alan Davis
Mark Farmer

Orig. Retail	Price Paid	Value
$1.99		$2.25

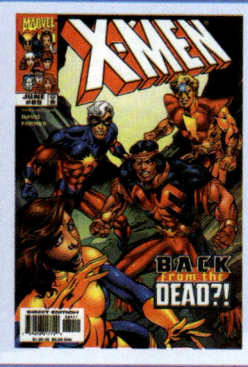

#89
Yesterday's News

June 1999

Terry Kavanaugh/Alan Davis
Alan Davis
Mark Farmer

Orig. Retail	Price Paid	Value
$1.99		$2

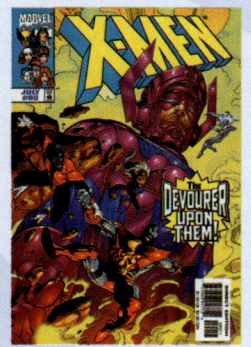

#90
Eve Of Destruction

July 1999

Terry Kavanaugh/Alan Davis
Alan Davis
Mark Farmer

Orig. Retail	Price Paid	Value
$1.99		$2

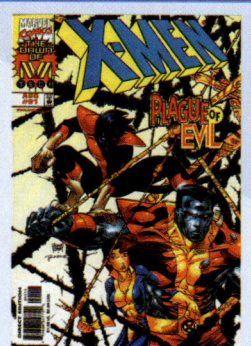

#91
Technical Difficulties

August 1999

Terry Kavanaugh/Alan Davis
Alan Davis
A. Robinson/D. Panosian

Orig. Retail	Price Paid	Value
$1.99		$2

#92
Pressure Points

September 1999

Terry Kavanaugh/Alan Davis
Jeff Johnson
Cam Smith

Orig. Retail	Price Paid	Value
$1.99		$2

COLLECTOR'S VALUE GUIDE™

Page Totals:

Price Paid	Total Value

Collector's Value Guide™ — X-Men®

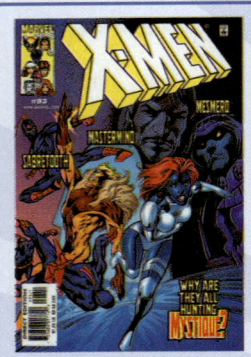

#93
Open Wounds

October 1999

Terry Kavanaugh/Alan Davis
Alan Davis
Mark Farmer

Orig. Retail	Price Paid	Value
$1.99		$2

#94
Pandora's Box

November 1999

Terry Kavanaugh/Alan Davis
Alan Davis
Mark Farmer

Orig. Retail	Price Paid	Value
$2.99		$3

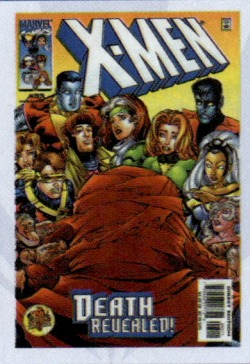

#95
Do Unto Others

December 1999

Alan Davis
Tom Raney
Scott Hanna

Orig. Retail	Price Paid	Value
$1.99		$3.50

#96
The Gathering

January 2000

Alan Davis
Alan Davis
Scott Hanna

Orig. Retail	Price Paid	Value
$1.99		$2.75

#97
The End Of The World As We Know It

February 2000

Terry Kavanaugh/Alan Davis
Alan Davis
Mark Farmer

Orig. Retail	Price Paid	Value
$1.99		$2.50

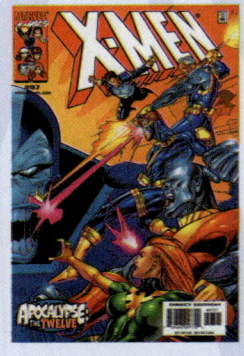

#97
The End Of The World As We Know It (Variant Cover)

February 2000

Terry Kavanaugh/Alan Davis
Alan Davis
Mark Farmer

Orig. Retail	Price Paid	Value
$1.99		$3.50

Page Totals: Price Paid | Total Value

COLLECTOR'S VALUE GUIDE™

Collector's Value Guide™ — X-Men®

#98
First And Last

March 2000

Terry Kavanaugh/Alan Davis
Alan Davis
Mark Farmer

Orig. Retail	Price Paid	Value
$1.99		$3.25

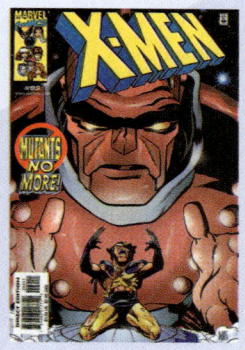

#99
Oh, The Humanity!

April 2000

Terry Kavanaugh/Alan Davis
Brett Booth
Sal Regla

Orig. Retail	Price Paid	Value
$1.99		$3

#100
End Of Days
(Cover By Arthur Adams)

May 2000

Chris Claremont
Leinil Francis Yu
Mark Morales

Orig. Retail	Price Paid	Value
$2.99		$3

#100
End Of Days
(Cover By Dave Cockrum)
May 2000

Chris Claremont
Leinil Francis Yu
Mark Morales

Orig. Retail	Price Paid	Value
N/A		$3

#100
End Of Days
(Cover By John Byrne)
May 2000

Chris Claremont
Leinil Francis Yu
Mark Morales

Orig. Retail	Price Paid	Value
N/A		$3

#100
End Of Days
(Cover By John Romita, Jr.)
May 2000

Chris Claremont
Leinil Francis Yu
Mark Morales

Orig. Retail	Price Paid	Value
N/A		$3

Page Totals: Price Paid / Total Value

Collector's Value Guide™ — X-Men®

#100
End Of Days
(Cover By
Leinil Francis Yu)
May 2000

Chris Claremont
Leinil Francis Yu
Mark Morales

Orig. Retail	Price Paid	Value
N/A		$3

#100
End Of Days
(Cover By
Leinil Francis Yu)
May 2000

Chris Claremont
Leinil Francis Yu
Mark Morales

Orig. Retail	Price Paid	Value
$2.99		$23

#100
End Of Days
(Cover By
Paul Smith)
May 2000

Chris Claremont
Leinil Francis Yu
Mark Morales

Orig. Retail	Price Paid	Value
N/A		$3

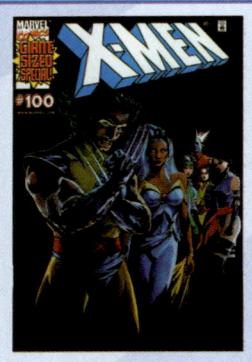

#100
End Of Days
(Dynamic Forces Exclusive
Cover by Jae Lee)
May 2000

Chris Claremont
Leinil Francis Yu
Mark Morales

Orig. Retail	Price Paid	Value
N/A		$9

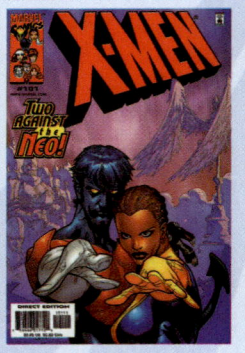

#101
Hard Landing

June 2000

Chris Claremont
Leinil Francis Yu
Mark Morales

Orig. Retail	Price Paid	Value
$2.25		$2.50

#102
The Cruelest Cut

July 2000

Chris Claremont
Leinil Francis Yu
Mark Morales

Orig. Retail	Price Paid	Value
$2.25		$2.50

Page Totals: Price Paid ___ Total Value ___

COLLECTOR'S VALUE GUIDE™

Collector's Value Guide™ — X-Men®

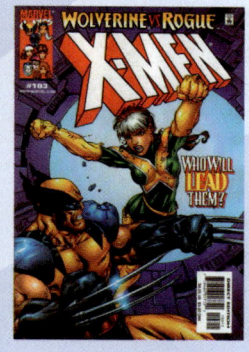

#103
The Goth

August 2000

Chris Claremont
Tom Rainey
Scott Hanna

Orig. Retail	Price Paid	Value
$2.50		$2.50

Future Releases

_____
_____
_____
_____
_____
_____
_____
_____
_____
_____
_____
_____

Annual #1
Various

1992

Various
Various
Various

Orig. Retail	Price Paid	Value
$2.25		$3.75

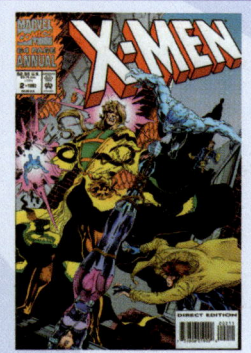

Annual #2
A Bluer Slice Of Heaven

1993

Fabian Nicieza
Aron Wiesenfeld
Various

Orig. Retail	Price Paid	Value
$2.95		$3.50

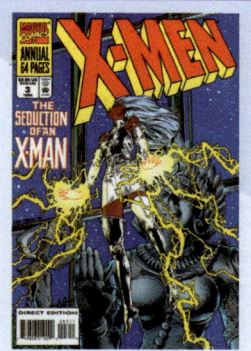

Annual #3
Heart & Soul

1994

Ian Edginton
Gene Ha
Various

Orig. Retail	Price Paid	Value
$2.95		$3.25

X-Men '95
N/A

1995

N/A

Orig. Retail	Price Paid	Value
N/A		$4

Value Guide — X-Men® (1991-Present)

Page Totals:

Price Paid	Total Value

Collector's Value Guide™ — X-Men®

X-Men '96
One Day At The Mansion

1996

Larry Hama
R. Flores/A. Castrillo
N. Massengill/A. Milgrom

Orig. Retail	Price Paid	Value
$2.95		$3.50

X-Men '97
Not A Cloud In The Sky

1997

John Francis Moore
Steve Epting
Dan Green

Orig. Retail	Price Paid	Value
$2.99		$3

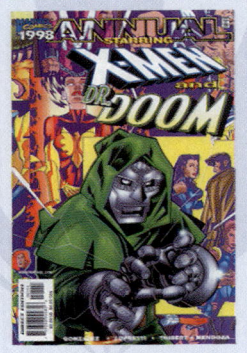

X-Men And Doctor Doom '98

1998

N/A

Orig. Retail	Price Paid	Value
N/A		$3.25

X-Men '99 Annual
Metal Works

August 1999

Alan Davis/Terry Kavanagh
Rick Leonardi
Bob Wiacek

Orig. Retail	Price Paid	Value
$3.50		$3.75

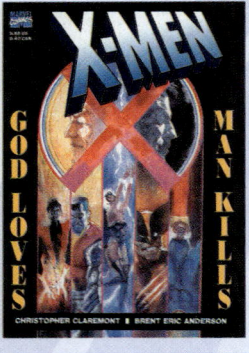

God Loves Man Kills
(Prestige Format)

August 1994

Chris Claremont
Brent Eric Anderson
Brent Eric Anderson

Orig. Retail	Price Paid	Value
$6.95		$7.50

Logan
Path Of The Warlord

February 1996

Howard Mackie
John Paul Leon
Shawn Martinbrough

Orig. Retail	Price Paid	Value
$5.95		$6.25

Page Totals:	Price Paid	Total Value

Collector's Value Guide™ — X-Men®

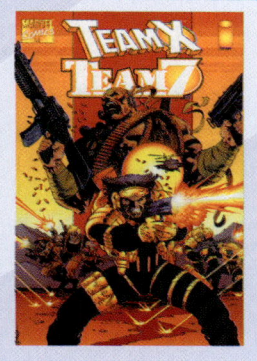

Team X Team 7
All Sold Out

November 1996

Larry Hama
Steve Epting
Klaus Janson

Orig. Retail	Price Paid	Value
$4.95		$6

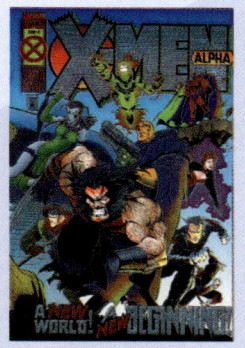

X-Men Alpha
Beginnings . . .

February 1995

Scott Lobdell/Mark Waid
Roger Cruz/Steve Epting
T. Townsend/D. Panosian

Orig. Retail	Price Paid	Value
$3.95		$8

X-Men Alpha
Beginnings . . .
(Gold Cover)

February 1995

Scott Lobdell/Mark Waid
Roger Cruz/Steve Epting
T. Townsend/D. Panosian

Orig. Retail	Price Paid	Value
N/A		$55

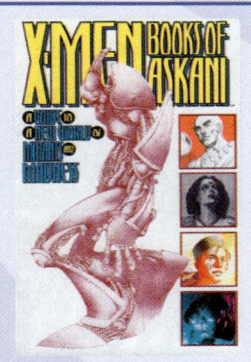

X-Men Books Of Askani
Various

1995

Scott Lobdell
Various
Various

Orig. Retail	Price Paid	Value
$2.95		$3.50

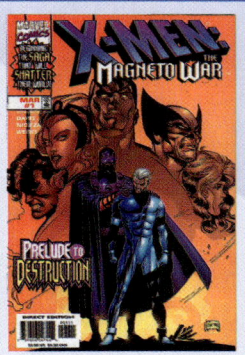

X-Men: The Magneto War
Savior Complex

March 1999

Alan Davis/Fabian Nicieza
Lee Weeks
Dan Green

Orig. Retail	Price Paid	Value
$2.99		$3.25

X-Men Omega
. . . Endings

June 1995

Scott Lobdell/Mark Waid
Roger Cruz
Various

Orig. Retail	Price Paid	Value
$3.95		$8

	Price Paid	Total Value
Page Totals:		

Collector's Value Guide™ — X-Men®

X-Men Omega
... Endings
(Gold Cover)

June 1995
Scott Lobdell/Mark Waid
Roger Cruz
Various

Orig. Retail	Price Paid	Value
N/A		$50

X-Men Prime
Racing The Night

July 1995
Scott Lobdell/Fabian Nicieza
Various
Various

Orig. Retail	Price Paid	Value
$4.95		$8

X-Men Rarities
Various

July 1995
Various
Various
Various

Orig. Retail	Price Paid	Value
$5.95		$6.25

X-Men Year In Review

N/A
N/A

Orig. Retail	Price Paid	Value
N/A		$3

The Age Of Apocalypse

The following section highlights the comics of *The Age Of Apocalypse* series. Each title is presented in alphabetical order (i.e. *The Amazing X-Men®*, *Factor X*™, *etc.*) and the comics within each of those titles are presented in numerical order.

#1
The Crossing Guards
(The Amazing X-Men®)

March 1995
Fabian Nicieza
Andy Kubert
Matt Ryan

Orig. Retail	Price Paid	Value
$1.95		$3.50

Page Totals: Price Paid | Total Value

Collector's Value Guide™ — X-Men®

#2
Sacrificial Lambs
(The Amazing X-Men®)

April 1995

Fabian Nicieza
Andy Kubert
Matt Ryan

Orig. Retail	Price Paid	Value
$1.95		$2.25

#3
Parents Of The Atom
(The Amazing X-Men®)

May 1995

Fabian Nicieza
Andy Kubert
Matt Ryan

Orig. Retail	Price Paid	Value
$1.95		$2.25

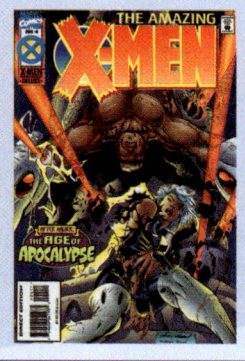

#4
On Consecrated Ground
(The Amazing X-Men®)

June 1995

Fabian Nicieza
Andy Kubert
Matt Ryan

Orig. Retail	Price Paid	Value
$1.95		$2.25

#1
Once More With Feeling
(The Astonishing X-Men®)

March 1995

Scott Lobdell
Joe Madureira
Dan Green/Tim Townsend

Orig. Retail	Price Paid	Value
$1.95		$4

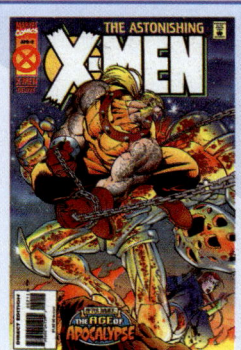

#2
No Exit
(The Astonishing X-Men®)

May 1995

Scott Lobdell/
Joe Madureira
Dan Green/Tim Townsend

Orig. Retail	Price Paid	Value
$1.95		$2.25

#3
In Excess
(The Astonishing X-Men®)

May 1995

Scott Lobdell/Jeph Loeb
Joe Madureira
Tim Townsend/Al Milgrom

Orig. Retail	Price Paid	Value
$1.95		$2.25

Value Guide — The Age Of Apocalypse

Page Totals:	Price Paid	Total Value

Collector's Value Guide™ — X-Men®

Value Guide — The Age Of Apocalypse

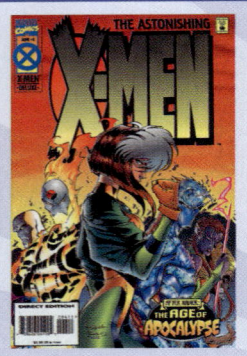

#4
Holocaust!
(The Astonishing X-Men®)
June 1995
Scott Lobdell
Joe Madureira
Tim Townsend/Al Milgrom

Orig. Retail	Price Paid	Value
$1.95		$2.25

#1
Sinister Neglect
(Factor X™)
March 1995
John Francis Moore
Steve Epting
Al Milgrom

Orig. Retail	Price Paid	Value
$1.95		$3.50

#2
Abandoned Children
(Factor X™)
April 1995
John Francis Moore
Steve Epting
Al Milgrom

Orig. Retail	Price Paid	Value
$1.95		$2

#3
Open Wounds
(Factor X™)
May 1995
John Francis Moore
Steve Epting/Terry Dodson
Al Milgrom

Orig. Retail	Price Paid	Value
$1.95		$2

#4
Reckonings
(Factor X™)
June 1995
John Francis Moore
Steve Epting/Terry Dodson
Al Milgrom

Orig. Retail	Price Paid	Value
$1.95		$2

#1
Some Of Us Looking To The Stars *(Gambit And The Xternals™)*
March 1995
Fabian Nicieza
Tony Daniel
Kevin Conrad

Orig. Retail	Price Paid	Value
$1.95		$3.25

Page Totals: | Price Paid | Total Value |

Collector's Value Guide™ — X-Men®

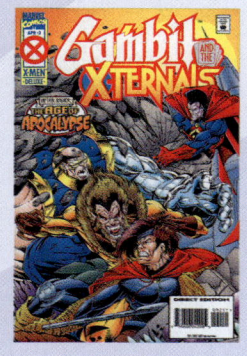

#2
Where No External Has Gone Before! *(Gambit And The Xternals™)*
April 1995
Fabian Nicieza
Tony Daniel
Various

Orig. Retail	Price Paid	Value
$1.95		$2

#3
To The Limits Of Infinity *(Gambit And The Xternals™)*
May 1995
Fabian Nicieza
Salvador Larroca
Al Milgrom

Orig. Retail	Price Paid	Value
$1.95		$2

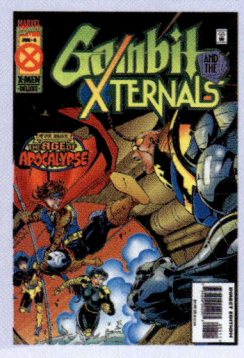

#4
The Maze *(Gambit And The Xternals™)*
June 1995
Fabian Nicieza
Salvador Larroca
Al Milgrom

Orig. Retail	Price Paid	Value
$1.95		$2

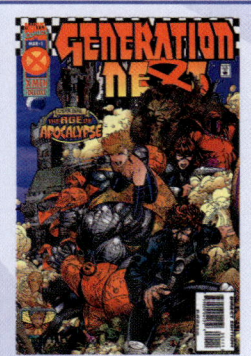

#1
From The Top *(Generation Next™)*
March 1995
Scott Lobdell
Chris Bachalo
Mark Buckingham

Orig. Retail	Price Paid	Value
$1.95		$4.75

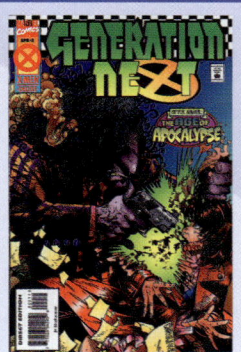

#2
Hither Comes The Sugar Man! *(Generation Next™)*
April 1995
Scott Lobdell
Chris Bachalo
Mark Buckingham

Orig. Retail	Price Paid	Value
$1.95		$3.25

#3
It Only Hurts When I Sing *(Generation Next™)*
May 1995
Scott Lobdell
Chris Bachalo
Mark Buckingham

Orig. Retail	Price Paid	Value
$1.95		$3

Value Guide – The Age Of Apocalypse

Page Totals:	Price Paid	Total Value

Collector's Value Guide™ — X-Men®

Value Guide — The Age Of Apocalypse

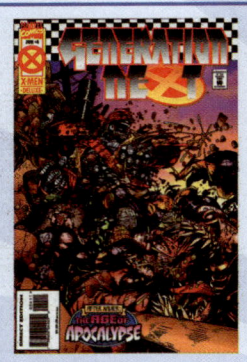

#4
Bye
(Generation Next™)

June 1995

Scott Lobdell
Chris Bachalo
Mark Buckingham

Orig. Retail	Price Paid	Value
$1.95		$3

#1
Unforgiven Trespasses
(Weapon X™)

March 1995

Larry Hama
Adam Kubert
Various

Orig. Retail	Price Paid	Value
$1.95		$4.50

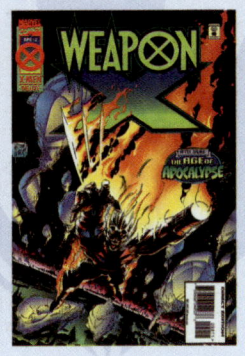

#2
Fire In The Sky!
(Weapon X™)

April 1995

Larry Hama
Adam Kubert
Dan Green

Orig. Retail	Price Paid	Value
$1.95		$3.50

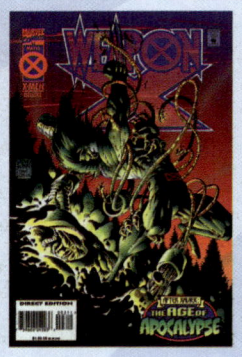

#3
The Common Right Of Toads And Men
(Weapon X™)

May 1995

Larry Hama
Adam Kubert
Dan Green/Mike Sellers

Orig. Retail	Price Paid	Value
$1.95		$3.25

#4
Into The Maelstrom!
(Weapon X™)

June 1995

Larry Hama
Adam Kubert
Dan Green

Orig. Retail	Price Paid	Value
$1.95		$3.25

#1
The Infernal Gallop
(X-Calibre™)

March 1995

Warren Ellis
Ken Lashley
Various

Orig. Retail	Price Paid	Value
$1.95		$3

Page Totals: Price Paid | Total Value

Collector's Value Guide™ — X-Men®

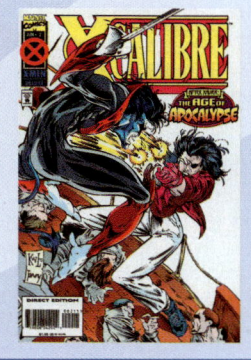

#2
Burn
(X-Calibre™)

April 1995

Warren Ellis
Roger Cruz/Renato Arlem
Various

Orig. Retail	Price Paid	Value
$1.95		$2

#3
Body Heat
(X-Calibre™)

May 1995

Warren Ellis
Ken Lashley
Tom Wegrzyn/Philip Moy

Orig. Retail	Price Paid	Value
$1.95		$2

#4
On Fire
(X-Calibre™)

June 1995

Warren Ellis
Ken Lashley
Tom Wegrzyn/Philip Moy

Orig. Retail	Price Paid	Value
$1.95		$2

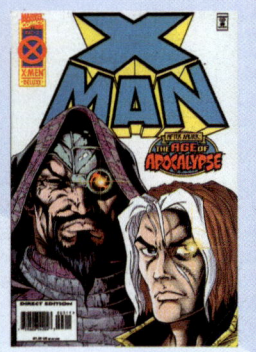

#1
Breaking Away
(X-Man™)

March 1995

Jeph Loeb
Steve Skroce
Various

Orig. Retail	Price Paid	Value
$1.95		$5.75

#2
Choosing Sides
(X-Man™)

April 1995

Jeph Loeb
Steve Skroce
Various

Orig. Retail	Price Paid	Value
$1.95		$4

#3
Turning Point
(X-Man™)

May 1995

Jeph Loeb
Steve Skroce
Bud Larosa/Mike Sellers

Orig. Retail	Price Paid	Value
$1.95		$3.75

Value Guide – The Age Of Apocalypse

COLLECTOR'S VALUE GUIDE™

Page Totals:	Price Paid	Total Value

Collector's Value Guide™ — X-Men®

#4
The Art Of War
(X-Man™)

June 1995

Jeph Loeb
Steve Skroce
Bud Larosa

Orig. Retail	Price Paid	Value
$1.95		$3.75

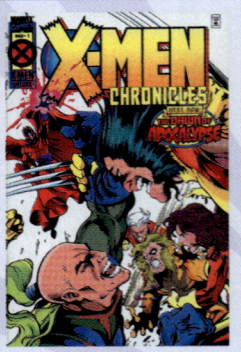

#1
Origins
(X-Men Chronicles)

March 1995

Howard Mackie
Terry Dodson
Klaus Janson

Orig. Retail	Price Paid	Value
$3.95		$6

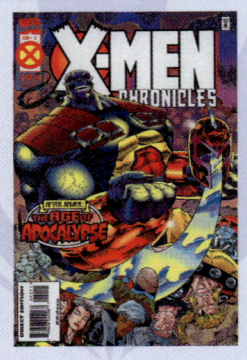

#2
Shattered Dreams
(X-Men Chronicles)

June 1995

Howard Mackie
Ian Churchill
Various

Orig. Retail	Price Paid	Value
$3.95		$6

#1
Last Stand
(X-Universe™)

May 1995

S. Lobdell/T. Kavanagh
Carlos Pacheco
Cam Smith

Orig. Retail	Price Paid	Value
$3.50		$5.25

#2
Last Stand
(X-Universe™)

June 1995

S. Lobdell/T. Kavanagh
C. Pacheco/T. Dodson
Cam Smith/Robin Riggs

Orig. Retail	Price Paid	Value
$3.50		$4.25

Mini Series

The following section highlights comics that were published in mini series. Each title is presented in alphabetical order (i.e. *Askani'son*™, *The Astonishing X-Men*®, *etc.*) and the comics within each of those titles are presented in numerical order.

Page Totals: Price Paid / Total Value

COLLECTOR'S VALUE GUIDE™

Collector's Value Guide™ — X-Men®

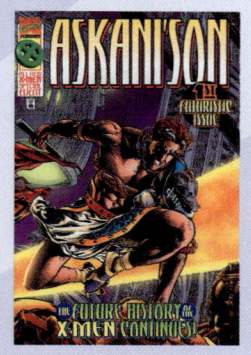

#1
The Shadow Lengthens
(Askani'son™)

February 1996

Scott Lobdell/Jeph Loeb
Gene Ha
Andrew Pepoy

Orig. Retail	Price Paid	Value
$2.95		$3

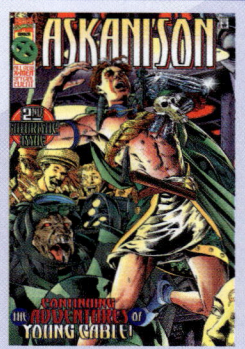

#2
A Tiny Spark
(Askani'son™)

March 1996

Scott Lobdell/Jeph Loeb
Gene Ha
Andrew Pepoy

Orig. Retail	Price Paid	Value
$2.95		$3

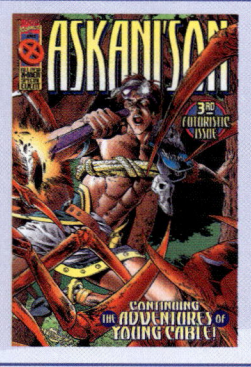

#3
An Ember Glows . . .
(Askani'son™)

April 1996

Scott Lobdell/Jeph Loeb
Gene Ha
Andrew Pepoy

Orig. Retail	Price Paid	Value
$2.95		$3

#4
A Bright And Shining Light
(Askani'son™)

May 1996

Scott Lobdell/Jeph Loeb
Gene Ha
Andrew Pepoy

Orig. Retail	Price Paid	Value
$2.95		$3

#1
Call To Arms!
(The Astonishing X-Men®)

September 1999

Howard Mackie
Brandon Peterson
T. Townsend/D. Panosian

Orig. Retail	Price Paid	Value
$2.50		$10

#1
**Call To Arms! (Dynamic Forces Printed Sketch Cover,
The Astonishing X-Men®)**

September 1999

Howard Mackie
Brandon Peterson
T. Townsend/D. Panosian

Orig. Retail	Price Paid	Value
N/A		$20

Page Totals: Price Paid / Total Value

Value Guide — Mini Series

Collector's Value Guide™ — X-Men®

#1
Call To Arms! (Dynamic Forces Printed Sketch Cover Limited Edition, *The Astonishing X-Men*®)
September 1999
Howard Mackie
Brandon Peterson
T. Townsend/D. Panosian

Orig. Retail	Price Paid	Value
N/A		$95

#1
Call To Arms! (Variant Cover, *The Astonishing X-Men*®)
September 1999
Howard Mackie
Brandon Peterson
T. Townsend/D. Panosian

Orig. Retail	Price Paid	Value
N/A		N/E

#2
The Trouble With Mannites (*The Astonishing X-Men*®)
October 1999
Howard Mackie
B. Peterson/B. Booth
T. Townsend/D. Panosian

Orig. Retail	Price Paid	Value
$2.50		$6.50

#3
In The Shadow Of Death! (*The Astonishing X-Men*®)
November 1999
Howard Mackie
Brandon Peterson
T. Townsend/D. Panosian

Orig. Retail	Price Paid	Value
$2.50		$6.50

#1
Mystery School (*Pryde*™ *And Wisdom*™)
September 1996
Warren Ellis
Terry Dodson/Karl Story
Various

Orig. Retail	Price Paid	Value
$1.95		$2

#2
Mystery Walk (*Pryde*™ *And Wisdom*™)
October 1996
Warren Ellis
T. Dodson/A. Lopresti
Various

Orig. Retail	Price Paid	Value
$1.95		$2

Page Totals: Price Paid ___ Total Value ___

Collector's Value Guide™ — X-Men®

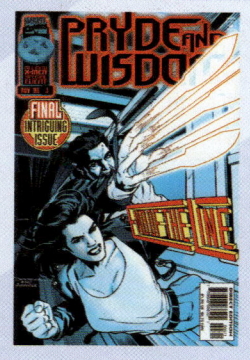

#3
Mystery Train
(Pryde™ And Wisdom™)
November 1996

Warren Ellis
T. Dodson/A. Lopresti
Various

Orig. Retail	Price Paid	Value
$1.95		$2

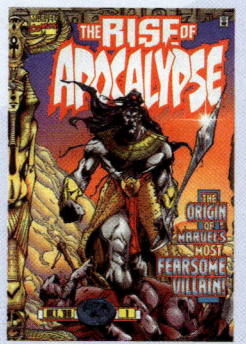

#1
Hammer & Chisel
(The Rise Of Apocalypse™)
October 1996

Terry Kavanagh
Adam Pollina
M. Morales/H. Candelario

Orig. Retail	Price Paid	Value
$1.95		$3.25

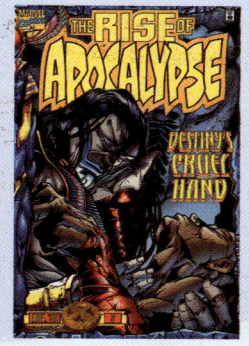

#2
Blood Of The Father
(The Rise Of Apocalypse™)
November 1996

T. Kavanagh/J. Felder
Adam Pollina
Mark Morales

Orig. Retail	Price Paid	Value
$1.95		$3.25

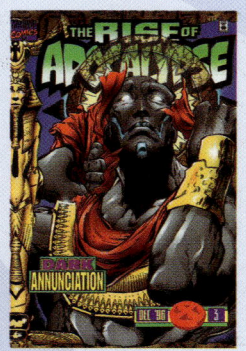

#3
The Face Of The Gods
(The Rise Of Apocalypse™)
December 1996

T. Kavanagh/J. Felder
Adam Pollina
Mark Morales

Orig. Retail	Price Paid	Value
$1.95		$3.25

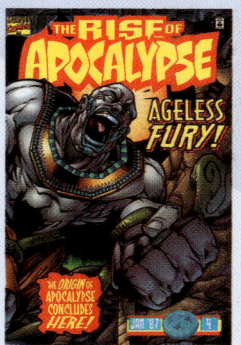

#4
The First Culling
(The Rise Of Apocalypse™)
January 1997

T. Kavanagh/J. Felder
A. Pollina/A. Williams
Mark Morales/Al Milgrom

Orig. Retail	Price Paid	Value
$1.95		$3.25

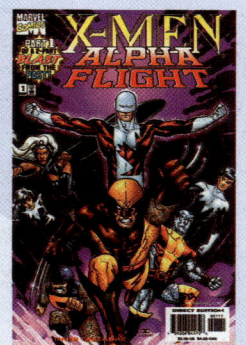

#1
Survivors
(X-Men: Alpha Flight®)
May 1998

Ben Raab/John Cassaday
John Cassaday
John Cassaday

Orig. Retail	Price Paid	Value
$2.99		$3.50

Page Totals: Price Paid / Total Value

Collector's Value Guide™ — X-Men®

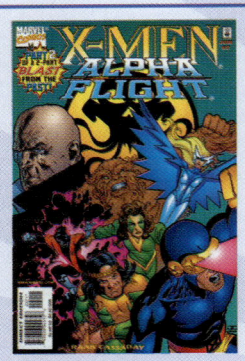

#2
Should Old Acquaintance Be Forgot... (X-Men: Alpha Flight®)
June 1998

John Cassaday/Ben Raab
John Cassaday
John Cassaday

Orig. Retail	Price Paid	Value
$2.99		$3

#1
The Gift (X-Men And Alpha Flight®)
December 1985

Chris Claremont
Paul Smith
Bob Wiacek

Orig. Retail	Price Paid	Value
$1.50		$5.50

#2
The Gift Part II (X-Men And Alpha Flight®)
January 1986

Chris Claremont
Paul Smith
Bob Wiacek & Friends

Orig. Retail	Price Paid	Value
$1.50		$5

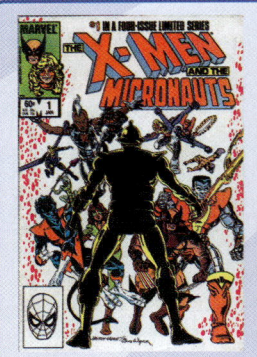

#1
First Encounter (X-Men And The Micronauts™)
January 1984

C. Claremont/B. Mantlo
Butch Guice
Bob Wiacek

Orig. Retail	Price Paid	Value
60¢		$4

#2
N/A (X-Men And The Micronauts™)
February 1984

B. Mantlo/C. Claremont
Butch Guice
Bob Wiacek/Kelley Jones

Orig. Retail	Price Paid	Value
60¢		$4

#3
Mine Eyes Have Seen The Gory! (X-Men And The Micronauts™)
March 1984

C. Claremont/B. Mantlo
Butch Guice
Bob Wiacek

Orig. Retail	Price Paid	Value
60¢		$4

Page Totals: Price Paid | Total Value

Value Guide – Mini Series

COLLECTOR'S VALUE GUIDE™

Collector's Value Guide™ — X-Men®

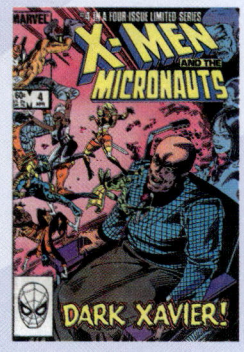

#4
Doppelganger!
(X-Men And The Micronauts™)
April 1984
C. Claremont/B. Mantlo
Butch Guice
Bob Wiacek

Orig. Retail	Price Paid	Value
60¢		$4

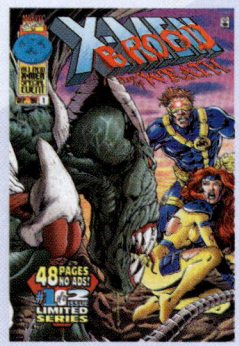

#1
Day Of Wrath Part 1
(X-Men: Brood Day Of Wrath™)
September 1996
John Ostrander
Bryan Hitch
Paul Neary

Orig. Retail	Price Paid	Value
$2.95		$3.25

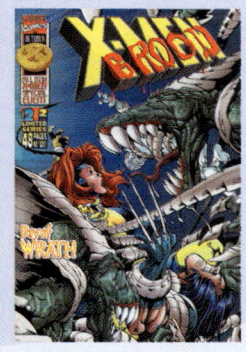

#2
Day Of Wrath Part 2
(X-Men: Brood Day Of Wrath™)
October 1996
John Ostrander
Bryan Hitch/Sal Velluto
Various

Orig. Retail	Price Paid	Value
$2.95		$3.25

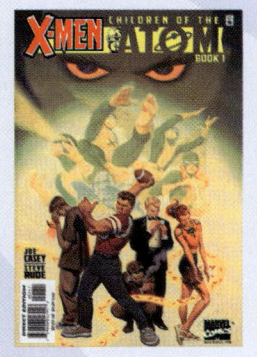

#1
Childhood's End
(X-Men: Children Of The Atom™)
November 1999
Joe Casey
Steve Rude
Andrew Pepoy

Orig. Retail	Price Paid	Value
$2.99		$4.25

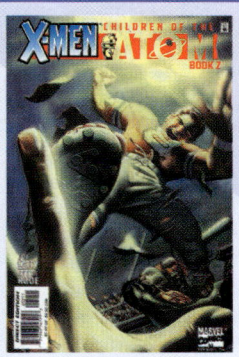

#2
All Children Wear The Sign *(X-Men: Children Of The Atom™)*
December 1999
Joe Casey
Steve Rude
Andrew Pepoy

Orig. Retail	Price Paid	Value
$2.99		$3

#3
Children Of A Lesser God *(X-Men: Children Of The Atom™)*
June 2000
Joe Casey
Steve Rude
Andrew Pepoy

Orig. Retail	Price Paid	Value
$2.99		$3

Value Guide — Mini Series

COLLECTOR'S VALUE GUIDE™

Page Totals:	Price Paid	Total Value

Collector's Value Guide™ — X-Men®

#4
Child's Play
(X-Men: Children Of The Atom™)
July 2000
Joe Casey
Paul Smith/Michael Ryan
Paul Smith/Andrew Pepoy

Orig. Retail	Price Paid	Value
$2.99		$3

#5
Where Your Children Are *(X-Men: Children Of The Atom™)*
August 2000
Joe Casey
Essad Ribic
Andrew Pepoy

Orig. Retail	Price Paid	Value
$2.99		$3

#6
N/A
(X-Men: Children Of The Atom™)
To Be Issued September 2000
N/A

Orig. Retail	Price Paid	Value
$____		$____

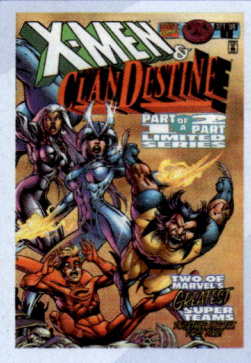

#1
Dreams Of Darkest Destiny *(X-Men & The Clandestine™)*
October 1996
Alan Davis
Alan Davis
Mark Farmer

Orig. Retail	Price Paid	Value
$2.95		$3.25

#2
The Destine's Darkest Dreams *(X-Men & The Clandestine™)*
November 1996
Alan Davis
Alan Davis
Mark Farmer

Orig. Retail	Price Paid	Value
$2.95		$3

#1
Witchhunt
(X-Men: The Hellfire Club™)
February 2000
Ben Raab
Charlie Adlard
Charlie Adlard

Orig. Retail	Price Paid	Value
$2.50		$2.75

Page Totals: Price Paid | Total Value

Collector's Value Guide™ — X-Men®

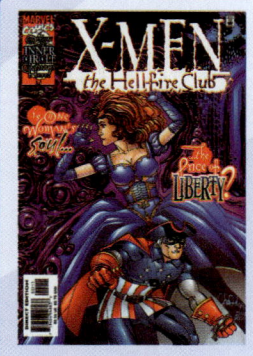

	#2 Toll The Bell Liberty (X-Men: The Hellfire Club™) February 2000 Ben Raab Charlie Adlard Charlie Adlard	#3 For Want Of A Soul (X-Men: The Hellfire Club™) March 2000 Ben Raab Charlie Adlard Charlie Adlard	#4 Also Sprach Sebastian (X-Men: The Hellfire Club™) April 2000 Ben Raab Charlie Adlard Charlie Adlard
Orig. Retail	$2.50	$2.50	$2.50
Price Paid			
Value	$2.50	$2.50	$2.50

	#1 Old Friends (X-Men: Liberators) November 1998 Joe Harris Phil Jimenez/Keith Aiken Various	#2 Home Is Where The Heart Is (X-Men: Liberators) December 1998 Joe Harris Phil Jimenez Various	#3 A Game Of Hide & Seek! (X-Men: Liberators) January 1999 Joe Harris Phil Jimenez/Keith Aiken Various
Orig. Retail	$2.99	$2.99	$2.99
Price Paid			
Value	$3.50	$3.50	$3.50

Page Totals:	Price Paid	Total Value

Collector's Value Guide™ — X-Men®

#4
Gifted Youngsters
(X-Men: Liberators)

February 1999

Joe Harris
Phil Jimenez
John Stokes

Orig. Retail	Price Paid	Value
$2.99		$3.50

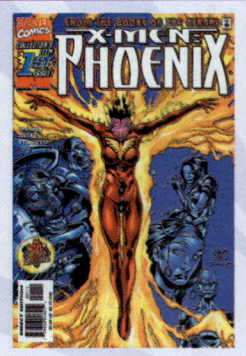

#1
Askani Rising
Part One
(X-Men: Phoenix®)

December 1999

John Francis Moore
Pascal Alixe
Various

Orig. Retail	Price Paid	Value
$2.50		$2.75

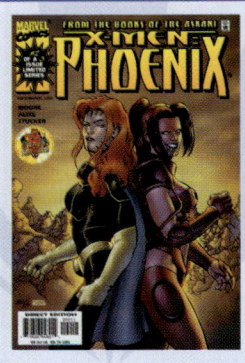

#2
Contagion
Askani Rising Part Two
(X-Men: Phoenix®)

January 2000

John Francis Moore
Pascal Alixe
Various

Orig. Retail	Price Paid	Value
$2.50		$2.75

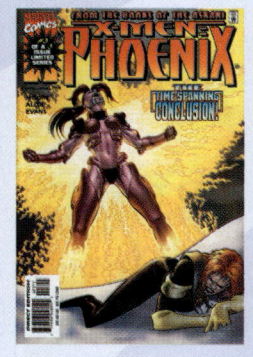

#3
Sacrifice
Askani Rising Conclusion
(X-Men: Phoenix®)

March 2000

John Moore
Pascal Alixe/Alan Evans
Various

Orig. Retail	Price Paid	Value
$2.50		$2.75

#1
Phalkon Quest
Part 1 *(X-Men Spotlight On . . . Starjammers™)*
1990

Terry Kavanagh
Dave Cockrum
Jeff Albrecht

Orig. Retail	Price Paid	Value
$4.50		$4.75

#2
Phalkon Quest
Part 2 *(X-Men Spotlight On . . . Starjammers™)*
1990

Terry Kavanagh
Dave Cockrum
Jeff Albrecht

Orig. Retail	Price Paid	Value
$4.50		$4.75

Page Totals:	Price Paid	Total Value

COLLECTOR'S
VALUE GUIDE™

Collector's Value Guide™ — X-Men®

#1
True Friends
(X-Men: True Friends)

September 1999

Chris Claremont
Rick Leonardi
Various

Orig. Retail	Price Paid	Value
$2.99		$3.50

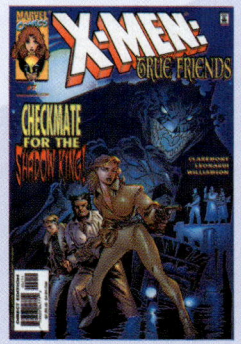

#2
Royal Hunt
(X-Men: True Friends)

October 1999

Chris Claremont
Rick Leonardi
A. Williamson/J. Palmiotti

Orig. Retail	Price Paid	Value
$2.99		$3.50

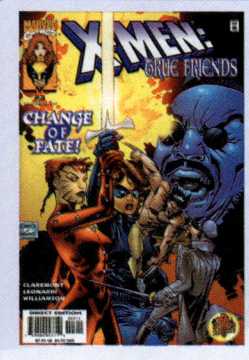

#3
Claiming The Clown
(X-Men: True Friends)

November 1999

Chris Claremont
Rick Leonardi
Al Williamson

Orig. Retail	Price Paid	Value
$2.99		$3.50

#1
Justice For All!
(The X-Men® Vs The Avengers®)
April 1987

Roger Stern
Marc Silvestri
Josef Rubinstein

Orig. Retail	Price Paid	Value
$1.50		$4.50

#2
Uneasy Allies
(The X-Men® Vs. The Avengers®)
May 1987

Roger Stern
Marc Silvestri
Josef Rubinstein

Orig. Retail	Price Paid	Value
$1.50		$3.50

#3
The Soviets Strike Back! *(The X-Men® Vs. The Avengers®)*
June 1987

Roger Stern
Marc Silvestri
Josef Rubinstein

Orig. Retail	Price Paid	Value
$1.50		$3.50

COLLECTOR'S
VALUE GUIDE™

Page Totals:	Price Paid	Total Value

Collector's Value Guide™ — X-Men®

#4
Day Of Judgement!
(The X-Men® Vs. The Avengers®)
July 1987
Tom DeFalco/Jim Shooter
Keith Pollard
Josef Rubinstein

Orig. Retail	Price Paid	Value
$1.50		$3.50

Other Uncanny X-Men® Comics

The following section highlights additional one shot comics based on the characters and intricate story lines of the *Uncanny X-Men* comic series. These issues offer a tangent to the on-going saga.

Special Edition X-Men
Second Genesis!
February 1983
Len Wein
Dave Cockrum
Dave Cockrum

Orig. Retail	Price Paid	Value
$2		$22

The Uncanny X-Men And The New Teen Titans
1982
Chris Claremont
Walter Simonson
Terry Austin

Orig. Retail	Price Paid	Value
$2		$22

The Uncanny X-Men At The State Fair Of Texas
1983
N/A

Orig. Retail	Price Paid	Value
N/A		$20

Future Releases

_____
_____
_____
_____
_____
_____
_____
_____
_____
_____
_____
_____

Page Totals:	Price Paid	Total Value

COLLECTOR'S VALUE GUIDE™

Collector's Value Guide™ — X-Men®

X-MEN® SPIN OFFS

Many of the most popular characters from the original *X-Men* series and new teams of X-related personnel started to emerge in the early 1980s with their own titles to capture readership and offer diverging storylines. *The New Mutants*™ was the first new team to debut in 1982 as a graphic novel which was then offered as a regular comic book series beginning in 1983.

Following the success of this superhero team spin off, *X-Factor*™ was introduced 1986 and featured many of the familiar old characters created by Lee and Kirby in 1963. *Excalibur*™, an *X-Men* title with a comedic slant, debuted in 1988 as well as the first *X-Men* character to get his own series, *Wolverine*®.

Other teams and single character series have followed including *X-Force*™ in 1991 and one of the more recent additions – *Bishop*™: *The Last X-Man*, which debuted in 1999. In the following lists, you will find the more popular of these X-generated spin offs each listed with its title and secondary market value.

Bishop™: The Last X-Man
(October 1999 to Present)

		Value
○ #1	Time Loves A Hero	$3.25
○ #2	Wish You Were Here	$2.75
○ #3	Walk This Way	$2.50
○ #4	Over The Hills And Far Away	$2
○ #5	In The Hall Of The Mountain King	$2
○ #6	The Battle Of Evermore!	$2
○ #7	A New Day Yesterday	$2
○ #8	Hello, Old Friend	$2
○ #9	Locomotive Breath	$2
○ #10	Gimme Shelter	$2
○ #11	Can't You Hear Me Knockin'?	N/E

Cable™
(October 1992 to Present)

		Value
○ #-1	The Devil's Herald	$2
○ #1	Rocks And Waves	$4.25
○ #2	Mired In Destiny	$2.50
○ #3	Twenty Questions	$2.50

Collector's Value Guide™ — X-Men®

Cable, cont.   Value
- #4   A Leader Among Men $2.50
- #5   Sinsearly Yours Sincerely Mine .. $2.50
- #6   Sunset Breaks $2.50
- #7   Illuminated Knights $2.50
- #8   Day Spring $2.50
- #9   In Humanity $2.25
- #10 Like Lambs To The Slaughter ... $2.25
- #11 Divide And Conquer $2.25
- #12 The Quick And The Dead $2.25
- #13 A Kiss Before Dying $2.25
- #14 Fear And Loathing $2.25
- #15 Shadows $2.25
- #16 The Phalanx Sanction $2.25
- #17 The Calling $2
- #18 Judgement Day $2
- #19 In The Name Of The Father $2
- #20 An Hour Of Last Things $2
- #21 . . . Our Regularly Scheduled
       Program $2.25
- #22 Sanctuary $2.25
- #23 Family Secrets $2.25
- #24 Lost Souls $2.25
- #25 What Was . . . What Is $4
- #26 The Long Way Home $2
- #27 Rebels $2
- #28 Tick . . . Tick . . . Tick! $2
- #29 Man In The Mirror $2
- #30 For Every Action $2
- #31 . . . There Is A Reaction! $2
- #32 Venting $2
- #33 Never Is A Very Short Time $2
- #34 Loose Cannons $2
- #35 It Is Always Darkest $2

Cable, cont.   Value
- #36 The Gift $2
- #37 True Lies $2
- #38 In Perspective $2
- #39 All Things Great And Small $2
- #40 Into The Dark $2
- #41 The Depths Of Time $2
- #42 Tolerance $2
- #43 Broken Soldiers $2
- #44 Temptation In The Wilderness .. $2
- #45 No Escape $2
- #46 Siege $2
- #47 Man To Man $2
- #48 Dirty Secrets $2
- #49 Weary Knights & Shabby Paladins .. $2
- #50 And He Shall Be Called . . . Man! . $3.25
- #51 Faith And Deception $2
- #52 Beyond Belief $2
- #53 Beautiful Friend $2
- #54 Jungle Action $2
- #55 Wiser Times $2
- #56 Bloodrite $2
- #57 Momentary Lapse $2
- #58 Busted! $2
- #59 Pressure Points $2
- #60 Atlas Burned $2
- #61 Captive Audience $2
- #62 Strange Agencies $2
- #63 Illusions Of Doom $2
- #64 'Twas The Night Before Dying .. $2
- #65 Acid Bath $2
- #66 Death From Above $2
- #67 God's Footsteps $2
- #68 Sign Of The Times $2
- #69 Millennium Storm Warning $2
- #70 The Ballad Of Karmic Retribution .. $2
- #71 Dreams, Nightmares & Prophecies . $2
- #72 Broken Pillars $2
- #73 Pestilence! $2
- #74 Mindgames $2
- #75 Who Is Worthy To Break
       The Seals . . . ? $3.50
- #76 In My Eyes $2
- #77 Falsehoods $2
- #78 I Still Believe I Cannot Be Saved .. $2
- #79 A Tale Of Revolution!: Fire Burn .. $2
- #80 . . . Cauldron Bubble $2

Collector's Value Guide™ — X-Men®

Cable, cont.
		Value
○	#81 The Nexus Of Time And Space	$2
○	#82 Irene Must Die!	N/E
○	Annual #1	$3.25
○	Annual #2	$3.25
○	Annual #3	$3.25
○	Annual #4	$3.50

Excalibur™
(October 1988 to October 1998)

		Value
○	#-1 A True And Terrible Sacrifice	$2
○	#1 Warwolves Of London	$6.50
○	#2 A Warwolf Possessed	$3.75
○	#3 Moving Day	$3.50
○	#4 Still Crazy After All These Years	$3.25
○	#5 Send In The Clowns!	$3.25
○	#6 Goblin Night	$3
○	#7 Goblin Morn	$3
○	#8 Excalibur's New York Adventure	$3
○	#9 The Two-Edged Sword	$3
○	#10 Widget	$3
○	#11 The Price	$2
○	#12 My Friends Call Me Billy The Kid	$2
○	#13 The Marriage Of True Minds	$2
○	#14 Too Many Heroes	$2
○	#15 Technet: Impossible Missions	$2
○	#16 Warlord	$1.75
○	#17 From The Crucible... A Captain?	$1.75
○	#18 Wild Wild Wheels	$1.75
○	#19 Madripoor Knights	$1.75
○	#20 The Eye Of The Beholder	$1.75
○	#21 Crusader X	$1.75
○	#22 Shadows Triumphant	$1.75
○	#23 Here Comes The Judge	$1.75
○	#24 Tempting Fates	$1.75
○	#25 Guess Who's Coming For Phoenix?	$1.75
○	#26 The Times They Are A-Changin	$1.75
○	#27 Reel People	$1.75
○	#28 The Night They Tore Down The Gilded Lady	$1.75
○	#29 Dream A Little Dream	$1.75
○	#30 Twas A Dark And Stormy Night	$1.75
○	#31 No Man Is An Island	$2

Excalibur, cont.
		Value
○	#32 Someone Will Die For This!	$2
○	#33 Cat On A Hot Tin Roof	$2
○	#34 School Spirit	$2
○	#35 Heartbreakers	$2
○	#36 Xs And Os	$2
○	#37 House Call	$2
○	#38 Out On A Limbo	$2
○	#39 Heart Of The Matter	$2
○	#40 The Trial Of Lockheed	$2
○	#41 At Last...The Reunion!	$2
○	#42 A Hatch Is Plotted	$2
○	#43 Home Comforts	$2
○	#44 Witless For The Prosecution	$2
○	#45 Nightcrawler's Technet	$2
○	#46 Colin The Barbarian	$2
○	#47 Come One And All To The Ugly Bug-Eyed Monster Ball	$2
○	#48 Irish Stew	$2
○	#49 Let There Be Dark	$2
○	#50 Winner Loses All	$2.25
○	#51 Don't Drink The Water	$2
○	#52 All You Ever Wanted To Know About Phoenix...But Were Afraid To Ask	$2
○	#53 The Litter	$2
○	#54 Curiouser And Curiouser	$2
○	#55 The Ghost Of Braddock Manor	$2
○	#56 Things That Go Shriek In The Night	$2
○	#57 For Whom The Bell Trolls	$2
○	#58 Troll Call	$2
○	#59 Enter...The Panther	$2
○	#60 Braddock Of The Jungle	$2
○	#61 Truth And Consequence	$2

Collector's Value Guide™ — X-Men®

Excalibur, cont.	Value
#62 Of Birth, Death And The Confused, Painful Bit In Between	$2
#63 Denial	$2
#64 Ascension	$2
#65 White Lies, Dark Truths	$2
#66 Back To The Present	$2
#67 Days Of Futures Yet To Come	$2
#68 Facades	$2
#69 Blight And Fog	$2
#70 Crime And Punishment	$2
#71 Crossing Swords	$4.25
#72 Ooohhh . . . Siena!	$2
#73 Memories Are Made Of This	$2
#74 In The Name Of Love	$2
#75 Hello, I Must Be Going	$2.50
#76 Dog Years	$2
#77 Lowest Common Denominator	$2
#78 Fire In The Wild	$2
#79 Twisted Logic	$2
#80 Out Of Time	$2
#81 Beginnings, Middles & Endings	$2
#82 The Light Of A Tainted Dawn	$3
#83 Bend Sinister	$2
#84 Dark Adapted Eye	$2
#85 Edge Of Night	$2
#86 Back To Life	$2
#87 Back To Reality	$2
#88 Dream Nails	$2
#89 Easy Tiger	$2
#90 Blood Eagle	$3
#91 Baby I Love You	$2
#92 I Want You	$2
#93 The Spire	$2
#94 Days Of Future Tense	$2

Excalibur, cont.	Value
#95 Amplified Heart	$2
#96 Fireback	$2
#97 Counterfire	$2
#98 Fireflies	$2
#99 Fire With Fire	$2
#100 London's Burning	$4
#101 Quiet	$2
#102 After The Bomb	$2
#103 Bend Sinister Reprise	$2
#104 Buried Secret	$2
#105 Hard Truths	$2
#106 A Portrait Of The Artist	$2
#107 Focus	$2
#108 The Old Ways	$2
#109 Dragon Moon Rising	$2
#110 Hearts Bled Crimson	$2
#111 Broken Vows	N/E
#112 Survival	$2
#113 Faith	$2
#114 For The One I Love	$2
#115 Missionaries	$2
#116 Death In Venice	$2
#117 Amendments	$2
#118 New Year's Evil	$2
#119 Preludes And Nightmares	$2
#120 Current Events	$2
#121 With Friends Like These	$2
#122 The Search Part 1	$2
#123 The Search Part 2	$2
#124 Someone	$2
#125 Tying The Knot	$3.50
Annual #1	$3.25
Annual #2	$3.25
Special Edition: Air Apparent	$7.50

Generation X™
(November 1994 to Present)

	Value
#-1 The Beginning Of A Beautiful Friendship	$2
#1/2 (San Diego Giveaway)	$12
#1/2 (*Wizard* Mail-Away)	N/E
#1/2 (*Wizard* Red Foil Edition)	N/E
#1 Third Genesis	$7
#2 Searching	$2.50
#2 Searching (Deluxe Edition)	$4.50

Collector's Value Guide™ — X-Men®

Generation X, cont.	Value
#3 Dead Silence	$2.25
#3 Dead Silence (Deluxe Edition)	$4.25
#4 Between the Cracks	$2.25
#4 Between the Cracks (Deluxe Edition)	$4.25
#5 Don't Touch That Dial!	$2.75
#6 Notes From The Underground	$2.75
#7 Nights and Bolts	$2.75
#8 What Happened To Cassidy Keep?!	$2.50
#9 Someplace Other Than Here	$2.50
#10 Death Wail	$2.50
#11 Death Wail Part Two	$2.50
#12 The Return Of Emplate	$2.50
#13 It's All Relative	$2.50
#14 Jubilee's Top Ten Reasons Why Emplate Is A Loser!	$2.50
#15 Death In the Family	$2.50
#16 Out of Sync!	$2.50
#17 The Teeth Of Our Skin	$2.50
#18 For The Sake Of The Children	$2.50
#19 Don't Wait Up	$2.50
#20 Bodies In Motion	$2.50
#21 To Live And Die And Molt In L.A.	$2.50
#22 All Hallows Eve	$2.50
#23 For All This We Give Thanks	$2.50
#24 Home For The Holidays	$2.50
#25 Chapter One The End	$3.75
#26 Adrift	$2.50
#27 The Last X-Man	$2.50
#28 Oh, Now I Get It	$2.25
#29 No Surrender	$2.25
#30 Some Things Hurt More Than Cars & Girls	$2.25
#31 Rites Of Passage	$2.25
#32 A Day At The Circus	$2.25
#33 Thieves In The Night	$2.25
#34 Guilty Secrets	$2.25
#35 Pool Of Tears	$2.25
#36 Strange Doings	$2.25
#37 In Dark Woods, The Right Road Lost	$2.25
#38 Mystery Train	$2.25
#39 Return From Forever	$2.25
#40 Pride And Penance	$2.25

Generation X, cont.	Value
#41 Massachusetts Chain-Saw Massacre	$2.25
#42 She Came From The Stars	$2.25
#43 An Eye For An Eye	$2.25
#44 Comings And Goings	$2.25
#45 Lost And Found	$2.25
#46 The Quality Of Mercy	$2.25
#47 She Got Game	$2.25
#48 Foxes And Scorpions	$2.25
#49 Trophies	$2.25
#50 Divided We Fall	$3
#51 The Rescuers	$2
#52 Secret Identities	$2
#53 Land Of The Rising Sons Part One	$2
#54 Land Of The Rising Sons Part Two	$2
#55 Another's Man Shoes	$2
#56 Heal Thyself	$2
#57 A Night To Remember	$2
#58 Something Wicked	$2
#59 Artie And Leech's Day Off	$2
#60 Christmas Fear	$2
#61 Christmas Fear Part Two	$2
#62 Prey	$2
#63 Correction Part One	$2
#64 Correction Part Two	$2
#65 Correction Part Three	$2
#66 Correction Part Four	N/E
Annual 1995	$3.75
Annual 1996	$3.25
Annual 1997	$3.25
Annual 1998	$3.50
Annual 1999	$3.50
Holiday Special #1	$3.75
Underground Special #1	$4

Collector's Value Guide™ — X-Men®

The New Mutants™
(March 1983 to April 1991)

		Value
#1	Initiation!	$6.25
#2	Sentinels	$3.75
#3	Nightmare	$3.50
#4	Who's Scaring Stevie?	$3.25
#5	Heroes	$3.25
#6	Road Warriors!	$3.25
#7	Flying Down to Rio!	$3.25
#8	The Road to . . . Rome?	$3.25
#9	Arena	$3.25
#10	Betrayal!	$3.25
#11	Magma	$3
#12	Sunstroke	$3
#13	School Dayze	$3
#14	Do You Believe in – Magik?	$3
#15	Scaredy Cat!	$3
#16	Away Game!	$3
#17	Getaway!	$3
#18	Death-Hunt	$5.75
#19	Siege	$3
#20	Badlands	$3
#21	Slumber Party!	$4
#22	The Shadow Within	$2.75
#23	Shadowman	$2.75
#24	The Hollow Heart	$2.75
#25	The Only Thing To Fear	$6
#26	Legion	$6
#27	Into The Abyss	$4
#28	Soulwar	$3.25
#29	Meanwhile, Back At The Mansion	$2.75
#30	The Singer And Her Song	$2.75
#31	Saturday Night Fight	$2.50
#32	To the Ends Of The Earth	$2.50
#33	Against All Odds	$2.50
#34	With A Little Bit of Luck!	$2.50
#35	The Times, They Are A'changin'!	$2.50
#36	Subway To Salvation!	$2.50
#37	If I Should Die	$2.50
#38	Aftermath	$2.50
#39	Pawns Of The White Queen	$2.50
#40	Avengers Assemble!	$2.50
#41	Way Of The Warrior	$2.25

The New Mutants, cont.

		Value
#42	New Song for Old	$2.25
#43	Getting Even	$2.25
#44	Runaway!	$2.50
#45	We Were Only Foolin'	$2.50
#46	Bloody Sunday	$2.50
#47	My Heart For The Highlands	$2.50
#48	Ashes Of The Heart	$2.50
#49	Ashes Of The Soul	$2.50
#50	Father's Day	$3
#51	Teacher's Choice	$2.75
#52	Grounded Forever	$2.75
#53	Seduced & Abandoned	$2.75
#54	Ratrace	$2.75
#55	Flying Wild!	$2.75
#56	Scavenger Hunt	$2.75
#57	Birds Of A Feather	$2.50
#58	A Bird In The Hand	$2.50
#59	Fang And Claw	$3.25
#60	Suspended Ani-mation	$3
#61	Our Way!	$2.75
#62	To Build A Fire	$2.25
#63	Redemption	$2.25
#64	Instant Replay!	$2.25
#65	Demons!	$2.25
#66	Sorcerer's Duel!	$2.25
#67	Promise	$2.25
#68	Illusion!	$2.25
#69	Bad Company	$2
#70	Self-Fulfilling Prophesy	$2
#71	Limbo	$2
#72	Demon Reign	$2
#73	The Gift	$2
#74	The Right Stuff	$2

Collector's Value Guide™ — X-Men®

The New Mutants, cont. — Value
- #75 King Of The Hill! $2.25
- #76 Splash! $2
- #77 Strange! $2
- #78 Let's Make A Deal $2
- #79 Asgard $2
- #80 Curse of the Valkyries $2
- #81 Faith $2
- #82 The Road To Hel $2
- #83 The Quick And The Dead $2
- #84 The Sword's Edge $2
- #85 The Killing Stroke $2.25
- #86 Bang! You're Dead $6
- #87 A Show Of Power! $17
- #88 The Great Escape $6.75
- #89 The Gift $5.25
- #90 To Hunt The Hunter $5.25
- #91 Prey For The Living $5.25
- #92 When The Carnival
       Comes To Town $3.75
- #93 Madripor $6
- #94 Lethal Weapons $6
- #95 Shell Game $6
- #96 United We Stand $6
- #97 War $6
- #98 The Beginning Of The End:
       Part One $9
- #99 The Beginning Of The End:
       Part Two $5.75
- #100 The End Of The Beginning .. $5
- Annual #1 .... $5
- Annual #2 .... $10
- Annual #3 .... $3.25
- Annual #4 .... $4
- Annual #5 .... $5.25
- Annual #6 .... $4
- Annual #7 .... $3.25
- Special #1: Home Is
       Where The Heart Is $4.75
- Summer Special #1:
       A Mutant In Megalopolis ... $3.25

Wolverine®
(November 1988 to Present) — Value
- #-1 A Whiff Of Satre's Madeleine! .. $2.50
- #1/2 (*Wizard* Exclusive) .... N/E
- #1 Sword Quest $26
- #2 Possession Is The Law $14
- #3 The Black Blade $10
- #4 Bloodsport $10
- #5 Hunter's Moon! $10
- #6 Roughouse! $9
- #7 Mr. Fixit Comes To Town $9
- #8 If It Ain't Broke – ! $9
- #9 Promises To Keep $9
- #10 24 Hours $22
- #11 Brother's Keeper $7
- #12 Straits Of San Francisco $7
- #13 Bloodties $7
- #14 Flying Wolves $7
- #15 Homecoming $7
- #16 Electric Warriors $7
- #17 Basics! $6.50
- #18 All At Sea $6.50
- #19 Heroes & Villains $6.50
- #20 Miracles $5
- #21 Battleground $4.25
- #22 Outburst! $4.25
- #23 Endings $4.25

- #24 Snow Blind $4.25
- #25 Heir Aid $4
- #26 Memory Of Peace $4
- #27 Predators And Prey! $4
- #28 The Stranger $4
- #29 The Road Back $4

Collector's Value Guide™ — X-Men®

Wolverine, cont.	Value
#30 Family Matters	$4
#31 Killing Zone	$3.25
#32 Terminal Trauma	$3.25
#33 Grave Undertakings	$3.25
#34 The Hunter In Darkness	$3.25
#35 Blood, Sand And Claws!	$3.25
#36 . . . It Tolls For Thee!	$3.25
#37 Fall Back & Spring Forward	$3
#38 See Venice & Die!	$3
#39 Deconstruction	$3
#40 Reconstruction	$3
#41 Down In The Bottoms	$6
#42 Papa Was A Rolling Stone!	$4.50
#43 Under The Skin	$4.25
#44 Babes At Sea	$3
#45 Claws Over Times Square!	$4
#46 Home Is The Hunter	$4
#47 Dog Day	$3.25
#48 Dreams Of Gore: Phase One	$4
#49 Dreams Of Gore: Phase Two	$4
#50 Dreams Of Gore: Phase Three	$4.50
#51 Heartbreak Motel!	$3.75
#52 Citadel At The End Of Time	$3
#53 The Chimerical Mystery Tour!	$3
#54 Station Identification	$3
#55 Thirty Slashes Over Tokyo Or "Sayonara Yellow Brick Road"	$3
#56 We Got Cylla, Can Mothra Be Far Behind?	$3
#57 Death In The Family!	$3
#58 Monkeywrenching!	$3
#59 Unnatural Resources	$3
#60 Counting Coup	$3
#61 Nightmare Quest!	$3

Wolverine, cont.	Value
#62 Reunion!	$3
#63 Bastions Of Glory!	$3
#64 What Goes Around	$3
#65 State Of Grace!	$3
#66 Prophecy	$3
#67 Valley O' Death	$3
#68 Epsilon Red!	$3
#69 Induction In The Savage Land!	$3
#70 Tooth And Nail	$3
#71 Triassic Park	$3
#72 Sleeping Giant	$3
#73 The Formicary Mound	$3
#74 Jubilee's Revenge	$3
#75 Nightmares Persist	$7.50
#76 Northern Dreams	$3
#77 The Lady Strikes	$3
#78 Deathstalk	$3
#79 Cyber! Cyber! Burning Bright!	$3
#80 . . . In The Forest Of The Night!	$3
#81 Storm Warning!	$3
#82 Omnia Mutantur	$3
#83 Cold Comfort	$3
#84 Things That Go Bump In The Night	$3
#85 Full Shred Thrash	$3
#86 Claws Along The Mohawk	$3
#87 Showdown In Lowtown	$2.50
#88 It's D-D-Deadpool, Folks!	$2.50
#89 The Mask Of Ogun	$2.50
#90 The Dying Game	$2.50
#91 Path Of Stones, Wood Of Thorns	$2.75
#92 A Northern Exposure	$2.75
#93 Tavern In The Town	$2.75
#94 The Lurker In The Machine	$2.75
#95 Manhattan Rhapsody	$2.75
#96 Campfire Tales	$2.75
#97 . . . . Bump In The Night	$2.75
#98 Fade To Black	$2.75
#99 Of Mythic Metal Forged	$2.75
#100 Furnace Of His Brain, Anvil Of His Heart	$4.25
#101 The Helix Of An Age Foretold	$2.75
#102 Unspoken Promises	$2.75
#103 Top Of The World, Ma!	$2.75

Collector's Value Guide™ — X-Men®

Wolverine, cont.	Value
#104 The Emperor Of The Realm Of Grief	$2.75
#105 Faces In The Fire	$2.75
#106 Openings And Closures	$2.75
#107 Once Upon A Time In Little Tokyo	$2.75
#108 East Is East	$2.75
#109 East Is East Part 2	$2.75
#110 Lesser Beasts	$2.75
#111 Restoration	$2.50
#112 The Light At The End Of The Day	$2.50
#113 The Wind From The East	$2.50
#114 For The Snark Was A Roojum, You See!	$2.50
#115 In The Face Of It	$2.50
#116 What The Blind Man Saw	$2.50
#117 A Divine Image	$2.50
#118 Out Of Darkness Into Light	$2.50
#119 Not Dead Yet: Part 1 of 4	$2.50
#120 Not Dead Yet: Part 2 of 4	$2.50
#121 Not Dead Yet: Part 3 of 4	$2.25
#122 Not Dead Yet: Part 4 of 4	$2.25
#123 Better Than Best!	$2.25
#124 Invisible Destroyers!	$2.25
#125 Logan's Run	$3.25
#126 Blood Wedding	$2.50
#127 I'm The King Of The World!	$2.25
#128 Green For Death	$2.25
#129 Whatever It Takes	$2.25
#130 . . . To Survive!	$2.25
#131 It Fell To Earth	$2.25
#132 A Rage In The Cage	$2.25
#133 Losing Control	$2.25
#134 Choice In The Matter	$2.25
#135 From Bad To Worse	$2.25
#136 Trust	$2.25
#137 Countdown To Destruction	$2.25
#138 Doomsday!	$2.25
#139 The Freaks Come Out At Night	$2.25
#140 Vengeance	$2.25
#141 Broken Dreams	$2.25
#142 Reunion!	$2.25
#143 Rebirth	$2.25
#144 First Cut!	$2.25
#145 On The Edge Of Darkness	$4

Wolverine, cont.	Value
#146 Through A Dark Tunnel	$2
#147 Into The Light	$2
#148 Same As It Never Was	$2
#149 Resurrection	$2
#150 Blood Debt	$3.50
#151 Blood Debt Part 2	$2
#152 Blood Debt Part 3	$2
#153 Blood Debt Conclusion	N/E
Annual '95	$4.25
Annual '96	$3.50
Annual '97	$3.50
Annual 1999	$3.75

X-Factor™
(January 1986 to September 1998)

#-1	A Summer's Tale	$2
#1	Third Genesis	$8
#2	Bless The Beasts And Children	$4.50
#3	Regression Obsession	$4.50
#4	Trials And Errors	$4.50
#5	Tapped Out	$6
#6	Apocalypse Now!	$12
#7	Fall Out!	$4
#8	Lost And Found!	$4
#9	Spots!	$4
#10	Falling Angel!	$4
#11	Redemption!	$3.50
#12	Boom Boom Boom!	$3.50
#13	Ghosts!	$3.50
#14	The Mutant Program!	$3.50
#15	Whose Death Is It, Anyway?	$3.50
#16	Playing With Fire!	$3.50

Value Guide — X-Men® Spin Offs

Collector's Value Guide — X-Men

X-Factor, cont.

		Value
○ #17	Die, Mutants, Die!	$3.50
○ #18	The Enemy Within!	$3.50
○ #19	All Together Now!	$3.50
○ #20	Children's Crusade	$3.50
○ #21	For Every Action	$3.50
○ #22	If I Should Die	$3.50
○ #23	You Say You Want Some Evolution?	$9
○ #24	Masks	$12
○ #25	Judgement Day!	$3.50
○ #26	Casualties	$3.50
○ #27	Gifts	$2.25
○ #28	Countdown!	$2.25
○ #29	Fame!	$2.25
○ #30	Kiss Of Death!	$2.25
○ #31	Kiss Off!	$2
○ #32	The Carbon Copy Avengers	$2
○ #33	For All The World To See	$2
○ #34	Death!	$2
○ #35	Go To The Orphan Maker!	$2
○ #36	Transformations!	$2
○ #37	A Matter Of Honor	$2
○ #38	Duet!	$2
○ #39	Ashes To Ashes	$2
○ #40	Dust To Dust	$3.50
○ #41	Golden Boy!	$2
○ #42	All That Glitters	$2
○ #43	Kidnapped!	$2
○ #44	Another World!	$2
○ #45	Arena!	$2
○ #46	Exchange	$2
○ #47	Guardian	$2
○ #48	Common Ground!	$2
○ #49	Power Struggle	$2
○ #50	Judgement Day	$3
○ #51	Home!	$3
○ #52	Celebrity!	$2.75
○ #53	Ghosts	$2.75
○ #54	Crimson	$2
○ #55	Desperately Seeking Vera	$2
○ #56	Ravens	$2
○ #57	Reflections	$2
○ #58	Nevermore	$2
○ #59	Yesterday's News	$2
○ #60	Brotherhood	$3.50
○ #61	Betrayal!	$3

X-Factor, cont.

		Value
○ #62	Capital Punishment	$3
○ #63	Family	$2.50
○ #64	The Price	$2.25
○ #65	Malign Influences	$2.25
○ #66	Heroic Effort	$2.25
○ #67	Lunar Opposition!	$2.25
○ #68	Finale	$2.50
○ #69	Clash Reunion	$2.25
○ #70	Ends And Odds	$2.25
○ #71	Cutting The Mustard	$3.25
○ #72	Multiple Homicide	$2
○ #73	Crowd Control	$2
○ #74	Politically Incorrect	$2
○ #75	The Nasty Boys	$2
○ #76	X-Communication	$2
○ #77	Great X-Pectations	$2
○ #78	Playing With Fire!	$2
○ #79	Rhapsody In Blue	$2
○ #80	Belles + Whistles	$2
○ #81	Belles Of The Ball	$2
○ #82	Sittin' By The Dock Of The Bay	$2
○ #83	Painting The Town	$2
○ #84	Tough Love	$2.25
○ #85	Snikts And Bones	$2.25
○ #86	One Of These Days . . . Pow! Zoom!	$2.25
○ #87	X-Aminations	$2
○ #88	. . . Random Violence	$2
○ #89	Dark Homecoming	$2
○ #90	A Green And Tender Place	$2
○ #91	Underpinnings	$2
○ #92	The Man Who Wasn't There	$5
○ #93	The Longest Day Part I	$2
○ #94	The Longest Day Part II	$2

Collector's Value Guide™ — X-Men®

X-Factor, cont.	Value
#95 Fatal Repulsions	$2
#96 In The Beginning	$2
#97 The New Humanity	$2
#98 Into Oblivion	$2
#99 The Cure!	$2
#100 Mahapralaya	$2
#101 Afterlives	$2
#102 The Polaris Plot!	$2
#103 Friends And Family	$2
#104 Malicious	$2
#105 Final Sacrifice	$2
#106 Life Signs	$2
#107 Punch-O-Rama	$2.25
#108 Promised Vengeance	$2.25
#109 The Waking	$2.25
#110 Creature On The Loose!	$2.25
#111 Explosive Performance	$2.25
#112 Unnecessary Evils	$2
#113 Impulsive Behavior	$2
#114 That Certain Mystique	$2
#115 Reaching Out To Yesterday	$2
#116 Home Comings	$2
#117 Adversaries . . . Old And New	$2
#118 Havok's Fall	$2
#119 The Best Offense	$2
#120 Meeting The Maker	$2
#121 The True Path	$2
#122 The Faces Of Truth	$2
#123 It Begins . . . Again!	$2
#124 Future Memories	$2
#125 The Ticking Clock	$3.75
#126 The Beast Within	$2
#127 Darker Destiny	$2
#128 Night Of The Hounds	$2
#129 Playing With Fire	$2
#130 A Mother's Eyes	$2
#131 Brotherhood	$2
#132 Breakaway	$2
#133 Down Under	$2
#134 Child	$2
#135 A Virtual Reality	$2
#136 Nothing Lasts Forever	$2
#137 It Was A Dark And Stormy Night	$2
#138 Fear Walks Amongst Us	$2
#139 The Enemy Within	$2
#140 Going Home	$2

X-Factor, cont.	Value
#141 Dreams Of Tomorrow	$2
#142 Give Me Shelter	$2
#143 The Fall Of The Brotherhood	$2
#144 Points Of View	$2
#145 Phantoms	$2
#146 Fairie Light	$2
#147 Bashed!	$2
#148 Sorry Is The Hardest Word!	$2
#149 Times Change	$2.50
Annual #1	$3.50
Annual #2	$3.50
Annual #3	$3.50
Annual #4	$3.50
Annual #5	$3
Annual #6	$3
Annual #7	$3
Annual #8	$3
Annual #9	$3

X-Force™
(August 1991 to Present)

		Value
#-1	The Brothers Proudstar	$2.25
#1	A Force To Be Reckoned With	$2.50
#2	The Blood Hunters	$3.50
#3	Battlecry	$3.25
#4	Sabotage: Part 2	$3.25
#5	Under The Magnifying Glass	$3
#6	Under The Gun	$3
#7	Under The Knife	$3
#8	Flashed Before My Eyes	$3
#9	Underground And Over The Top	$3
#10	Answers (And Questions)	$2.75
#11	Friendly Reminders	$2.25

Value Guide — X-Men® Spin Offs

Collector's Value Guide™ — X-Men®

X-Force, cont.

	Value
#12 Traitors To The Cause	$2
#13 Everything Hits The Fan	$2
#14 Payback!	$2
#15 To The Pain	$2
#16 Jacklightning	$2.25
#17 Sleeping With The Enemy	$2.25
#18 Ghosts In The Machine	$2.25
#19 The Open Hand . . . The Closed Fist	$2
#20 Assault On Greymalkin	$2
#21 War Machines	$2
#22 Ordinance Weighed In Blood	$2
#23 Compromising Positions	$2
#24 Prisoners Of Fate	$2
#25 Back To Front	$4
#26 Shadows On The Rock	$2.25
#27 Liberation Through Subjugation	$2
#28 The Axe Falls	$2
#29 Toy Soldiers	$2
#30 Something Worth Fighting For	$2
#31 Cry Uncle!	$2
#32 With A Roll Of The Dice	$2
#33 Rules Were Made To Be Broken	$2
#34 Guns And Roses	$2.25
#35 Beg Tomorrow	$2
#36 Genocidal Tendencies	$2
#37 The Young And The Restless	$2
#38 The Faith Dancers	$2.25
#39 Letting Go	$2
#40 Holding On	$2
#41 The Fun House	$2
#42 A Lie Of The Mind	$2
#43 Teapot In A Tempest	$2
#44 . . . Already In Progress	$2

X-Force, cont.

	Value
#45 Under One Roof	$2
#46 Behind Closed Doors	$2
#47 Breakout	$2
#48 Intervention	$2
#49 Target: X-Force	$2
#50 Target: Cable	$3.75
#51 Reflections In The Night	$2
#52 Bad Girls	$2
#53 Even An X-Ternal Can Die!	$2
#54 Q & A	$2
#55 Without A Net	$2
#56 Crazy For You	$2.75
#57 The Best Laid Plans	$2
#58 . . . Before The Dawn	$2
#59 Are You Now Or Have You Ever Been?	$2
#60 I Know You Are But What Am I?	$2
#61 Ask Me No More Questions And I'll Tell You No More Lies!	$2
#62 Human Nature	$2
#63 Wish You Were Here	$2
#64 The Haunting Of Castle Doom	$2
#65 Lower East Side Story	$2
#66 Tragic Kingdom	$2
#67 Stand-Off	$2
#68 Girl Talk	$2
#69 Roadside Attractions	$2
#70 Transitions	$2
#71 Destination: Unknown	$2
#72 Lies And Deception	$2
#73 Stop Motion	$2
#74 Afterlife	$2
#75 Convergence	$2.75
#76 Bittersweet Reunions	$2
#77 City Of Lost Children	$2
#78 Burning Desires	$2
#79 Set My Soul On Fire	$2
#80 The Fire Within	$2
#81 Hot Lava	$2
#82 The Gryphon Agenda	$2
#83 Homefront	$2
#84 By The Sword	$2
#85 Possessions	$2
#86 Experimental Living	$2
#87 Family Matters	$2
#88 Blood & Betrayal	$2

Page Total: Total Value

COLLECTOR'S VALUE GUIDE™

Collector's Value Guide — X-Men

X-Force, cont.	Value
#89 Hellions Triumphant!	$2
#90 Rude Awakening	$2
#91 Fallout	$2
#92 Strange Interlude	$2
#93 Temple Of The Dying Sun	$2
#94 Artifacts & Apocrypha	$2
#95 Magnetic Distraction	$2
#96 Family Secrets	$2
#97 Cracked Foundation	$2
#98 Temptation	$2
#99 Bad Company	$2
#100 Dark Cathedral	$2.75
#101 Learning To Fly	$2
#102 Games Without Frontiers	$2
#103 Games Without Frontiers Part 2	$2
#104 Games Without Frontiers Part 3	$2
Annual #1	$3
Annual #2	$3
Annual #3	$3
X-Force And Cable '95 Annual	$4
X-Force And Cable '96 Annual	$3
X-Force And Cable '97 Annual	$3
X-Force And Champions '98 Annual	$3.50
X-Force '99 Annual	$3.50

X-Man
(March 1995 to Present)

	Value
#-1 Breeding Ground	$2
#1 Breaking Away	$5.75
#2 Choosing Sides	$4
#3 Turning Point	$3.75
#4 The Art Of War	$3.75
#5 The Man Who Fell To Earth	$2.25
#6 Earthly Delights	$2
#7 Whispers In The Night	$2
#8 Hitting Bottom	$2
#9 A Question Of Power	$2
#10 Confrontation	$2.50
#11 The X-Cutioner's Song!	$2
#12 Trust	$2
#13 The Hunted Below	$2
#14 Fallen From Grace	$2
#15 Turning Point	$2.75
#16 Survivors Of The Storm	$2.25

X-Man, cont.	Value
#17 One Step Forward	$2.25
#18 In The Company Of Strangers	$2.25
#19 Shades Of Grey	$2.25
#20 The Mourning After	$2.25
#21 Open Cage	$2
#22 Falling Up	$2
#23 Crash Course	$2
#24 First Noel	$2
#25 Closer To The Flame	$3.50
#26 Down To Earth	$2
#27 Blood Brothers	$2
#28 Dance With The Devil	$2
#29 Dead Ahead	$2
#30 Coming Home	$2
#31 The Last Innocent Mind	$2
#32 Catching Up From Behind	$2
#33 Blood Will Tell	$2
#34 The Ride	$2
#35 Media Blitz	$2
#36 Falling Star	$2
#37 Breaking Point	$2
#38 Nowhere To Run, Nowhere To Hide	$2
#39 If Tomorrow Never Comes	$2
#40 Nothing Left But The Screaming	$2
#41 Outta Nowhere	$2
#42 Rainbow's End	$2
#43 Inside Out	$2
#44 Nowhere To Hide	$2
#45 Crossing Borders	$2
#46 Stormfront	$2
#47 Dreams End	$2
#48 The Blood Of The Righteous	$2
#49 Skyfall	$2

Collector's Value Guide™ — X-Men®

X-Man, cont.
	Value
#50 New Blood	$2.75
#51 Uninvited Guests	$2
#52 All Fall Down	$2
#53 In Cold Blood	$2
#54 A Little Piece Of Home	$2
#55 Trouble On The Homefront	$2
#56 Greyville	$2
#57 Behind The Curtain	$2
#58 The Heart Of Darkness	$2
#59 The Ties That Bond	$2
#60 Out Of The Loop	$2
#61 Falling Forward	$2
#62 The Dark Side Of The Sun	$2
#63 No Direction Home Part One	$2
#64 No Direction Home Part Two	$2
#65 No Direction Home Part Three	$2

X-Men Hidden Years
(October 1998 to Present)

	Value
#1 Once More The Savage Land	$3.25
#2 The Ghost And The Darkness	$2.75
#3 On Wings Of Angels	$2.50
#4 Escape To Oblivion	$2.50
#5 Riders On The Storm	$2.50
#6 Behold A Goddess Rising!	$2.50
#7 Power Play	$2.50
#8 Shadow On The Stars	$2.50
#9 Dark Destiny	$2.50
#10 Home Is Where The Hurt Is	N/E

X-Men Unlimited™
(June 1993 to Present)

	Value
#1 Follow The Leader	$6
#2 Point Blank	$5
#3 The Whispers Scream	$6
#4 Theories Of Relativity	$4.50

	Value
#5 Hard Promises	$4.25
#6 Primal Scream	$4.25
#7 Memories	$4.25
#8 First Contact	$4.25
#9 Horse Latitudes	$4.25
#10 Need To Know	$6
#11 Adrift	$5.50
#12 The Once And Future Juggernaut	$3.25
#13 Fugitive From Space	$3
#14 Innocence Lost	$3
#15 Second Contact	$3
#16 Primal	$3
#17 Alone In His Head	$3
#18 Once An X-Man	$3
#19 Unforgiven	$3
#20 Where The Wild Things Were	$3
#21 Devil's Haircut	$3
#22 Cat & Mouse	$3
#23 Lessons	$3
#24 Search & Destroy	$3
#25 In Remembrance	$3
#26 Day Of Judgement	$3
#27 New Dawn Rising	$3

Collector's Value Guide™ — X-Men®

ACTION FIGURES

Toy Biz is the primary producer of Marvel action figures and released the first X-Men series in 1991. This section lists the Toy Biz X-Men action figures in alphabetical order from Ahab to X-Cutioner, with all the figures for each character listed together.

1
Ahab
Series 5
5" · 1993
Value: $8

2
Apocalypse
2nd Edition
Series 4
5" · 1993
Value: $9
Reissued 1996
Value: N/E

3
Apocalypse
The Age Of Apocalypse
5" · 1995
Value: $10

4
Apocalypse
Deluxe Edition
10" · 1994
Value: $20

5
Apocalypse
Projectors
7" · 1994
Value: $10

6
Apocalypse
Series 1
5" · 1991
Value: $23
Reissued 1993 – Series 3
Value: $12

7
Apocalypse
Super Shooters
5" · 1997
Value: $7

8
Apocalypse Rising
Onslaught
5" · 1997
Value: $12

9
Future Apocalypse
Missile Flyers
5" · 1997
Value: $7

10
Archangel
Battle Brigade
5" · 1996
Value: $9
Repaint – red & white costume
Value: $12

11
Archangel
Series 1
5" · 1991
Value: $23
Reissued 1993 – Series 3
Value: $10
Variation – gray wings
Value: $11

12
Archangel II
Deluxe Edition
10" · 1995
Value: $14

Action Figures

	Price Paid	Value
1.		
2.		
3.		
4.		
5.		
6.		
7.		
8.		
9.		
10.		
11.		
12.		
Totals		

Collector's Value Guide™ — X-Men®

1
Archangel II
Invasion Series
5" · 1995
Value: $17

2
Banshee
Series 2
5" · 1992
Value: $15

3
Beast
Battle Blaster
5" · 1998
Value: N/E

4
Beast
Classics
5" · 1995
Value: $11

5
Beast
Deluxe Edition
10" · 1994
Value: $16

6
Beast
Deluxe Edition
10" · 1995
Value: $17

7
Beast
Projectors
7" · 1995
Value: $11

8
Beast
Series 6
5" · 1994
Value: $18

9
Beast
Space Riders
5" · 1997
Value: $9

10
Beast
Super Shooters
5" · 1997
Value: $7.50

11
Dark Beast
Mutant Monsters Series
6" · 1996
Value: $12

12
Heavy Metal Beast
Mutant Armor Series
5" · 1996
Value: $8.50

13
Post Apocalypse Beast
Battle Brigade
5" · 1996
Value: $8
Repaint – blue & yellow costume
Value: $8

Action Figures

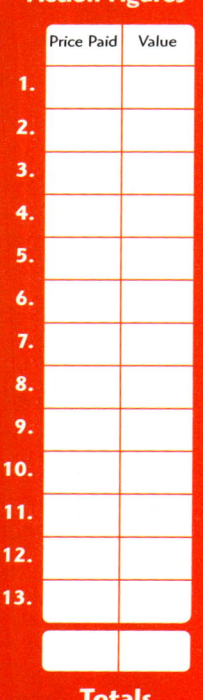

	Price Paid	Value
1.		
2.		
3.		
4.		
5.		
6.		
7.		
8.		
9.		
10.		
11.		
12.		
13.		
Totals		

Collector's Value Guide™ — X-Men®

1
Bishop
Deluxe Edition
10" · 1994
Value: $11

2
Bishop
Projectors
7" · 1995
Value: $11

3
Bishop
Series 4
5" · 1993
Value: $15
Reissued 1998 – Kay-Bee
Value: N/E

4
Bishop II
Flashback Series
5" · 1996
Value: $8.50
Variation – red body
Value: $7

5
Future Bishop
Missile Flyers
5" · 1997
Value: $7.50

6
Bonebreaker
Series 7
5" · 1994
Value: $8

7
Brood
Series 5
5" · 1993
Value: $10

8
Cable
Projectors
7" · 1995
Value: $11

9
Cameron Hodge
Mutant Genesis Series
5" · 1995
Value: $6.50

10
Ch'od
Series 7
5" · 1994
Value: $8

11
Colossus
Battle Brigade
5" · 1996
Value: $8
Repaint – purple & red body
Value: $9

12
Colossus
Series 1
5" · 1991
Value: $24
Reissued 1993 – Series 3
Value: $17
Reissued 1998 – Kay-Bee
Value: $7

13
Colossus
Super Shooters
5" · 1997
Value: $7

14
Corsair
Phoenix Saga
5" · 1994
Value: $8
Reissued 1995 – larger card
Value: $8.50

Action Figures

	Price Paid	Value
1.		
2.		
3.		
4.		
5.		
6.		
7.		
8.		
9.		
10.		
11.		
12.		
13.		
14.		
Totals		

Collector's Value Guide™ — X-Men®

1

Cyclops
The Age Of Apocalypse
5" · 1995
Value: $10

2

Cyclops
Battle Blaster
5" · 1998
Value: $7

3

Cyclops
Classics
5" · 1995
Value: $8

4

Cyclops
Deluxe Edition
10" · 1993
Value: $25

5

Cyclops
Flying Fighters
5" · 1998
Value: $7

6

Cyclops
Metallic Mutants
10" ·1994
Value: $13

7

Cyclops
Monster Armor Series
5" · 1997
Value: $7

8

Cyclops
Projectors
7" · 1994
Value: $10

9
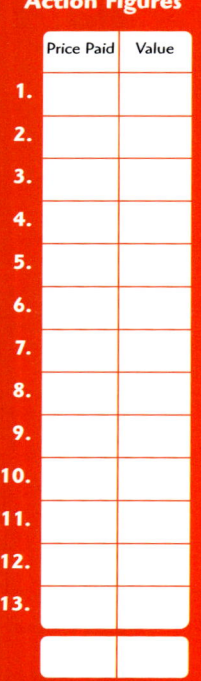
Cyclops
Robot Fighters
5" · 1997
Value: $7.50

10

Cyclops
Series 1
5" · 1991
Value: $23
Reissued 1993 – Series 3
Value: $12
Variation – yellow & blue costume
Value: $11

11

Cyclops
Series 5
5" · 1993
Value: $9

12

Cyclops
Space Riders
5" · 1997
Value: $10

13

Cyclops
X-Men: The Movie
6" · 2000
Value: N/E

Action Figures

	Price Paid	Value
1.		
2.		
3.		
4.		
5.		
6.		
7.		
8.		
9.		
10.		
11.		
12.		
13.		
Totals		

Collector's Value Guide™ — X-Men®

Value Guide — Action Figures

1
Cyclops
To Be Released

2
Cyclops
To Be Released

3
Space Ninja Deathbird
Ninja Force
5" · 1996
Value: $12

4
Elektra
Classics: Light Up Weapon
5" · 1996
Repaint – Psylocke in red costume
Value: $11

5
Eric The Red
Invasion Series
5" · 1995
Value: $7

6
Forge
Series 2
5" · 1992
Value: $48
Variation – yellow holster
Value: $22

7
Gambit
Classics
5" · 1995
Value: $8

8
Gambit
Classics: Light Up Weapon
5" · 1996
Value: $7.50
Repaint – yellow & blue costume
Value: $8

9
Gambit
Deluxe Edition
10" · 1994
Value: $12

10
Gambit
Power Slammers
5" · 1998
Value: $7

11
Gambit
Robot Fighters
5" · 1997
Value: $8

12
Gambit
Series 2
5" · 1992
Value: $12

13
Gladiator
Phoenix Saga
5" · 1994
Value: $10
Reissued 1995 – larger card
Value: $9

14
Havok
Invasion Series
5" · 1995
Value: $6.50

Action Figures

	Price Paid	Value
1.		
2.		
3.		
4.		
5.		
6.		
7.		
8.		
9.		
10.		
11.		
12.		
13.		
14.		

Totals

COLLECTOR'S VALUE GUIDE™

Collector's Value Guide™ — X-Men®

1
Iceman
Mutant Armor Series
5" · 1996
Value: $8.50

2
Iceman
Series 2
5" · 1992
Value: $40

3
Iceman
Series 3
5" · 1993
Value: $9

4
Iceman (#2)
N/A
5" · 1994
Value: $12
Variation – clear with blue tint
Value: $11
Reissued 1998 – Kay-Bee
Value: N/E

5
Iceman II
Invasion Series
5" · 1995
Value: $6.50

6
Ultimate Iceman
Water Wars
5" · 1997
Value: $8

7
Jean Grey
Battle Blaster
5" · 1998
Value: $8

8
Jean Grey
Flying Fighters
5" · 1998
Value: $9

9
Jean Grey
Onslaught
5" · 1997
Value: $11

10
Jean Grey
Space Riders
5" · 1997
Value: $10

11
Jean Grey
X-Men: The Movie
6" · 2000
Value: N/E

12
Jubilee
Robot Fighters
5" · 1997
Value: $7.50

13
Juggernaut
Classics: Light Up Weapon
5" · 1996
Value: $7.50
Repaint
Value: $7.50

Action Figures

	Price Paid	Value
1.		
2.		
3.		
4.		
5.		
6.		
7.		
8.		
9.		
10.		
11.		
12.		
13.		
Totals		

Collector's Value Guide™ — X-Men®

Value Guide — Action Figures

1
Juggernaut
Series 1
5" · 1991
Value: $20
Reissued 1993 – Series 3
Value: $12

2
Juggernaut
Shape Shifters
7" · 1998
Value: $6.50

3
Kylun
Series 7
5" · 1994
Value: $8

4
Lady Deathstrike
Battle Brigade
5" · 1996
Value: $11
Repaint – dark brown costume
Value: N/E

5
Logan
X-Men: The Movie
6" · 2000
Value: N/E

6
Logan
To Be Released

7
Longshot
Series 5
5" · 1993
Value: $9

8
Maggot
Flying Fighters
5" · 1998
Value: $7

9
Magneto
N/A
5" · 1993
Value: $7

10
Magneto
The Age Of Apocalypse
5" · 1995
Value: $8.50
Reissued 1998 – Kay-Bee
Value: N/E

11
Magneto
Battle Bases
5" · 1998
Value: N/E

12
Magneto
Battle Talkers
7" · 1998
Value: $9

13
Magneto
Classics
5" · 1995
Value: $10

14
Magneto
Deluxe Edition
10" · 1995
Value: $14

Action Figures

	Price Paid	Value
1.		
2.		
3.		
4.		
5.		
6.		
7.		
8.		
9.		
10.		
11.		
12.		
13.		
14.		
Totals		

Collector's Value Guide™ — X-Men®

1
Magneto
Metallic Mutants
10" · 1994
Value: $14

2
Magneto
Projectors
7" · 1994
Value: $10

3
Magneto
Series 1
5" · 1991
Value: $21
Reissued 1993 – Series 3
Value: $18

4
Magneto
Series 2
5" · 1992
Value: $11
Variation – striped gloves
Value: $11

5
Magneto
Supersize
15" · N/A
Value: N/E

6
Magneto
X-Men: The Movie
6" · 2000
Value: N/E

7
Magneto
To Be Released

8
Master Mold
Power Slammers
5" · 1998
Value: $7

9
Maverick
Mutant Genesis Series
5" · 1995
Value: $10

10
Morph
Series 6
5" · 1994
Value: $14

11
Morph
Shape Shifters
7" · 1998
Value: $6.50

12
Mr. Sinister
Deluxe Edition
10" · 1994
Value: $9

13
Mr. Sinister
Flying Fighters
5" · 1998
Value: $8

Action Figures

	Price Paid	Value
1.		
2.		
3.		
4.		
5.		
6.		
7.		
8.		
9.		
10.		
11.		
12.		
13.		
Totals		

Collector's Value Guide™ — X-Men®

Value Guide – Action Figures

1
Mr. Sinister
Projectors
7" · 1995
Value: $11

2
Mr. Sinister
Series 2
5" · 1992
Value: $11
Reissued 1996 – Series 8
Value: $10

3
Sinister
Monster Armor Series
5" · 1997
Value: $7

4
Mystique
Deluxe Edition
10" · 1996
Value: $17

5
Mystique
Monster Armor
5" · 1997
Value: $7.50

6
Mystique
X-Men: The Movie
6" · 2000
Value: N/E

7
Dark Nemesis
Ninja Force
5" · 1996
Value: $8

8
Aqua Attack Nightcrawler
Water Wars
5" · 1997
Value: $8

9
Nightcrawler
Classics: Light Up Weapon
5" · 1996
Value: $7
Repaint
Value: $7.50

10
Nightcrawler
Series 1
5" · 1991
Value: $32
Reissued 1993 – Series 3
Value: $14

11
Omega
Battle Blaster
5" · 1998
Value: $7

12
Omega Red
Metallic Mutants
10" · 1994
Value: $15

13
Omega Red
Series 4
5" · 1993
Value: $14

14
Omega Red II
Flashback Series
5" · 1996
Value: $9
Variation – black costume
Value: $9

Action Figures

	Price Paid	Value
1.		
2.		
3.		
4.		
5.		
6.		
7.		
8.		
9.		
10.		
11.		
12.		
13.		
14.		
Totals		

Collector's Value Guide™ — X-Men®

Value Guide — Action Figures

1
Onslaught
Onslaught
5" · 1997
Value: $11

2
Phoenix
Phoenix Saga
5" · 1994
Value: $22
Reissued 1995 – larger card
Value: $18

3
Polaris
Flashback Series
5" · 1996
Value: $7.50

4
Professor X
Series 5
5" · 1993
Value: $9

5
Professor X
Space Riders
5" · 1997
Value: $10

6
Professor X
X-Men: The Movie
6" · 2000
Value: N/E

7
Professor X
To Be Released

8
Professor Xavier
Mutant Armor Series
5" · 1996
Value: $11

9
Ninja Psylocke
Ninja Force
5" · 1996
Value: $9

10
Psylocke
Classics: Light Up Weapon
5" · 1996
Value: $9

11
Quicksilver
Mutant Armor Series
5" · 1996
Value: $8
Variation – gray body
Value: $8

12
Random
Series 6
5" · 1994
Value: $7.50

13
Raza
Series 7
5" · 1994
Value: $7

14
Rogue
N/A
5" · 1994
Value: $32

Action Figures

	Price Paid	Value
1.		
2.		
3.		
4.		
5.		
6.		
7.		
8.		
9.		
10.		
11.		
12.		
13.		
14.		
Totals		

Collector's Value Guide™ — X-Men®

1. Rogue
Collector Hero
12" · 1996
Value: N/E

2. Rogue
Deluxe Edition
10" · 1996
Value: $16

3. Rogue
Monster Armor
5" · 1997
Value: $7

4. Rogue
Power Slammers
5" · 1998
Value: $7

5. Rogue
X-Men: The Movie
6" · 2000
Value: N/E

6. Rogue
To Be Released

7. Captive Sabretooth
Invasion Series
5" · 1995
Value: $9

8. Ninja Sabretooth
Ninja Force
5" · 1996
Value: $8

9. Sabretooth
The Age Of Apocalypse
N/A · 1995
Value: $9

10. Sabretooth
Battle Blaster
5" · 1998
Value: $11

11. Sabretooth
Battle Talkers
7" · 1998
Value: $8

12. Sabretooth
Deluxe Edition
10" · 1993
Value: $20

13. Sabretooth
Metallic Mutants
10" · 1994
Value: $15

14. Sabretooth
Projectors
7" · 1994
Value: $11

Action Figures

	Price Paid	Value
1.		
2.		
3.		
4.		
5.		
6.		
7.		
8.		
9.		
10.		
11.		
12.		
13.		
14.		
Totals		

Collector's Value Guide™ — X-Men®

1
Sabretooth
Series 2
5" · 1992
Value: $12

2
Sabretooth
Series 5
5" · 1993
Value: $10
Reissued 1998 – Kay-Bee
Value: $10

3
Sabretooth
X-Men: The Movie
6" · 2000
Value: N/E

4 Future Release
Sabretooth
To Be Released

5
Sauron
Series 2
5" · 1992
Value: $12

6
Sentinel Test Robot
Water Wars
5" · 1997
Value: $9

7
Senyaka
Toys "R" Us Exclusive
5" · 1994
Value: $11
Reissued 1995
Value: $9

8
Future Shard
Missile Flyers
5" · 1997
Value: $8.50

9
Silver Samurai
Series 6
5" · 1994
Value: $12

10
Spiral
Invasion Series
5" · 1995
Value: $11

11
Storm
Battle Action Mega-Armor
9" · 1997
Value: $11

12
Storm
Battle Blaster
5" · 1998
Value: N/E

13
Storm
Classics
5" · 1995
Value: $12

14
Storm
Collector Hero
12" · 1996
Value: N/E

Action Figures

	Price Paid	Value
1.		
2.		
3.		
4.		
5.		
6.		
7.		
8.		
9.		
10.		
11.		
12.		
13.		
14.		
Totals		

Collector's Value Guide™ — X-Men®

1
Storm
Robot Fighters
5" · 1997
Value: $12
Variation – short hair with two long strands
Value: $10

2
Storm
Series 1
5" · 1991
Value: $45
Reissued 1993 – Series 3, silver costume
Value: N/E

3
Storm
X-Men: The Movie
6" · 2000
Value: N/E

4
Weather Fury Storm
Water Wars
5" · 1997
Value: $9

5
Strong Guy
Series 4
5" · 1993
Value: $11
Reissued 1998 – Kay-Bee
Value: $10

6
Sugar Man
Mutant Monsters Series
6" · 1996
Value: $12

7
Sunfire
Mutant Genesis Series
5" · 1995
Value: $7

8
Toad
X-Men: The Movie
6" · 2000
Value: N/E

9
Future Release
Toad
To Be Released

10
Trevor Fitzroy
Series 6
5" · 1994
Value: $9

11
Tusk
Series 4
5" · 1993
Value: $14

12
Warstar
Phoenix Saga
5" · 1994
Value: $10
Reissued 1995 – larger card
Value: $10

13
Weapon X
The Age Of Apocalypse
5" · 1995
Value: $7.50

14
Weapon X (Wolverine)
Deluxe Edition
10" · 1994
Value: $16

Value Guide – Action Figures

Action Figures

	Price Paid	Value
1.		
2.		
3.		
4.		
5.		
6.		
7.		
8.		
9.		
10.		
11.		
12.		
13.		
14.		
Totals		

Collector's Value Guide™ — X-Men®

1

Battle Armor Wolverine
Mutant Armor Series
5" · 1996
Value: $8.50

2

Battle Ravaged Wolverine
Invasion Series
5" · 1995
Value: $7

3

Civilian Wolverine
Projectors
8" · 1995
Value: $10

4

Electronic Talking Wolverine
N/A
15" · 1995
Value: N/E

5

Future Wolverine
Missile Flyers
5" · 1997
Value: $8

6

Hydro Blast Wolverine
Water Wars
5" · 1997
Value: $8

7

Ninja Wolverine
Ninja Force
5" · 1996
Value: $7.50

8

Robot Wolverine
Series 6
5" · 1994
Value: $9
Reissued 1998 – Kay-Bee
Value: N/E

9

Savage Land Wolverine
Flashback Series
5" · 1996
Value: $8
Variation
Value: $8

10

Space Wolverine
8th Edition
Phoenix Saga
5" · 1994
Value: $12
Reissued 1995 – larger card
Value: $10
Reissued 1998 – Kay-Bee
Value: N/E

11

Spy Wolverine
Deluxe Edition
10" · 1995
Value: $22
Variation – 1996, blue
Value: $10

12

Spy Wolverine
Metallic Mutants
10" · 1994
Value: $21

13

"Weapon X" Wolverine
Series 2
5" · 1992
Value: $16
Reissued – Kay-Bee, red cables
Value: $16
Reissued – silver cables
Value: $20

14

Werewolf Wolverine
Mutant Monsters Series
6" · 1996
Value: $12

Action Figures

	Price Paid	Value
1.		
2.		
3.		
4.		
5.		
6.		
7.		
8.		
9.		
10.		
11.		
12.		
13.		
14.		
Totals		

Collector's Value Guide™ — X-Men®

1
Wolverine
2nd Edition
Series 2
5" • 1992
Value: $23

2
Wolverine
3rd Edition
Series 2
5" • 1992
Value: $33

3
Wolverine
5th Edition
Series 4
5" • 1993
Value: $20
Variation – Kay-Bee green costume
Value: $14

4
Wolverine
Battle Blasters
5" • 1998
Value: $10

5
Wolverine
Battle Talkers
7" • 1998
Value: N/E

6
Wolverine
Classics
5" • 1995
Value: $7

7
Wolverine
Classics: Light Up Weapon
5" • 1996
Value: $7
Repaint – yellow & navy blue costume
Value: $7

8
Wolverine
Deluxe Edition
10" • 1993
Value: $24

9
Wolverine
Deluxe Edition
10" • 1995
Value: $12

10
Wolverine
Electronic Big Time Action Hero
13" • 1998
Value: $22

11
Wolverine
Metallic Mutants
10" • 1994
Value: $12

12
Wolverine
Monster Armor
5" • 1997
Value: $8

13
Wolverine
Power Slammers
5" • 1998
Value: $7.50

14
Wolverine
Projectors
7" • 1994
Value: $10

Action Figures

	Price Paid	Value
1.		
2.		
3.		
4.		
5.		
6.		
7.		
8.		
9.		
10.		
11.		
12.		
13.		
14.		
Totals		

Value Guide – Action Figures

COLLECTOR'S
VALUE GUIDE™

Collector's Value Guide™ — X-Men®

Value Guide — Action Figures

1
Wolverine
Robot Fighters
5" • 1997
Value: $7

2
Wolverine
Series 1
5" • 1991
Value: $25
Reissued 1993 – Series 3
Value: $21

3
Wolverine
Shape Shifters
7" • 1998
Value: $7

4
Wolverine
Space Riders
N/A • 1997
Value: $10

5
Wolverine
Super Shooters
5" • 1998
Value: $7

6
Wolverine
Supersize
15" • N/A
Value: N/E

7
Wolverine
X-Men: The Movie
6" • 2000
Value: N/E

8 Future Release
Wolverine
To Be Released

Action Figures

	Price Paid	Value
1.		
2.		
3.		
4.		
5.		
6.		
7.		
8.		
9.		
10.		
11.		
12.		
13.		
Totals		

9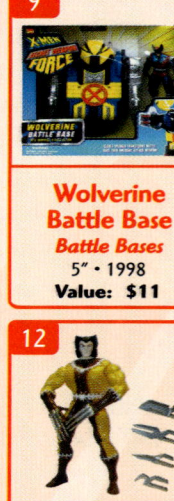
Wolverine Battle Base
Battle Bases
5" • 1998
Value: $11

10
Wolverine (Battle Ravage)
Deluxe Edition
10" • 1995
Value: $11

11
Wolverine Classic
Deluxe Edition
10" • 1996
Value: $13

12
Wolverine Fang
Mutant Genesis Series
5" • 1995
Value: $7

13
Wolverine Patch
Battle Brigade
5" • 1996
Value: $7
Repaint
Value: $8

Collector's Value Guide™ — X-Men®

1
Wolverine Space
Deluxe Edition
10" • 1995
Value: $14

2
Wolverine – Street Clothes
7th Edition
Series 7
5" • 1994
Value: $8

3
Wolverine Unleashed
Onslaught
5" • 1997
Value: $11

4
X-Cutioner
Mutant Genesis
Series
5" • 1995
Value: N/E

Twin Packs
Some X-Men action figures come as sets, providing for double the fun.

5
Angel & Sauron
Savage Land
5" • 1997
Value: $8.50

6
Apocalypse vs. Archangel
Steel Mutants
2" • 1994
Value: $7

7
Beast vs. Evil Morph
Steel Mutants
2" • 1994
Value: $8

8
Cable vs. Stryfe
Steel Mutants
2" • N/A
Value: $6

9
Civilian Wolverine vs. Silver Samurai
Steel Mutants
2" • 1994
Value: $8

10
Cyclops vs. Mr. Sinister
Steel Mutants
2" • N/A
Value: $6

11
Gambit vs. Bishop
Steel Mutants
2" • N/A
Value: $6

12
Joseph & Amphibious
Savage Land
5" • 1997
Value: $8

13
Juggernaut vs. Cyclops
Steel Mutants
2" • 1994
Value: $8

Action Figures

	Price Paid	Value
1.		
2.		
3.		
4.		
5.		
6.		
7.		
8.		
9.		
10.		
11.		
12.		
13.		
Totals		

Value Guide — Action Figures

COLLECTOR'S VALUE GUIDE™

Collector's Value Guide™ — X-Men®

Value Guide – Action Figures

1. Ka-Zar & Zabu

Savage Land
5" • 1997
Value: $7.50

2. Logan vs. Rogue

X-Men: The Movie
6" • 2000
Value: N/E

3. Logan vs. Magneto

X-Men: The Movie
6" • 2000
Value: N/E

4. Longshot vs. Mojo

Steel Mutants
2" • 1994
Value: $8

5. Professor X vs. Magneto

Steel Mutants
2" • N/A
Value: $7

6. Rogue vs. Pyro

Steel Mutants
2" • 1994
Value: $8

7. Savage Storm & Colossus

Savage Land
5" • 1997
Value: $9

8. Savage Wolverine & Crawler-Rex

Savage Land
5" • 1997
Value: $8

9. Spy Wolverine vs. Omega Red

Steel Mutants
2" • 1994
Value: $7

10. Storm

To Be Released

11. Toad

To Be Released

12. Wolverine
To Be Released

13. Wolverine vs. Sabretooth

Steel Mutants
2" • 1994
Value: $8

14. Wolverine vs. Sabretooth

X-Men: The Movie
6" • 2000
Value: N/E

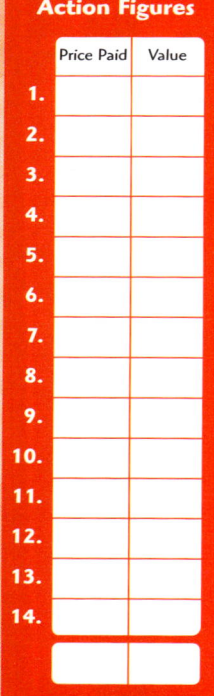

Action Figures

	Price Paid	Value
1.		
2.		
3.		
4.		
5.		
6.		
7.		
8.		
9.		
10.		
11.		
12.		
13.		
14.		
Totals		

COLLECTOR'S VALUE GUIDE™

Collector's Value Guide™ — X-Men®

Accessories

A variety of vehicles and scenes have been issued that allow you to set the stage for new adventures.

1
Battle Blaster Bomber
Battle Blaster
N/A • N/A
Value: N/E

2
Cyclops Light Force Arena
Series 1
N/A • 1991
Value: $13

3
Electronic X-Jet
X-Men: The Movie
N/A • 2000
Value: N/E

4
Lady Liberty Playset
X-Men: The Movie
N/A • 2000
Value: N/E

5
Magneto Magnetron
N/A • N/A
Value: $15

6
Magneto's Mutant Machine
X-Men: The Movie
N/A • 2000
Value: N/E

7
The Space Lab: Cyclops vs. Magneto
N/A
Various • N/A
Value: N/E

8
The Striker: Wolverine vs. Sabretooth
N/A
Various • N/A
Value: N/E

9
Wolverine 4x4
N/A
N/A • N/A
Value: N/E

10
Wolverine Combat Cave
N/A
N/A • 1991
Value: $15

11
Wolverine Mutantcycle
Series 1
N/A • 1991
Value: N/E

12
Wolverine Remote Control 4x4
N/A
N/A • N/A
Value: N/E

13
Wolverine Remote Control Cycle
N/A
N/A • N/A
Value: N/E

Action Figures

	Price Paid	Value
1.		
2.		
3.		
4.		
5.		
6.		
7.		
8.		
9.		
10.		
11.		
12.		
13.		
Totals		

Collector's Value Guide™ — X-Men®

1
Wolverine X-Cycle
X-Men: The Movie
Various • 2000
Value: N/E

2
X-Men Battle Cycle
N/A
N/A • N/A
Value: N/E

3
X-Men Blackbird Jet
N/A
N/A • 1994
Value: $20

4
X-Men Headquarters Playset
N/A
N/A • 1995
Value: N/E

5
X-Men Mini Blackbird Jet
N/A
N/A • N/A
Value: N/E

6
X-Men Power Slammers Assault Vehicle
Power Slammers
N/A • 1998
Value: $16

7
X-Men Sentinel
N/A
N/A • N/A
Value: N/E

8
X-Men Water Wars Playset
Water Wars
N/A • 1997
Value: $25

9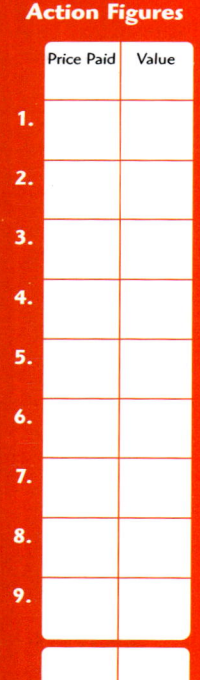
X-Men Wolverine Jeep
N/A
N/A • N/A
Value: N/E

Action Figures

	Price Paid	Value
1.		
2.		
3.		
4.		
5.		
6.		
7.		
8.		
9.		
Totals		

COLLECTOR'S VALUE GUIDE™

Collector's Value Guide™ — X-Men®

X-Men® Trading Card Game
Starter Set

Wizards of the Coast® has produced a trading card game featuring the X-Men® characters. Following is a list of the cards included in the *Starter Set*. The information provided includes the card title, the card number, the card type (Lightning, Mission, Momentum, Power-Up, Villain or X-Man), the card rarity (Holo-Rare, Rare, Uncommon, Common or Starter) and the name of the card's theme deck (*Slashburn* or *Powerhouse*). As these cards were released in July 2000, card values have not yet been established.

Agility Trial
#81/131
Mission • Common
Slashburn

How Many	Price Paid	Value
		$

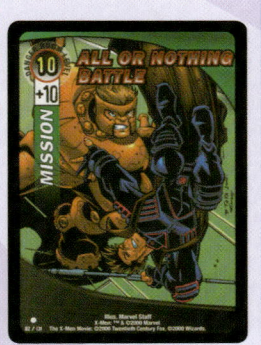

All Or Nothing Battle
#82/131
Mission • Common
Slashburn

How Many	Price Paid	Value
		$

Bad Blood
#83/131
Mission • Common
Slashburn

How Many	Price Paid	Value
		$

Baptism By Fire
#41/131
Momentum • Uncommon
Slashburn

How Many	Price Paid	Value
		$

Page Totals: | Price Paid | Total Value |

Collector's Value Guide™ — X-Men®

Berserker Rage

#42/131
Mission • Uncommon
Slashburn

How Many	Price Paid	Value
		$

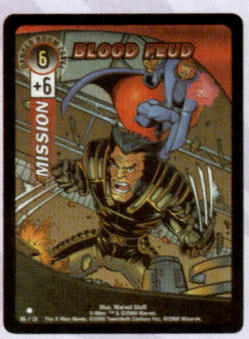

Blood Feud

#86/131
Mission • Common
Slashburn

How Many	Price Paid	Value
		$

Combat Training

#89/131
Mission • Common
Slashburn

How Many	Price Paid	Value
		$

Cry For Help

#92/131
Mission • Common
Powerhouse

How Many	Price Paid	Value
		$

Cyclops

#122/131
X-Man • Starter
Powerhouse

How Many	Price Paid	Value
		$

Death Trap

#93/131
Mission • Common
Slashburn

How Many	Price Paid	Value
		$

Page Totals:

Price Paid	Total Value

COLLECTOR'S VALUE GUIDE™

Collector's Value Guide™ — X-Men®

Dogfight

#94/131
Mission • Common
Powerhouse

How Many	Price Paid	Value
		$____

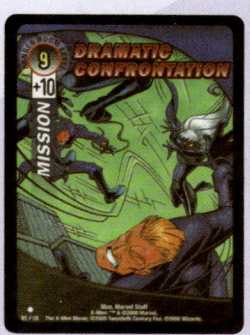

Dramatic Confrontation

#95/131
Mission • Common
Powerhouse

How Many	Price Paid	Value
		$____

Dramatic Escape

#96/131
Momentum • Common
Powerhouse

How Many	Price Paid	Value
		$____

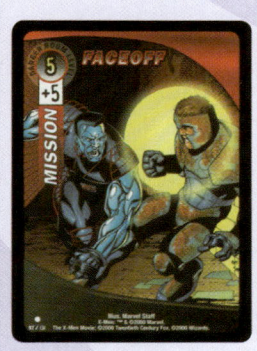

Faceoff

#97/131
Mission • Common
Slashburn

How Many	Price Paid	Value
		$____

Finishing Blow

#100/131
Momentum • Common
Slashburn

How Many	Price Paid	Value
		$____

Firefight

#101/131
Mission • Common
Powerhouse

How Many	Price Paid	Value
		$____

Page Totals:

Price Paid	Total Value

Collector's Value Guide™ — X-Men®

First Aid!

#102/131
Lightning • Common
Powerhouse

How Many	Price Paid	Value
		$

Follow Me!

#54/131
Lightning • Uncommon
Powerhouse

How Many	Price Paid	Value
		$

Goddess!

#56/131
Lightning • Uncommon
Powerhouse

How Many	Price Paid	Value
		$

Hold Your Fire!

#57/131
Lightning • Uncommon
Powerhouse

How Many	Price Paid	Value
		$

Jean Grey

#123/131
X-Man • Starter
Slashburn

How Many	Price Paid	Value
		$

Last Stand

#104/131
Mission • Common
Powerhouse

How Many	Price Paid	Value
		$

Page Totals: | Price Paid | Total Value |

Collector's Value Guide™ — X-Men®

Magneto

#124/131
Villain • Starter
Powerhouse

How Many	Price Paid	Value
		$____

Mental Probe

#105/131
Momentum • Common
Powerhouse

How Many	Price Paid	Value
		$____

Mystique

#125/131
Villain • Starter
Powerhouse

How Many	Price Paid	Value
		$____

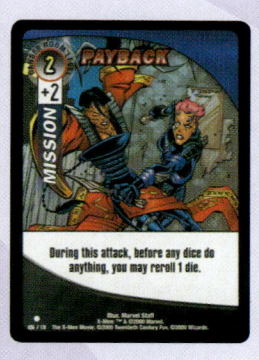

Payback

#106/131
Mission • Common
Powerhouse

How Many	Price Paid	Value
		$____

Pounce

#107/131
Momentum • Common
Powerhouse

How Many	Price Paid	Value
		$____

Precision Fire

#108/131
Momentum • Common
Slashburn

How Many	Price Paid	Value
		$____

Page Totals:

Price Paid	Total Value

COLLECTOR'S VALUE GUIDE™

Collector's Value Guide™ — X-Men®

Professor X

#126/131
X-Man • Starter
Powerhouse

How Many	Price Paid	Value
		$

Protection Of The Innocent

#109/131
Mission • Common
Powerhouse

How Many	Price Paid	Value
		$

Psi-Shield

#67/131
Momentum • Uncommon
Slashburn

How Many	Price Paid	Value
		$

Psychic Boost

#110/131
Momentum • Common
Powerhouse

How Many	Price Paid	Value
		$

Reality Shift
(Starter Set Promo)

#121/131
Power-Up • Holo-Rare
N/A

How Many	Price Paid	Value
		$

Rogue

#127/131
X-Man • Starter
Slashburn

How Many	Price Paid	Value
		$

Page Totals:

Price Paid	Total Value

COLLECTOR'S VALUE GUIDE™

Collector's Value Guide™ — X-Men®

Sabretooth

#128/131
Villain • Starter
Slashburn

How Many	Price Paid	Value
		$____

Showdown

#113/131
Mission • Common
Slashburn

How Many	Price Paid	Value
		$____

Storm

#129/131
X-Man • Starter
Powerhouse

How Many	Price Paid	Value
		$____

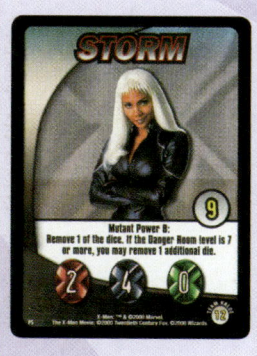

Storm
(Top Deck Promo)

#P5
N/A

How Many	Price Paid	Value
		$____

Surprise Assault

#117/131
Mission • Common
Slashburn

How Many	Price Paid	Value
		$____

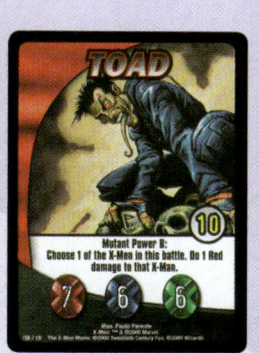

Toad

#130/131
Villain • Starter
Slashburn

How Many	Price Paid	Value
		$____

Page Totals:	Price Paid	Total Value

Collector's Value Guide™ — X-Men®

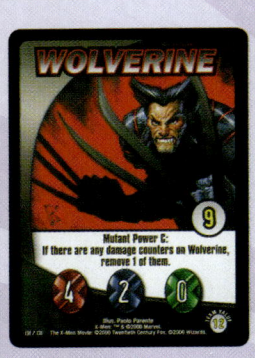

Wolverine
#131/131
X-Men • Starter
Slashburn

How Many	Price Paid	Value
		$

You Can Make It!
#120/131
Lightning • Common
Slashburn

How Many	Price Paid	Value
		$

Future Releases

Future Releases

Future Releases

Future Releases

Page Totals:

Price Paid	Total Value

COLLECTOR'S VALUE GUIDE™

Collector's Value Guide™ — X-Men®

BOOSTER PACKS

The following is a list of additional cards that are included in the Booster Packs for the X-Men® Trading Card Game.

Rarity Key

H .... Holo-Rare   R .... Rare
U .... Uncommon   C .. Common

	Value			
☐ Alien Invasion (Mission)	R	#21/131	$___
☐ Ambush (Mission)	R	#22/131	$___
☐ Angel (X-Man)	H	#1/131	$___
☐ Apocalypse (Villain)	H	#2/131	$___
☐ Back Alley Brawl (Mission)	R	#23/131	$___
☐ Bait And Switch (Mission)	C	#84/131	$___
☐ Battle Simulation (Mission)	C	#85/131	$___
☐ Bewilder (Power-Up)	U	#43/131	$___
☐ Bishop (X-Man)	H	#3/131	$___
☐ Blend In (Power-Up)	U	#44/131	$___
☐ Block (Power-Up)	U	#45/131	$___
☐ Braindrain (Power-Up)	U	#46/131	$___
☐ Brainwashed! (Lightning)	U	#47/131	$___
☐ Brood (Villain)	H	#4/131	$___
☐ Call Down The Heavens (Power-Up)	U	#48/131	$___
☐ Call The Cops (Power-Up)	U	#49/131	$___
☐ Close Call (Power Up)	C	#87/131	$___
☐ Collision Course (Momentum)	C	#88/131	$___
☐ Come Out Wherever You Are! (Lightning)	U	#50/131	$___
☐ Concentrate (Power-Up)	U	#51/131	$___
☐ Controlled Burst (Power-Up)	C	#90/131	$___
☐ Cross Dimensional Raid (Mission)	C	#91/131	$___
☐ Crossfire (Mission)	R	#24/131	$___
☐ Deadly Dance (Mission)	R	#25/131	$___
☐ DMZ (Mission)	R	#26/131	$___
☐ Dodge This! (Lightning)	U	#52/131	$___
☐ Don't Give Up (Lightning)	R	#27/131	$___
☐ Double Team (Power-Up)	U	#53/131	$___
☐ Fastball Special (Momentum)	C	#98/131	$___
☐ Fight To The Finish (Mission)	C	#99/131	$___
☐ Fly Away! (Power-Up)	R	#28/131	$___
☐ Focus (Power-Up)	R	#29/131	$___
☐ Fusillade (Power-Up)	U	#55/131	$___
☐ Get To The Truth! (Lightning)	R	#30/131	$___
☐ Inferno (Mission)	C	#103/131	$___
☐ Juggernaut (Villain)	H	#7/131	$___
☐ Kiss For Luck (Power-Up)	U	#58/131	$___
☐ Kra-ka-thoom! (Lightning)	U	#59/131	$___
☐ Lend Moral Support (Power-Up)	R	#31/131	$___
☐ Lure Them In (Power-Up)	U	#60/131	$___
☐ Marrow (X-Man)	H	#9/131	$___
☐ Mojo (Villain)	H	#10/131	$___

	Value			
☐ Moment Of Reflection (Momentum)	U	#61/131	$___
☐ Moment Of Truth (Lightning)	R	#32/131	$___
☐ Natural Disaster (Mission)	R	#33/131	$___
☐ Nice Shot! (Lightning)	U	#62/131	$___
☐ No Way Out (Power-Up)	U	#63/131	$___
☐ Obstacle Course (Mission)	R	#34/131	$___
☐ Outflank (Power-Up)	U	#64/131	$___
☐ Out Of Control (Mission)	U	#65/131	$___
☐ Practical Joke (Power-Up)	U	#66/131	$___
☐ Practice, Practice, Practice (Power-Up)	R	#35/131	$___
☐ Press Gang (Mission)	R	#36/131	$___
☐ Psychic Showdown (Mission)	C	#111/131	$___
☐ Psylocke (X-Man)	H	#13/131	$___
☐ Read The Riot Act (Power-Up)	U	#68/131	$___
☐ Ready Or Not (Power-Up)	R	#37/131	$___
☐ Reprieve (Power-Up)	U	#69/131	$___
☐ Rescue Mission (Mission)	C	#112/131	$___
☐ Scientific Solution (Power-Up)	U	#70/131	$___
☐ Sentinels (Villains)	H	#16/131	$___
☐ Shhhhh ... (Lightning)	U	#71/131	$___
☐ Shrapnel Blast (Power-Up)	R	#114/131	$___
☐ Sinister (Villain)	H	#17/131	$___
☐ Slugfest (Mission)	R	#38/131	$___
☐ Snikt! (Lightning)	R	#39/131	$___
☐ Spinal Tap (Momentum)	U	#72/131	$___
☐ Stay Out Of Reach (Power-Up)	C	#115/131	$___
☐ Sucker Punch (Momentum)	C	#116/131	$___
☐ Swipe (Power-Up)	U	#73/131	$___
☐ Take It To The Sky (Power-Up)	U	#74/131	$___
☐ Take The Hit (Power-Up)	U	#75/131	$___
☐ Take Your Best Shot (Power-Up)	C	#118/131	$___
☐ Teach Some Manners (Power-Up)	U	#76/131	$___
☐ Team Work (Mission)	U	#77/131	$___
☐ Ugh ... Take It! (Lightning)	U	#78/131	$___
☐ Underground Menace (Mission)	R	#40/131	$___
☐ Vendetta (Mission)	C	#119/131	$___
☐ Work as a Team (Power-Up)	U	#79/131	$___
☐ Workout (Mission)	U	#80/131	$___

COLLECTOR'S VALUE GUIDE™

Page Totals:	Price Paid	Total Value

Total Value Of My Collection

Record your collection here by adding the totals from the bottom of each Value Guide page.

Comic Books			Comic Books, cont.		
Page Number	Price Paid	Total Value	Page Number	Price Paid	Total Value
Page 33			Page 60		
Page 34			Page 61		
Page 35			Page 62		
Page 36			Page 63		
Page 37			Page 64		
Page 38			Page 65		
Page 39			Page 66		
Page 40			Page 67		
Page 41			Page 68		
Page 42			Page 69		
Page 43			Page 70		
Page 44			Page 71		
Page 45			Page 72		
Page 46			Page 73		
Page 47			Page 74		
Page 48			Page 75		
Page 49			Page 76		
Page 50			Page 77		
Page 51			Page 78		
Page 52			Page 79		
Page 53			Page 80		
Page 54			Page 81		
Page 55			Page 82		
Page 56			Page 83		
Page 57			Page 84		
Page 58			Page 85		
Page 59			Page 86		
Subtotal:			Subtotal:		

Page Totals:	Price Paid	Total Value

TOTAL VALUE OF MY COLLECTION

Record your collection here by adding the totals from the bottom of each Value Guide page.

Comic Books, cont.			Comic Books, cont.		
Page Number	Price Paid	Total Value	Page Number	Price Paid	Total Value
Page 87			Page 114		
Page 88			Page 115		
Page 89			Page 116		
Page 90			Page 117		
Page 91			Page 118		
Page 92			Page 119		
Page 93			Page 120		
Page 94			Page 121		
Page 95			Page 122		
Page 96			Page 123		
Page 97			Page 124		
Page 98			Page 125		
Page 99			Page 126		
Page 100			Page 127		
Page 101			Page 128		
Page 102			Page 129		
Page 103			Page 130		
Page 104			Page 131		
Page 105			Page 132		
Page 106			Page 133		
Page 107			Page 134		
Page 108			Page 135		
Page 109			Page 136		
Page 110			Page 137		
Page 111			Page 138		
Page 112			Page 139		
Page 113			Page 140		
Subtotal:			Subtotal:		

Page Totals:	Price Paid	Total Value

Total Value Of My Collection

Record your collection here by adding the totals from the bottom of each Value Guide page.

Comic Books, cont.

Page Number	Price Paid	Total Value
Page 141		
Page 142		
Page 143		
Page 144		
Page 145		
Page 146		
Page 147		
Page 148		
Page 149		
Page 150		
Page 151		
Page 152		
Page 153		
Page 154		
Page 155		
Page 156		
Page 157		
Page 158		
Page 159		
Page 160		
Page 161		
Page 162		

Action Figures

Page Number	Price Paid	Total Value
Page 163		
Page 164		
Page 165		
Page 166		
Subtotal:		

Action Figures, cont.

Page Number	Price Paid	Total Value
Page 167		
Page 168		
Page 169		
Page 170		
Page 171		
Page 172		
Page 173		
Page 174		
Page 175		
Page 176		
Page 177		
Page 178		
Page 179		
Page 180		
Page 181		
Page 182		

Trading Card Game

Page Number	Price Paid	Total Value
Page 183		
Page 184		
Page 185		
Page 186		
Page 187		
Page 188		
Page 189		
Page 190		
Page 191		
Subtotal:		

	Price Paid	Total Value
Grand Total:		

SECONDARY MARKET OVERVIEW

Collecting comics can be a time-consuming hobby. Hunting down early issues can prove difficult – and costly! Since comics are such a fragile medium, it could take a lot of footwork to find the comic you want, in the condition you want and for a price you're willing to pay.

The Hunt Begins . . .

The best place to start your search is at the local comic book store. Comics are usually released in a monthly format. At the end of the month, any left-over books are typically moved to the "back issues" section of the store. This section contains all of the store's older comics, including some that may have been acquired through other dealers or private collections. It can also be helpful to talk with the retailers and fellow collectors who are very knowledgeable about the industry and might be able to provide you with additional information. If your local store doesn't have what you're looking for, the next step would be to call other comic stores in the area. If you still can't locate those coveted comics, it's time for a more aggressive plan of action.

Another way to find comics is to attend conventions or shows. These events bring in dealers from all over the country who will have different merchandise to offer. You might even have the chance to meet some of your favorite comic creators! To locate these shows, check the community calendar in your local paper or talk to your retailer.

If you'd rather not leave the comfort of your own home, check the newspaper and the Internet. It never hurts to look at the classified section of the newspaper. You never know when someone could be selling exactly what you want. The Internet is also a great tool for collectors. Stores from all over the country, and sometimes even the world, now sell their inventory on-line. Remember, before purchasing over the Internet, be sure that it is a reputable and secure web site. You can also try bidding on on-line auctions. Read the rules and regulations carefully and make sure that the seller has a good feedback rating from other customers. By visiting personal web sites, chat rooms, discussion groups and bulletin boards, you may find someone looking to sell comics from their personal collection.

Making The Grade

As with most other collectible items, condition matters to the secondary market value of your comics. Before purchasing a comic, it is important to know its "grade." This system assigns a condition to a comic depending on its overall appearance. Grades include: Mint (new with no flaws), Near Mint (one or two minor stress lines), Very Fine (minor signs of wear), Fine (several minor flaws), Very Good (average condition with creases and minor tears), Good (worn but intact), Fair (a few loose pages or bits missing off the cover) and Poor (missing pages or covers). Often in-between grades are used like Near Mint/Mint, Very Fine/Near Mint, Fine/Very Fine, Very Good/Fine, Good/Very Good, and Fair/Good.

Unfortunately, grading is very subjective. A comic that you consider Mint might only be Near Mint to someone else.  One solution to this dilemma could be to use a professional grading service. For a fee, these companies will grade your comics and place them in a protective holder. This certification is a good way to prevent potential disputes between buyers and sellers. It should also be noted that a new comic purchased directly from the store may not be in Mint condition. Shipping and other handling may cause minor damage.

Proper storage and handling are the best ways to keep your comics looking their best. Search for a cool, dry place to store your collection. Heat and humidity will eventually destroy your comics and exposure to direct sunlight will fade the covers. Because of these conditions, it is not recommended that you store your collection in the basement, attic or garage. To help prevent them from wear and tear, your comics should be protected from exposure to oxygen, which will cause them to decompose more quickly. Each comic should be stored in a bag or protective sleeve with a backing board. You may want to invest in archival, acid-free boards and boxes and Mylar® sleeves for the ultimate protection. If you want to keep your comics in Mint condition, you should avoid handling them. The less exposure to air, and to the oil on your hands, the better. This will also prevent accidental creases and tears.

The same general rules of care that apply to comics also apply to cards and action figures. Cards should be stored individually in card pages and in a binder. This will help prevent creasing and worn edges. Action figures are more valuable if they remain in their original packaging. Removing a figure from its packaging can significantly reduce its value. So store your action figures carefully and you will also want to avoid shaking the packages. Also be careful if you try to remove a price tag from a package as in doing so, you may damage the packaging.

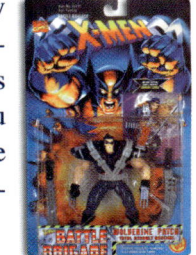

Protecting Your Investment

Once you have determined the value of your collection, check if your homeowner's policy will cover the amount that you have determined your collection to be worth. If you discover that your existing homeowner's policy is not sufficient, you may want to consider purchasing special insurance. There are several companies that specialize in collectibles insurance. You should also keep an itemized list of your collection and store a copy in a safe deposit box or with a trusted friend or relative. It is also helpful to photograph the items and keep the original receipts.

Other X-Men® Merchandise

Wolverine, Magneto and the rest of the mutant forces behind the X-Men have come a long way from appearing only as one dimensional figures in comic books. In addition to the action figures from Toy Biz, you can find your favorite Marvel mutant on everything from board games and posters to apparel and sculptures.

Toad On The Boardwalk

X-Men® Collector's Edition Monopoly® game by Parker Brothers® is one that is sure to please both X-Men and *Monopoly* fans. The basic rules of *Monopoly* still apply but, with the mutant heroes battling the villains, there are some interesting differences! Instead of play money, you will collect Mutant Power Points to strengthen your team. Chance Cards, Community Chest Cards and railroads are replaced by Evil Mutant Cards, Good Mutant Cards and X-Men transports. The traditional *Monopoly* green houses and red hotels are now training bases and headquarters for the X-Men recruits. It gives you the whole X-Universe at the roll of a die.

Lenticular X

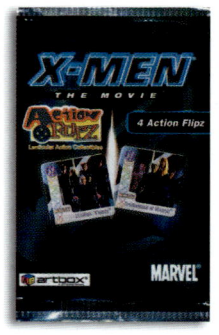

Art Box® has joined the mutant melee with a new set of lenticular action collectible cards, the X-Men® Action Flipz™ cards. These 40 Action Flipz cards, four 3-D Chase cards and one 3-D Rare card feature the X-Men characters and teams in transforming poses that make Mystique turn green with envy. Watch for these entertaining cards in your local hobby shop.

By The Book

For the collector who prefers having their favorite mutants together in a large collection, Marvel produces a series of books featuring X-Men stories from a variety of comic books including *Cable*™, *Wolverine*®, *Generation X*™ and *X-Force*™, among others. One of these is *X-Men*®: *Zero Tolerance,* an anthology of the history of the X-Men. For the more artistically inclined, *How To Draw X-Men*® is also available from Marvel. Its step-by-step instructions on the basics of drawing the characters include hints on the importance of attending to detail. For example, it is suggested that Wolverine's size be kept to scale since he is only 5 feet, 2 inches in height!

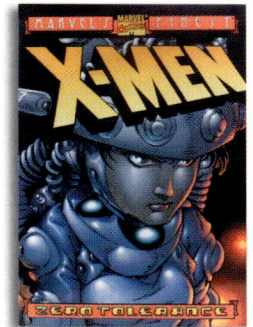

Against The Wall & On The Shelf

If you are looking to "color your world" with X-Men, the variety of decorating paraphernalia will leave you eXtra happy. Numerous colorful and artistic posters, lithographs and wall plaques are on the X-Men market. For adult collectors who wish to display their X-Men fascination, the X-Men six-inch ceramic Marvel Mini-Busts™ by Bowen Designs may be eXactly what you are looking for! Much like sculptures, these small busts portray the mutants so life-like that you can see the bulging muscles of Wolverine and the organic steel skin of Colossus. Put your favorite mutant on display to show you have X-mania.

Wear X-Men With Pride!

Shirts, neckties and hats featuring X-Men are available to X-maniacs who are looking to wear their favorite characters. A wide variety of T-shirts and long sleeve shirts that showcase the X-Men logo, the original mutants and the X-Men movie characters are available in your local comic book and department stores and through the Internet. Choose a shirt that best fits your very own X-Men fascination and style. A X-Men silk necktie featuring the original X-Men in classic 60s artwork might be a great choice for the X-maniac with an interest in nostalgia. Wear your necktie to the office, to a party or to a special gathering to show off your passion for the X-Men.

Small Cheese & A Cyclops To Go!

Hardee's® Food Systems, Inc. and Marvel Comics joined forces in 1995 to offer exclusive limited edition X-Men figurines in their Hardee's restaurants. The X-Men collector sets were available for 99¢ with the purchase of a combo meal and featured two action figures on a plastic base. The rivalries include Cyclops vs. Commando, Wolverine vs. The Blob, Rogue vs. Avalanche and Phantasia vs. Storm. A Certificate of Authenticity and a collector card was included with each packaged set.

In 1993, Pizza Hut® participated in a special promotion with *X-Men* comic books. The promotion consisted of four special custom-designed *X-Men* comic books and were available with the purchase of a kid's pizza pack meal.

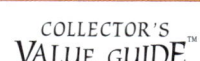

Comic Book Index & Checklist

X-Men (1963-1981)

	Page #
○ #-1 (Flashback Issue)	.33
○ #-1 (American Entertainment Cover)	.33
○ #1	.33
○ #2	.34
○ #3	.34
○ #4	.34
○ #5	.34
○ #6	.34
○ #7	.34
○ #8	.35
○ #9	.35
○ #10	.35
○ #11	.35
○ #12	.35
○ #13	.35
○ #14	.36
○ #15	.36
○ #16	.36
○ #17	.36
○ #18	.36
○ #19	.36
○ #20	.37
○ #21	.37
○ #22	.37
○ #23	.37
○ #24	.37
○ #25	.37
○ #26	.38
○ #27	.38
○ #28	.38
○ #29	.38
○ #30	.38
○ #31	.38
○ #32	.39
○ #33	.39
○ #34	.39
○ #35	.39
○ #36	.39
○ #37	.39
○ #38	.40
○ #39	.40
○ #40	.40
○ #41	.40
○ #42	.40
○ #43	.40
○ #44	.41
○ #45	.41
○ #46	.41
○ #47	.41
○ #48	.41
○ #49	.41
○ #50	.42
○ #51	.42
○ #52	.42
○ #53	.42
○ #54	.42
○ #55	.42
○ #56	.43
○ #57	.43
○ #58	.43
○ #59	.43
○ #60	.43
○ #61	.43
○ #62	.44
○ #63	.44

X-Men (1963-1981), cont.

	Page #
○ #64	.44
○ #65	.44
○ #66	.44
○ #67	.44
○ #68	.45
○ #69	.45
○ #70	.45
○ #71	.45
○ #72	.45
○ #73	.45
○ #74	.46
○ #75	.46
○ #76	.46
○ #77	.46
○ #78	.46
○ #79	.46
○ #80	.47
○ #81	.47
○ #82	.47
○ #83	.47
○ #84	.47
○ #85	.47
○ #86	.48
○ #87	.48
○ #88	.48
○ #89	.48
○ #90	.48
○ #91	.48
○ #92	.49
○ #93	.49
○ #94	.49
○ #95	.49
○ #96	.49
○ #97	.49
○ #98	.50
○ #99	.50
○ #100	.50
○ #101	.50
○ #102	.50
○ #103	.50
○ #104	.51
○ #105	.51
○ #106	.51
○ #107	.51
○ #108	.51
○ #109	.51
○ #110	.52
○ #111	.52
○ #112	.52
○ #113	.52
○ #114	.52
○ #115	.52
○ #116	.53
○ #117	.53
○ #118	.53
○ #119	.53
○ #120	.53
○ #121	.53
○ #122	.54
○ #123	.54
○ #124	.54
○ #125	.54
○ #126	.54
○ #127	.54
○ #128	.55
○ #129	.55

X-Men (1963-1981), cont.

	Page #
○ #130	.55
○ #131	.55
○ #132	.55
○ #133	.55
○ #134	.56
○ #135	.56
○ #136	.56
○ #137	.56
○ #138	.56
○ #139	.56
○ #140	.57
○ #141	.57

Uncanny X-Men (1981-Present)

	Page #
○ #142	.57
○ #143	.57
○ #144	.57
○ #145	.57
○ #146	.58
○ #147	.58
○ #148	.58
○ #149	.58
○ #150	.58
○ #151	.58
○ #152	.59
○ #153	.59
○ #154	.59
○ #155	.59
○ #156	.59
○ #157	.59
○ #158	.60
○ #159	.60
○ #160	.60
○ #161	.60
○ #162	.60
○ #163	.60
○ #164	.61
○ #165	.61
○ #166	.61
○ #167	.61
○ #168	.61
○ #169	.61
○ #170	.62
○ #171	.62
○ #172	.62
○ #173	.62
○ #174	.62
○ #175	.62
○ #176	.63
○ #177	.63
○ #178	.63
○ #179	.63
○ #180	.63
○ #181	.63
○ #182	.64
○ #183	.64
○ #184	.64
○ #185	.64
○ #186	.64
○ #187	.64
○ #188	.65
○ #189	.65
○ #190	.65
○ #191	.65
○ #192	.65

Uncanny X-Men (1981-Present), cont.

- #193 65
- #194 66
- #195 66
- #196 66
- #197 66
- #198 66
- #199 66
- #200 67
- #201 67
- #202 67
- #203 67
- #204 67
- #205 67
- #206 68
- #207 68
- #208 68
- #209 68
- #210 68
- #211 68
- #212 69
- #213 69
- #214 69
- #215 69
- #216 69
- #217 69
- #218 70
- #219 70
- #220 70
- #221 70
- #222 70
- #223 70
- #224 71
- #225 71
- #226 71
- #227 71
- #228 71
- ○ #229 71
- #230 72
- #231 72
- #232 72
- #233 72
- #234 72
- #235 72
- #236 73
- #237 73
- #238 73
- #239 73
- #240 73
- #241 73
- #242 74
- #243 74
- #244 74
- #245 74
- #246 74
- #247 74
- #248 75
- #248 (2nd Printing) .75
- #249 75
- #250 75
- #251 75
- #252 75
- #253 76
- #254 76
- #255 76
- #256 76
- #257 76

Uncanny X-Men (1981-Present), cont.

- #258 76
- #259 77
- #260 77
- #261 77
- #262 77
- #263 77
- #264 77
- #265 78
- #266 78
- #267 78
- #268 78
- #268 (2nd Printing) .78
- #269 78
- #270 79
- #270 (2nd Printing, Gold Version) 79
- #271 79
- #272 79
- #273 79
- #274 79
- #275 80
- #275 (2nd Printing, Gold Version) 80
- #276 80
- #277 80
- #278 80
- #279 80
- #280 81
- #281 81
- #281 (2nd Printing, Red Logo) 81
- #282 81
- #282 (2nd Printing) .81
- #283 81
- #284 82
- #285 82
- #286 82
- #287 82
- #288 82
- #289 82
- #290 83
- #291 83
- #292 83
- #293 83
- #294 83
- #295 83
- #296 84
- #297 84
- #298 84
- #299 84
- #300 84
- #301 84
- #302 85
- #303 85
- #303 (Gold Cover) ..85
- #304 85
- #305 85
- #306 85
- #307 86
- #308 86
- #309 86
- #310 86
- #311 86
- #312 86
- #313 87
- #314 87

Uncanny X-Men (1981-Present), cont.

- #315 87
- #316 87
- #316 (Foil Cover) ..87
- #317 87
- #317 (Foil Cover) ...88
- #318 88
- #318 (Foil Cover) ..88
- #319 88
- #319 (Foil Cover) ..88
- #320 88
- #320 (Deluxe Edition) ..89
- #320 (Gold Edition, Wizard Exclusive) ..89
- #321 89
- #321 (Deluxe Edition w/card) ...89
- #322 89
- #323 89
- #324 90
- #325 90
- #326 90
- #327 90
- #328 90
- #329 90
- #330 91
- #331 91
- #332 91
- #333 91
- #334 91
- #335 91
- #336 92
- #337 92
- #338 92
- #339 92
- #340 92
- #341 92
- #342 93
- #342 (Variant Cover) .93
- #343 93
- #344 93
- #345 93
- #346 93
- #347 94
- #348 94
- #349 94
- #350 94
- #350 94
- #351 94
- #352 95
- #353 95
- #354 95
- #354 (Variant Cover) .95
- #355 95
- #356 95
- #357 96
- #358 96
- #359 96
- #360 96
- #360 (Dynamic Forces Exclusive Cover) ...96
- ○ #360 (Prismatic Cover) .96
- #361 97
- #362 97
- #363 97

Comic Book Index & Checklist

Uncanny X-Men (1981-Present), cont.

- #364 97
- #365 97
- #366 97
- #367 98
- #368 98
- #369 98
- #370 98
- #371 98
- #372 98
- #373 99
- #374 99
- #375 99
- #375 (Variant Cover) . 99
- #376 99
- #377 99
- #377 (Variant Cover) . . 100
- #378 100
- #379 100
- #380 100
- #381 100
- #381 (Variant Cover) . . 100
- #382 101
- #383 101
- Annual #1 101
- Annual #2 101
- Annual #3 101
- Annual #4 102
- Annual #5 102
- Annual #6 102
- Annual #7 102
- Annual #8 102
- Annual #9 102
- Annual #10 103
- Annual #11 103
- Annual #12 103
- Annual #13 103
- Annual #14 103
- Annual #15 103
- Annual #16 104
- Annual #17 104
- Annual #18 104
- Uncanny X-Men Annual '95 104
- Uncanny X-Men Annual '96 104
- Uncanny X-Men Annual '97 104
- Uncanny X-Men Fantastic Four Annual 105
- Uncanny X-Men Annual 105
- Giant X-Men #1 . . . 105
- Giant X-Men #2 . . . 105
- Phoenix: The Untold Story . . . 105
- Pint-Sized X-Babies . 105
- Tales From The Age Of Apocalypse . . . 106
- X-Babies Reborn . . . 106
- Yearbook 1999 106

X-Men (1991-Present)

- #-1 106
- #-1 (*Wizard* Exclusive) . . 106
- #0 107
- #1/2 107
- #1 107
- #1 (Variant Cover) . 107
- #1 (Variant Cover) . 107
- #1 (Variant Cover) . 107
- #1 (Deluxe Edition) . 108
- #2 108
- #3 108
- #4 108
- #5 108
- #6 108
- #7 109
- #8 109
- #9 109
- #10 109
- #11 109
- #12 109
- #13 110
- #14 110
- #15 110
- #16 110
- #17 110
- #18 110
- #19 111
- #20 111
- #21 111
- #22 111
- #23 111
- #24 111
- #25 112
- #25 (Black & White Cover) 112
- #25 (Gold Cover) . . 112
- #26 112
- #27 112
- #28 112
- #29 113
- #30 113
- #31 113
- #32 113
- #33 113
- #34 113
- #35 114
- #36 114
- #36 (Foil Cover) . . . 114
- #37 114
- #37 (Foil Cover) . . . 114
- #38 114
- #38 (Deluxe Cover) 115
- #39 115
- #39 (Deluxe Cover) 115
- #40 115
- #40 (Deluxe Cover) 115
- #41 115
- #41 (Deluxe Cover) . 116
- #42 116
- #43 116
- #44 116
- #45 116
- #46 116
- #47 117
- #48 117

X-Men (1991-Present), cont.

- #49 117
- #50 117
- #50 (American Entertainment Exclusive) 117
- #50 (Deluxe Cover) . 117
- #50 (Gold Cover) . . 118
- #51 118
- #52 118
- #53 118
- #54 118
- #54 (Prismatic Cover) . 118
- #54 (Silver Cover) . . 119
- #55 119
- #56 119
- #57 119
- #58 119
- #59 119
- #60 120
- #61 120
- #62 120
- #62 120
- #63 120
- #64 120
- #65 121
- #66 121
- #67 121
- #68 121
- #69 121
- #70 121
- #71 122
- #72 122
- #73 122
- #74 122
- #75 122
- #76 122
- #77 123
- #78 123
- #79 123
- #80 123
- #80 (Dynamic Forces Exclusive Cover) . . 123
- #80 (Foil Cover) . . . 123
- #81 124
- #82 124
- #83 124
- #84 124
- #85 124
- #86 124
- #87 125
- #88 125
- #89 125
- #90 125
- #91 125
- #92 125
- #93 126
- #94 126
- #95 126
- #96 126
- #97 126
- #97 (Variant Cover) . 126
- #98 127
- #99 127
- #100 (Cover By Arthur Adams) . . 127

Comic Book Index & Checklist

X-Men (1991-Present), cont.

- #100 (Cover By Dave Cockrum) .127
- #100 (Cover By John Byrne) 127
- #100 (Cover By John Romita, Jr.) .127
- #100 (Cover By Leinil Francis Yu) .128
- #100 (Cover By Leinil Francis Yu) .128
- #100 (Cover By Paul Smith) 128
- #100 (Dynamic Forces Exclusive Cover By Jae Lee) 128
- #101 128
- #102 128
- #103 129
- Annual #1 129
- Annual #2 129
- Annual #3 129
- X-Men '95 129
- X-Men '96 130
- X-Men '97 130
- X-Men And Doctor Doom '98 130
- X-Men '99 Annual .130
- God Loves Man Kills 130
- Logan 130
- Team X Team 7 ...131
- X-Men Alpha 131
- X-Men Alpha (Gold Cover) 131
- X-Men Books Of Askani 131
- X-Men: The Magneto War ...131
- X-Men Omega 131
- X-Men Omega (Gold Cover) 132
- X-Men Prime 132
- X-Men Rarities 132
- X-Men Year In Review 132

The Age Of Apocalypse

The Amazing X-Men
- #1 132
- #2 133
- #3 133
- #4 133

The Astonishing X-Men
- #1 133
- #2 133
- #3 133
- #4 134

Factor X
- #1 134
- #2 134
- #3 134
- #4 134

Gambit And The Xternals
- #1 134
- #2 135
- #3 135
- #4 135

The Age Of Apocalypse, cont.

Generation Next
- #1 135
- #2 135
- #3 135
- #4 136

Weapon X
- #1 136
- #2 136
- #3 136
- #4 136

X-Calibre
- #1 136
- #2 137
- #3 137
- #4 137

X-Man
- #1 137
- #2 137
- #3 137
- #4 138

X-Men Chronicles
- #1 138
- #2 138

X-Universe
- #1 138
- #2 138

Mini Series

Askani'son
- #1 139
- #2 139
- #3 139
- #4 139

The Astonishing X-Men
- #1 139
- #1 (Dynamic Forces Printed Sketch Cover) ...139
- #1 (Dynamic Forces Printed Sketch Cover, Limited Edition) 140
- #1 (Variant Cover) ...140
- #2 140
- #3 140

Pryde And Wisdom
- #1 140
- #2 140
- #3 141

The Rise Of Apocalypse
- #1 141
- #2 141
- #3 141
- #4 141

X-Men: Alpha Flight
- #1 141
- #2 142

X-Men And Alpha Flight
- #1 142
- #2 142

Mini Series, cont.

X-Men And The Micronauts
- #1 142
- #2 142
- #3 142
- #4 143

X-Men: Brood Days Of Wrath
- #1 143
- #2 143

X-Men: Children Of The Atom
- #1 143
- #2 143
- #3 143
- #4 144
- #5 144

X-Men And The Clandestine
- #1 144
- #2 144

X-Men: The Hellfire Club
- #1 144
- #2 145
- #3 145
- #4 145

X-Men: Liberators
- #1 145
- #2 145
- #3 145
- #4 146

X-Men: Phoenix
- #1 146
- #2 146
- #3 146

X-Men: Spotlight On . . . Starjammers
- #1 146
- #2 146

X-Men: True Friends
- #1 147
- #2 147
- #3 147

X-Men Vs. The Avengers
- #1 147
- #2 147
- #3 147
- #4 148

Other Uncanny X-Men Comics

- Special Edition X-Men 148
- The Uncanny X-Men And The New Teem Titans 148
- The Uncanny X-Men At The State Fair Of Texas 148

Action Figure Index & Checklist

The following checklist lists action figures by year of release and the number refers to the page on which the figure is found. Following the name is an abbreviation of the series that the piece belongs to (see key below). **Note:** Reissues, variations and future releases are not listed.

AA .. The Age Of Apocalypse	EH .... Electronic Big Time	PR .... Projectors
BA .... Battle Action	Action Hero	RF .... Robot Fighters
Mega Armor	FL .... Flashback Series	S__ .... Series __
BB .... Battle Brigade	IN .... Invasion Series	SH .... Shape Shifters
BL .... Battle Blasters	MA .... Mutant Armor Series	SL .... Savage Land
BS .... Battle Bases	MF .... Missle Flyers	SM .... Steel Mutants
BT .... Battle Talkers	MG .. Mutant Genesis Series	SR .... Space Riders
CH .... Collector Hero	MM ...... Metallic Mutants	SS .... Super Shooters
CL .... Classics	MO .. Mutant Monster Series	SU .... Supersize
CW .... Classics: Light	NF. .... Ninja Force	WW. .... Water Wars
Up Weapon	ON .... Onslaught	XM .... X-Men: The Movie
DE .... Deluxe Edition	PH .... Phoenix Saga	

1991   Page
- Apocalypse (S1)....................163
- Archangel (S1).....................163
- Colossus (S1)......................165
- Cyclops (S1).......................166
- Cyclops Light Force Arena (S1)........181
- Juggernaut (S1)....................169
- Magneto (S1).......................170
- Nightcrawler (S1)..................171
- Storm (S1).........................175
- Wolverine (S1).....................178
- Wolverine Combat Cave (N/A).........181
- Wolverine Mutantcycle (S1)..........181

1992
- Banshee (S2).......................164
- Forge (S2).........................167
- Gambit (S2)........................167
- Iceman (S2)........................168
- Magneto (S2).......................170
- Mr. Sinister (S2)..................171
- Sabretooth (S2)....................174
- Sauron (S2)........................174
- Wolverine (2nd Ed., S2)............177
- Wolverine (3rd Ed., S2)............177
- "Weapon X" Wolverine (S2)..........176

1993
- Ahab (S5).........................163
- Apocalypse (2nd Ed., S4)...........163
- Bishop (S3).......................165
- Brood (S5)........................165
- Cyclops (DE)......................166
- Cyclops (S5)......................166
- Iceman (S3).......................168
- Longshot (S5).....................169
- Magneto (N/A).....................169
- Omega Red (S4)....................171
- Professor X (S5)..................172
- Sabretooth (DE)...................173
- Sabretooth (S5)...................174
- Strong Guy (S4)...................175
- Tusk (S4).........................175
- Wolverine (DE)....................177
- Wolverine (5th Ed., S4)...........177

1994
- Apocalypse (PR)...................163
- Apocalypse (DE)...................163
- Apocalypse vs. Archangel (SM).....179
- Beast (S6).......................164
- Beast (DE).......................164
- Beast vs. Morph (SM).............179
- Bishop (DE).......................165
- Bonebreaker (S7)..................165
- Ch'od (S7).......................165
- Civilian Wolverine vs. Silver Samurai (SM)....179
- Corsair (PH).....................165
- Cyclops (MM).....................166
- Cyclops (PR)......................166
- Cyclops vs. Mr. Sinister (SM).....179

1994, cont.   Page
- Gambit (DE)......................167
- Gambit vs. Bishop (SM)...........179
- Gladiator (PH)...................167
- Iceman (#2)......................168
- Juggernaut vs. Cyclops (SM)......179
- Kylun (S7).......................169
- Longshot vs. Mojo (SM)...........180
- Magneto (MM).....................170
- Magneto (PR).....................170
- Morph (S6).......................170
- Mr. Sinister (DE)................170
- Omega Red (MM)...................171
- Phoenix (PH).....................172
- Professor X vs. Magneto (SM).....180
- Random (S6)......................172
- Raza (S7)........................172
- Robot Wolverine (S6).............176
- Rogue (N/A)......................172
- Rogue vs. Pyro (SM)..............180
- Sabretooth (MM)..................173
- Sabretooth (PR)..................173
- Senyaka (Toys "R" Us)............174
- Silver Samurai (S6)..............174
- Space Wolverine (8th, PH)........176
- Spy Wolverine (MM)...............176
- Spy Wolverine vs. Omega Red (SM).180
- Trevor Fitzroy (S6)..............175
- Warstar (PH).....................175
- Weapon X (Wolverine, DE).........175
- Wolverine (MM)...................177
- Wolverine (PR)...................177
- Wolverine–Street Clothes (7th Ed., S7)....179
- Wolverine vs. Sabretooth (XM)....180
- X-Men Blackbird Jet (N/A)........182

1995
- Apocalypse (AA)..................163
- Archangel II (DE)................163
- Archangel II (IN)................164
- Battle Ravaged Wolverine (IN)....176
- Beast (CL).......................163
- Beast (PR).......................164
- Beast (DE).......................164
- Bishop (PR)......................165
- Cable (PR).......................165
- Cameron Hodge (MG)...............165
- Captive Sabretooth (IN)..........173
- Civilian Wolverine (PR)..........176
- Cyclops (AA).....................166
- Cyclops (CL).....................166
- Electronic Talking Wolverine (NA)....176
- Eric the Red (IN)................167
- Havok (IN).......................167
- Iceman II (IN)...................168
- Gambit (CL)......................167
- Magneto (AA).....................169
- Magneto (CL).....................169
- Magneto (DE).....................169
- Maverick (MG)....................170
- Mr. Sinister (PR)................171

1995, cont.

	Page #
○ Sabretooth (AA)	173
○ Spiral (IN)	174
○ Spy Wolverine (DE)	176
○ Storm (CL)	174
○ Sunfire (MG)	175
○ Weapon X (AA)	175
○ Wolverine (CL)	177
○ Wolverine (DE)	177
○ Wolverine (Battle Ravage, DE)	178
○ Wolverine Fang (MG)	178
○ Wolverine Space (DE)	179
○ X-Cutioner (MG)	179
○ X-Men Headquarters Playset (N/A)	182

1996

	Page #
○ Archangel (BB)	163
○ Battle Armor Wolverine (IN)	176
○ Bishop II (FL)	165
○ Colossus (BB)	165
○ Dark Beast (MO)	164
○ Dark Nemesis (NF)	171
○ Electra (CW)	167
○ Gambit (CW)	167
○ Heavy Metal Beast (MA)	164
○ Iceman (MA)	168
○ Juggernaut (CW)	168
○ Lady Deathstrike (BB)	169
○ Longshot vs. Mojo (SM)	180
○ Mystique (DE)	171
○ Nightcrawler (CW)	171
○ Ninja Psylocke (NF)	172
○ Ninja Sabretooth (NF)	173
○ Ninja Wolverine (NF)	176
○ Omega Red II (FL)	171
○ Polaris (FL)	172
○ Post Apocalypse Beast (BB)	164
○ Professor Xavier (MA)	172
○ Psylocke (CW)	172
○ Quicksilver (MA)	172
○ Rogue (CH)	173
○ Rogue (DE)	173
○ Rogue vs. Pyro (SM)	180
○ Savage Land Wolverine (FL)	176
○ Space Ninja Deathbird (NF)	167
○ Storm (CH)	174
○ Sugar Man (MO)	175
○ Werewolf Wolverine (MM)	176
○ Wolverine (CW)	177
○ Wolverine Classic (DE)	178
○ Wolverine Patch (BB)	178

1997

	Page #
○ Angel & Sauron (SL)	179
○ Apocalypse (SS)	163
○ Apocalypse Rising (ON)	163
○ Aqua Attack Nightcrawler (WW)	171
○ Beast (SS)	164
○ Beast (SR)	164
○ Colossus (SS)	165
○ Cyclops (MA)	166
○ Cyclops (RF)	166
○ Cyclops (SR)	166
○ Future Apocalypse (MF)	163
○ Future Bishop (MF)	165
○ Future Shard (MF)	174
○ Future Wolverine (MF)	176
○ Gambit (RF)	167
○ Hydro Blast Wolverine (WW)	176
○ Jean Grey (FF)	168
○ Jean Grey (ON)	168
○ Jean Grey (SR)	168
○ Joseph & Amphibious (SL)	179
○ Jubilee (RF)	168
○ Ka-Zar & Zabu (SL)	180
○ Mystique (MA)	171
○ Onslaught (ON)	172
○ Professor X (SR)	172
○ Rogue (MA)	173
○ Sabletooth (BT)	173

1997, cont.

	Page #
○ Savage Storm & Colossus (SL)	180
○ Savage Wolverine & Crawler-Rex (SL)	180
○ Sentinel Test Robot (WW)	174
○ Sinister (MA)	171
○ Storm (BA)	174
○ Storm (BL)	174
○ Storm (RF)	175
○ Ultimate Iceman (WW)	168
○ Weather Fury Storm (WW)	175
○ Wolverine (MA)	177
○ Wolverine (RF)	178
○ Wolverine (SR)	179
○ Wolverine Unleashed (ON)	179
○ X-Men Water Wars Playset (WW)	182

1998

	Page #
○ Beast (BL)	164
○ Cyclops (FF)	166
○ Cyclops (BL)	166
○ Gambit (PS)	167
○ Jean Grey (BL)	168
○ Juggernaut (SH)	169
○ Maggot (FF)	169
○ Magneto (BT)	169
○ Magneto (BS)	169
○ Master Mold (PS)	170
○ Morph (SH)	170
○ Mr. Sinister (FF)	171
○ Omega (BL)	171
○ Rogue (PS)	173
○ Sabretooth (BL)	173
○ Wolverine (BL)	177
○ Wolverine (BT)	177
○ Wolverine (PS)	177
○ Wolverine (SH)	178
○ Wolverine (SS)	178
○ Wolverine Battle Base (BS)	178
○ Wolverine (EH)	177
○ X-Men Power Slammers Assault Vehicle (PS)	182

2000

	Page #
○ Cyclops (XM)	166
○ Electronic X-Jet (XM)	181
○ Jean Grey (XM)	168
○ Lady Liberty Playset (XM)	181
○ Logan (XM)	169
○ Logan vs. Magneto (XM)	180
○ Logan vs. Rogue (XM)	180
○ Magneto (XM)	170
○ Mutant Machine (XM)	181
○ Mystique (XM)	171
○ Professor X (XM)	172
○ Rogue (XM)	173
○ Sabretooth (XM)	174
○ Storm (XM)	175
○ Toad (XM)	175
○ Wolverine (XM)	178
○ Wolverine vs. Sabretooth (XM)	180
○ Wolverine X-Cycle (XM)	182

Undetermined Release Dates

	Page #
○ Battle Blaster Bomber (BL)	181
○ Cable vs. Stryfe (SM)	179
○ Cyclops vs. Mr. Sinister (SM)	179
○ Gambit vs. Bishop (SM)	179
○ Magneto (SU)	170
○ Magneto Magnatron (N/A)	181
○ Professor X vs. Magneto (SM)	180
○ The Space Lab: Cyclops vs. Magneto (N/A)	181
○ The Striker: Wolverine vs. Sabretooth (N/A)	181
○ Wolverine (SU)	178
○ Wolverine 4 x 4 (SL)	181
○ Wolverine Remote Control 4 x 4 (N/A)	181
○ Wolverine Remote Control Cycle (N/A)	181
○ X-Men Battle Cycle (N/A)	182
○ X-Men Mini Blackbird Jet (N/A)	182
○ X-Men Sentinel (N/A)	182
○ X-Men Wolverine Jeep (N/A)	182

Trading Card Game Index & Checklist

Card Title and Number	Page #
Agility Trial (#81/131)	183
Alien Invasion (#21/131)	191
All Or Nothing Battle (#82/131)	183
Ambush (#22/131)	191
Angel (#1/131)	191
Apocalypse (#2/131)	191
Back Alley Brawl (#23/131)	191
Bad Blood (#83/131)	183
Bait And Switch (#84/131)	191
Baptism By Fire (#41/131)	183
Battle Simulation (#85/131)	191
Berserker Rage (#42/131)	184
Bewilder (#43/131)	191
Bishop (#3/131)	191
Blend In (#44/131)	191
Block (#45/131)	191
Blood Feud (#86/131)	184
Braindrain (#46/131)	191
Brainwashed! (#47/131)	191
Brood (#4/131)	191
Call Down The Heavens (#48/131)	191
Call The Cops (#49/131)	191
Close Call (#87/131)	191
Collision Course (#88/131)	191
Combat Training (#89/131)	184
Come Out Wherever You Are! (#50/131)	191
Concentrate (#51/131)	191
Controlled Burst (#90/131)	191
Cross-Dimensional Raid (#91/131)	191
Crossfire (#24/131)	191
Cry For Help (#92/131)	184
Cyclops (#5/131)	191
Cyclops (#122/131)	184
Deadly Dance (#25/131)	191
Death Trap (#93/131)	184
DMZ (#26/131)	191
Dodge This! (#52/131)	191
Dogfight (#94/131)	185
Don't Give Up! (#27/131)	191
Double Team (#53/131)	191
Dramatic Confrontation (#95/131)	185
Dramatic Escape (#96/131)	185
Faceoff (#97/131)	185
Fastball Special (#98/131)	191
Fight To The Finish (#99/131)	191
Finishing Blow (#100/131)	185
Firefight (#101/131)	185
First Aid! (#102/131)	186
Fly Away (#28/131)	191
Follow Me! (#54/131)	186
Focus (#29/131)	191
Fusillade (#55/131)	191
Get To The Truth! (#30/131)	191
Goddess! (#56/131)	186
Hold Your Fire! (#57/131)	186
Inferno (#103/131)	191
Jean Grey (#123/131)	186
Juggernaut (#7/131)	191
Kiss For Luck (#58/131)	191
Kra-ka-thoom! (#59/131)	191
Last Stand (#104/131)	186
Lend Moral Support (#31/131)	191
Lure Them In (#60/131)	191
Magneto (#124/131)	187
Marrow (#9/131)	191
Mental Probe (#105/131)	187
Mojo (#10/131)	191
Moment Of Reflection (#61/131)	191
Moment Of Truth (#32/131)	191

Card Title and Number	Page #
Mystique (#125/131)	187
Natural Disaster (#33/131)	191
Nice Shot! (#62/131)	191
No Way Out (#63/131)	191
Obstacle Course (#34/131)	191
Outflank (#64/131)	191
Out Of Control (#65/131)	191
Payback (#106/131)	187
Pounce (#107/131)	187
Practical Joke (#66/131)	191
Practice, Practice, Practice (#35/131)	191
Precision Fire (#108/131)	187
Press Gang (#36/131)	191
Professor X (#126/131)	188
Protection Of The Innocent (#109/131)	188
Psi-Shield (#67/131)	188
Psychic Boost (#110/131)	188
Psychic Showdown (#111/131)	191
Psylocke (#13/131)	191
Read The Riot Act (#68/131)	191
Reality Shift (#121/131)	188
Reprieve (#69/131)	191
Rescue Mission (#112/131)	191
Rogue (#14/131)	191
Rogue (#127/131)	188
Sabretooth (#128/131)	189
Scientific Solution (#70/131)	191
Sentinels (#16/131)	191
Shhhhh . . . (#71/131)	191
Showdown (#113/131)	189
Shrapnel Blast (#114/131)	191
Sinister (#17/131)	191
Slugfest (#38/131)	191
Snikt! (#39/131)	191
Spinal Tap (#72/131)	191
Stay Out Of Reach (#115/131)	191
Storm (#18/131)	191
Storm (#129/131)	189
Storm (#P5)	189
Sucker Punch (#116/131)	191
Surprise Assault (#117/131)	189
Swipe (#73/131)	191
Take It To The Sky (#74/131)	191
Take the Hit (#75/131)	191
Take Your Best Shot (#118/131)	191
Teach Some Manners (#76/131)	191
Team Work (#77/131)	191
Toad (#130/131)	189
Ugh . . . Take It! (#78/131)	191
Vendetta (#119/131)	191
Wolverine (#131/131)	190
Work As A Team (#79/131)	191
Workout (#80/131)	191
You Can Make It (#120/131)	191

ACKNOWLEDGEMENTS

CheckerBee Publishing would like to extend a special thanks to Jim MacLeod, Eric Setreus. And also to Mike Cote and Kevin Hall of DJ's Comics in Meriden, CT and Brian Kozicki of Buried Under in Manchester, CT. In addition, we would like to thank Jamie Coville, James Denis, Wayne Hogan, Dan Interlandi, Beth Jarvis, Mikhail Suvorov and all the X-Men fans and retailers who contributed their valuable time to assist us with this book.

X-PERIENCE Our Hottest Guides

CheckerBee PUBLISHING

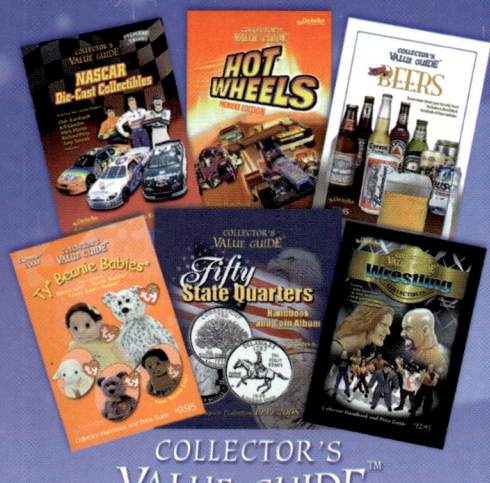

Digimon™
Fifty State Quarters
Harry Potter™
Hot Wheels®
NASCAR®
Dale Earnhardt®
Jeff Gordon®
Pokémon™
Ty® Beanie Babies®
Wrestling
X-Men®

COLLECTOR'S VALUE GUIDE™

And that's not all! We have 27 great titles available in stores everywhere. They're out of this universe! To find out more, call toll free: **800.746.3686** or visit **CollectorBee.com**

Enter The Magnificent World Of Superheroes

If you're a fan of X-Men, our website is for you! Conquer it today, Bub!

CollectorBee.com

- Keep up with the latest X-Men news!
- Meet other comic fans on our free Bulletin Board!
- Try your luck with our contests & giveaways!

306 Industrial Park Road   Middletown, CT 06457   800.746.3686   www.collectorbee.com